ARENA TRACKS

A Rider, Trainer, and Instructor's Reference for Dressage, Jumping, and Cavalletti Exercises

Christian Baier

Foreword by Ulf Wadeborn | Afterword by Albert Voorn

TRAFALGAR SQUARE
North Pomfret, Vermont

First published in 2023 by
Trafalgar Square Books
North Pomfret, Vermont 05053

Disclaimer of Liability
The author and publisher shall have neither liability nor responsibility to any person or entity with respect to any loss or damage caused or alleged to be caused directly or indirectly by the information contained in this book. While the book is as accurate as the author can make it, there may be errors, omissions, and inaccuracies.

Trafalgar Square Books encourages the use of approved safety helmets in all equestrian sports and activities.

Library of Congress Cataloging-in-Publication Data
Names: Baier, Christian, 1975- author.
Title: Arena tracks : an international reference for dressage, jumping, and cavalletti
  exercises / Christian Baier.
Description: North Pomfret, Vermont : Trafalgar Square Books, 2022. | Includes index. |
  Summary: "Rider and trainer Christian Baier has been educated in horses and equitation in
  Sweden, England, Bermuda, Germany, and the United States. It is his mission to provide an
  accurate international resource on the correct arena tracks for training and riding, as well as
  select exercises for using them in the development of a sport horse. In this book readers find
  an easy-to-use reference for learning the arena tracks, and a second part that helps you
  apply them to dressage, jumping, and cavalletti training scenarios"-- Provided by publisher.
Identifiers: LCCN 2022011193 (print) | LCCN 2022011194 (ebook) | ISBN
  9781646011179 (hardback) | ISBN 9781646011186 (epub)
Subjects: LCSH: Horse arenas. | Courses (Horse sports)
Classification: LCC SF294.35 .B35 2022 (print) | LCC SF294.35 (ebook) |
  DDC 636.1/0811--dc23/eng/20220601
LC record available at https://lccn.loc.gov/2022011193
LC ebook record available at https://lccn.loc.gov/2022011194

Diagrams by Christian Baier
Book design by Lauryl Eddlemon
Cover design by RM Didier

Printed in China

10 9 8 7 6 5 4 3 2 1

Thank you to everyone for

continuing to learn in order to be

better humans for the horses.

CONTENTS

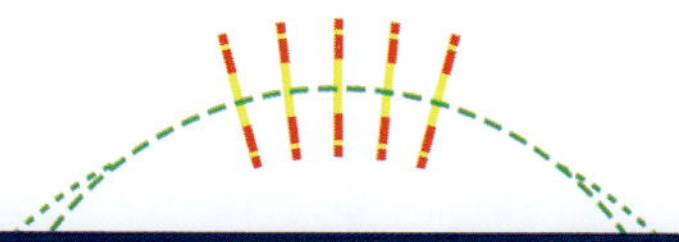

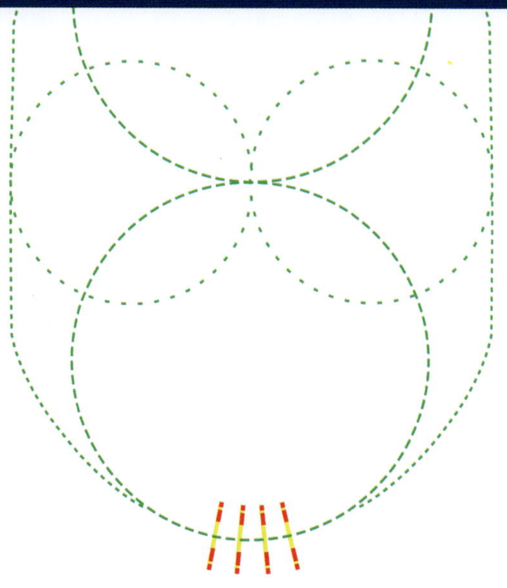

Jumping Exercises   81

A FORMULA FOR SUCCESS—JUMPING   81

SUPPLENESS, RHYTHM, AND CONTROL—JUMPING EXERCISES   106

GRIDS AND COMBINATIONS   133

FOREWORD

I was very happy when I was asked to say something about this book that Christian Baier has written, which, for me, is something I think is very important for riders to know. I was brought up in Europe, and this system was taught to us at the riding schools all over Sweden. All the patterns and lines of travel included here were always used during lessons. I still use most of them in my teaching because riding is about building up a feel of what's going on underneath us. To be precise in following these patterns and lines really helps with rider development and also in keeping the horse between the aids. Using these patterns and lines helps to work on suppleness and alignment, which is a requirement for balance, and later, collection. A balanced horse will stay healthier and last longer for us to enjoy.

All these patterns can be found in various old military instruction books and have been used for many hundreds of years. I'm happy now that they can be found in one place with very nice, modern, and clear illustrations.

Ulf Wadeborn

Ulf Wadeborn is a native of Sweden and now an almost 30-year resident of California. One of his most important mentors was the legendary dressage trainer Bo Tibblin. Ulf has himself successfully competed up to Grand Prix dressage. He is an "R"-rated dressage judge and a breeding judge in Sweden, a USEF "S"-rated dressage judge in the United States, and a former president of the Swedish Warmblood Association of North America. He has an enormous passion for education, which makes him a highly sought-after instructor and judge. When Ulf is not traveling for judging or teaching, he is running H&W Dressage together with Lars Holmberg in Los Angeles. You can read more about him at www.hwdressage.com.

INTRODUCTION

The reason for writing this book is that through my years as a teacher of the art of riding, I would always be asked the question, *"Where can I look up these tracks?"* This was in reference to the figures one rides, or is directed to ride by a trainer or instructor, on a horse in an arena. I would always give a recommendation that consisted of several books and additional websites.

While in the process of creating a new rider's educational system for use in Asia, I realized just how challenging it was to find information about the classical arena tracks. This was when I decided to do something about it: I created a simple overview of the common arena tracks so that, at the very least, I would have something I knew was correct to recommend to my own students.

These classical tracks are ultimately at the foundation of *everything* we are doing in the arena with the horse. It starts with the beginner rider just off the longe line learning the most basic tracks all the way to the most experienced rider working a horse at the highest level of equestrianism. Jumping courses even consist of a combination (or variation) of classical arena tracks strung together from start to finish marker!

The classical arena tracks that I outline in Part One (p. 3) guide the rider in how to safely navigate the arena in an organized way (starting with the most basic, progressing to intermediate, and finishing with the most advanced tracks), in addition to being a useful tool in the physical development of the horse. For the instructor, they are an important tool for communicating with the student.

The purpose of Part Two (p. 27) is to tie in jumping tracks and exercises in a way that correlates to the classical arena tracks on the flat and the escalating levels of difficulty they represent (from most basic to most advanced). The goal with the jumping exercises in this book is to serve both rider and trainer with a set of helpful tools for training the horse in a classical way. Even if these exercises are not physically ridden by the reader, the hope is to inspire individual creativity within the parameters of physics and ethics that classical horsemanship has developed over thousands of years. The encouragement of continuing studies is what has the potential to make us into better humans for our horses.

PART ONE

THE ARENA TRACKS

Why Do We Have Tracks?

- To ride in an organized and safe way in an arena.

- To change direction with many options from basic to more advanced.

- To make it easier to deal with other horses in the arena.

- Basic tracks are of great help to the novice rider and inexperienced horse.

- They are excellent help in training accuracy.

- Riding tracks support and demonstrate the suppleness of the horse.

The tracks described in the pages that follow are in reference to the standard dressage arenas, which come in two sizes:

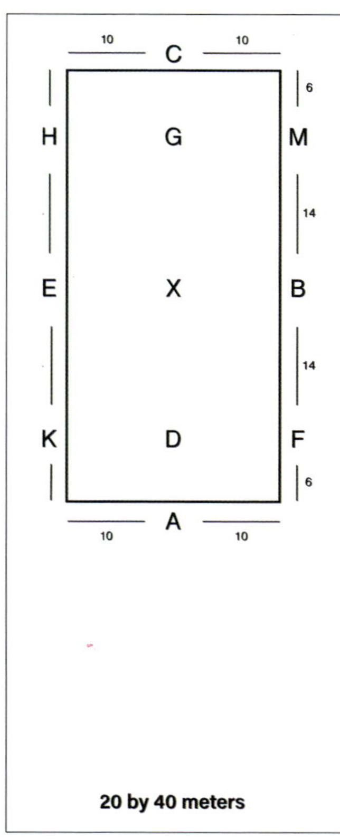

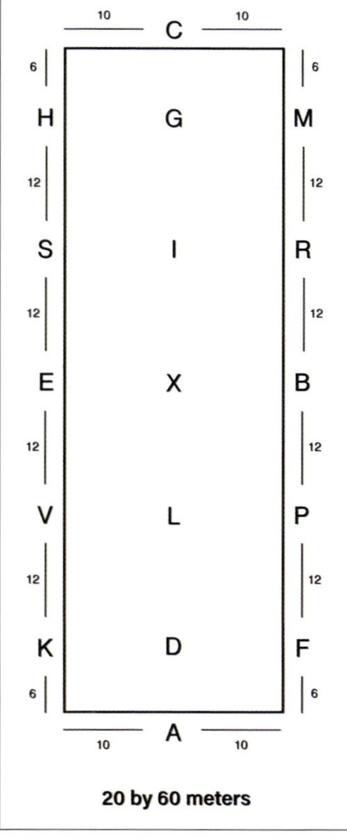

Long and Short Sides

- **Purpose:** Terminology

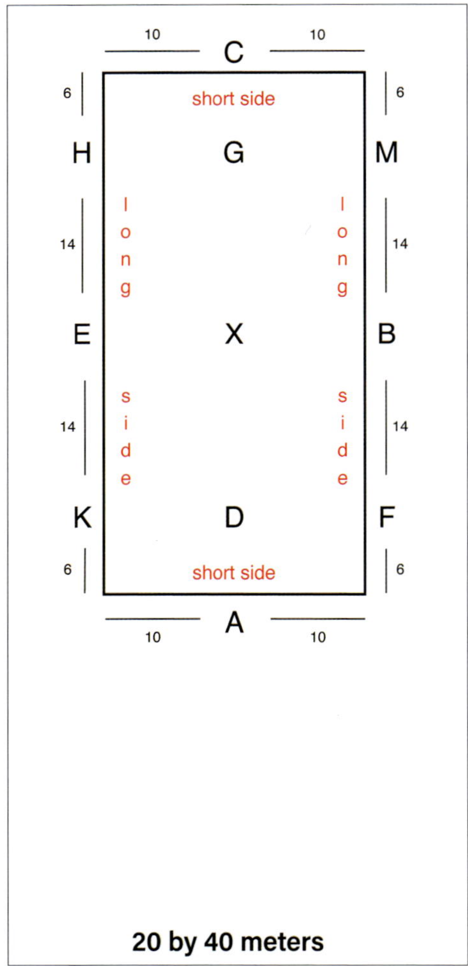

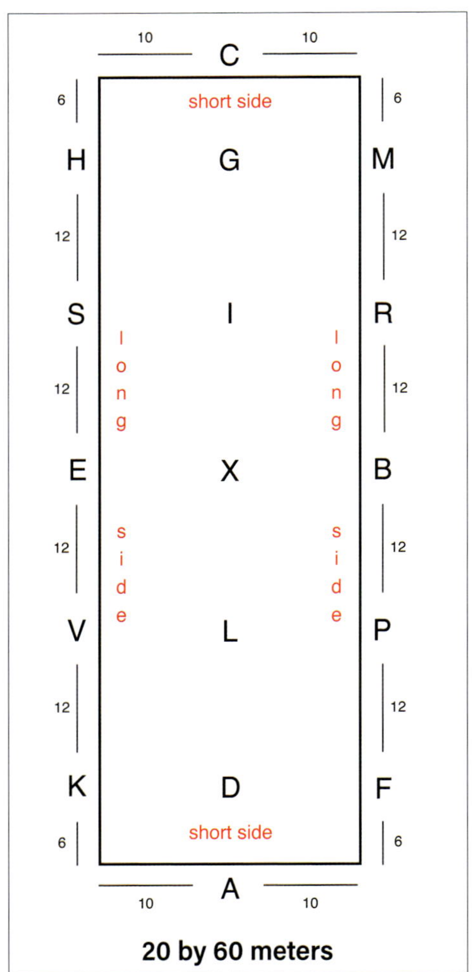

Straight Ahead

- **Purpose:** Using maximum space in the arena.

- **Possible tracks:** Tracking left or right.

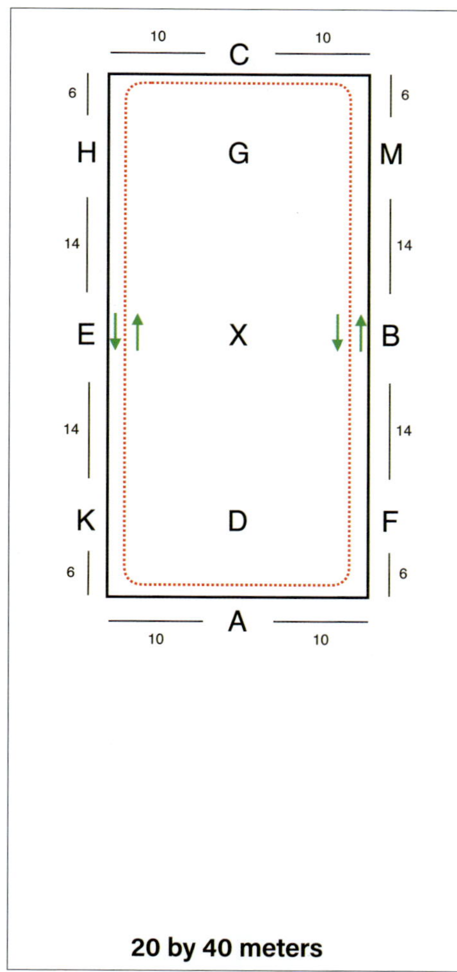

20 by 40 meters

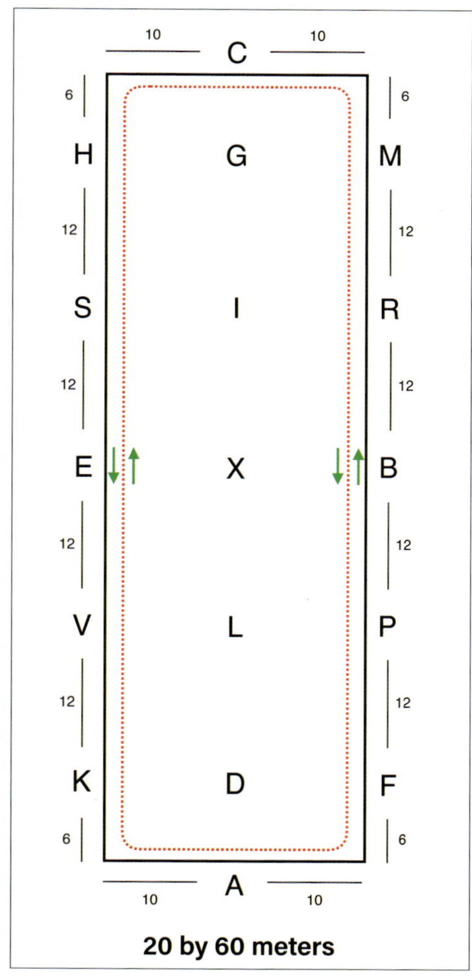

20 by 60 meters

Corners

- **Purpose:** Turning the horse, and developing bend, engagement, and balance as the depth of corner increases with training.
- **Possible tracks:** Tracking left or right.

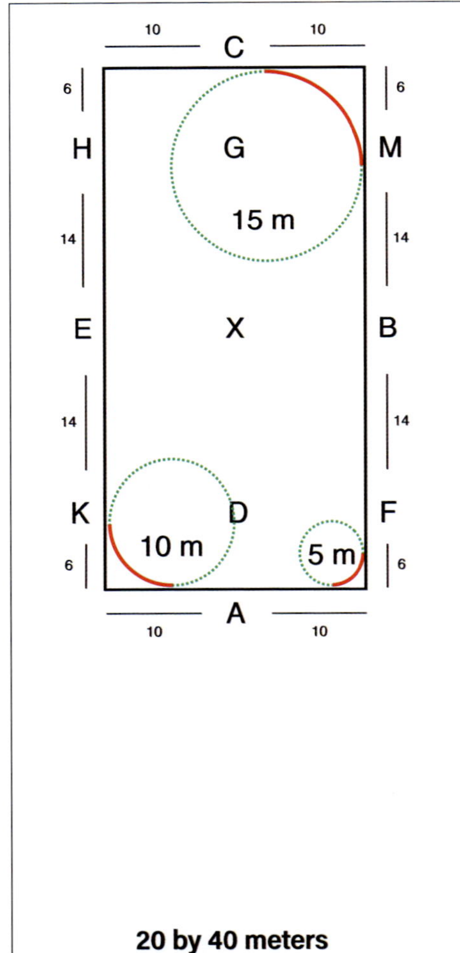

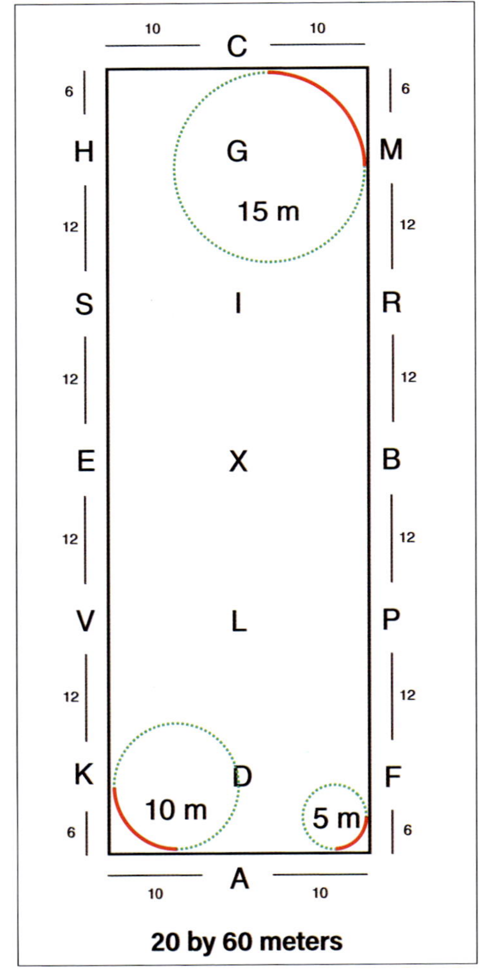

Note: The corners are not a specific track but still require explanation of how to ride them. Thinking of a corner as a part of a smaller circle helps. In Grand Prix dressage, corners will match a significantly smaller circle.

Changing Direction Across the Diagonal

- **Purpose:** Used to change direction.

- **Possible tracks:** K–M and M–K; F–H and H–F.

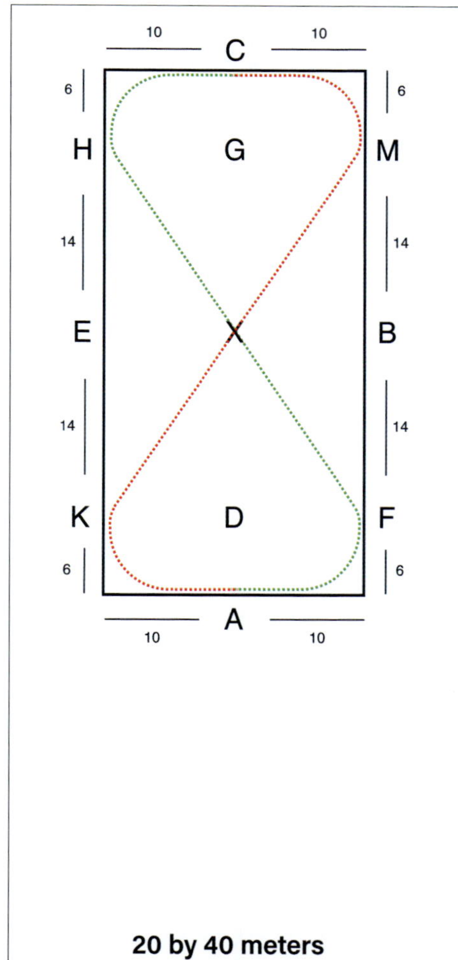

20 by 40 meters

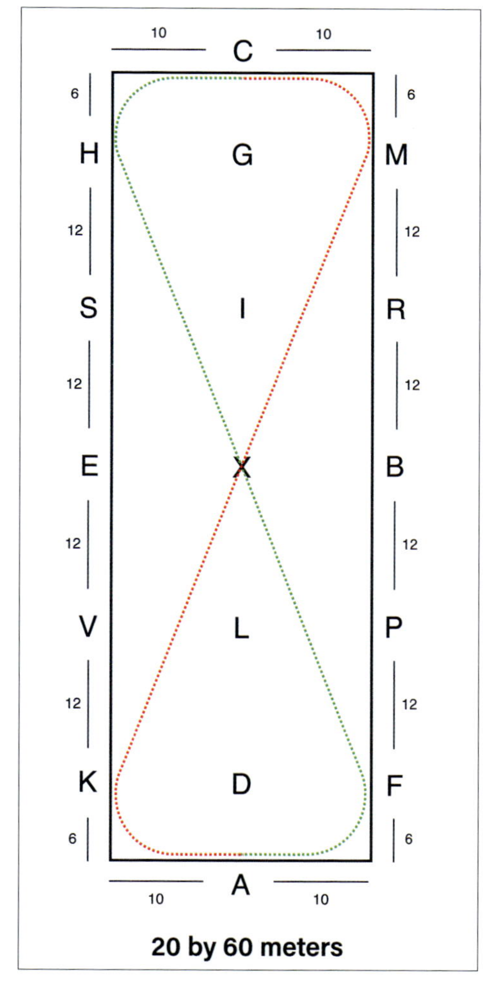

20 by 60 meters

Note: Always turn from the second corner after the long side (so not the first corner on the short side, but the second corner on the short side).

Centerline

- **Purpose:** To change direction; to train riding straight.
- **Possible tracks:** Approach centerline from left or right and finish left or right.

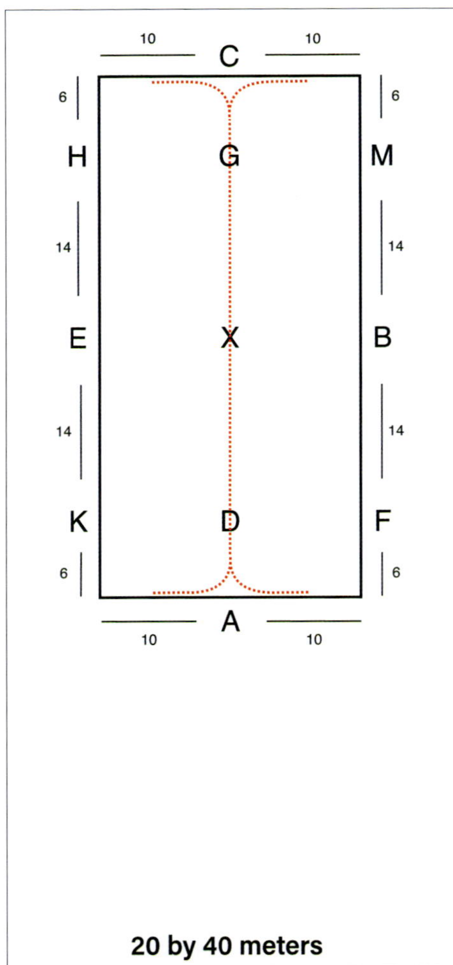

20 by 40 meters

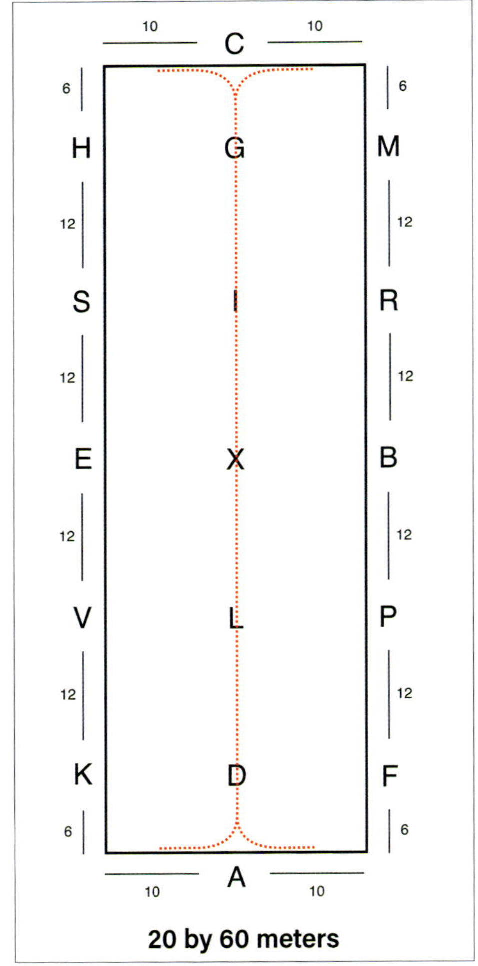

20 by 60 meters

Note: Dressage tests start and end on the centerline.

Quarterline

- **Purpose:** Training to ride straight.

- **Possible tracks:** The approach and the finish are usually made from and end in the same direction. Typically, riding the quarterline does not involve a change of direction.

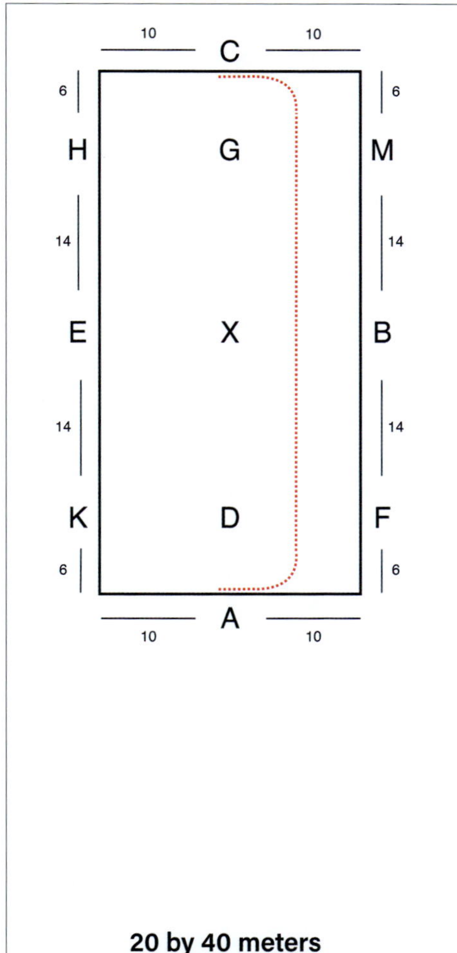

20 by 40 meters

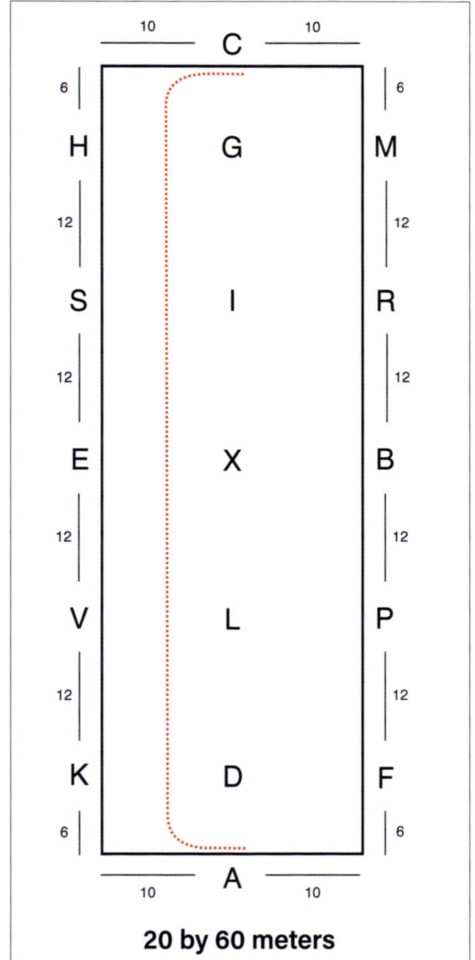

20 by 60 meters

Note: The quarterlines are the tracks between the centerline and the track on both long sides. There is one quarterline per long side.

Turning Across the Arena

- **Purpose:** Used to change direction.

- **Possible tracks:** Starts from left or right, and usually finishes in the opposite direction from the start.

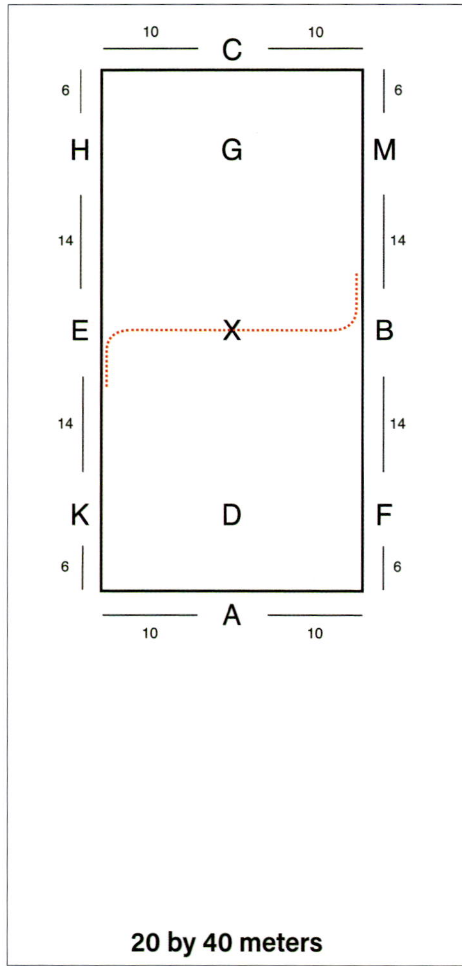

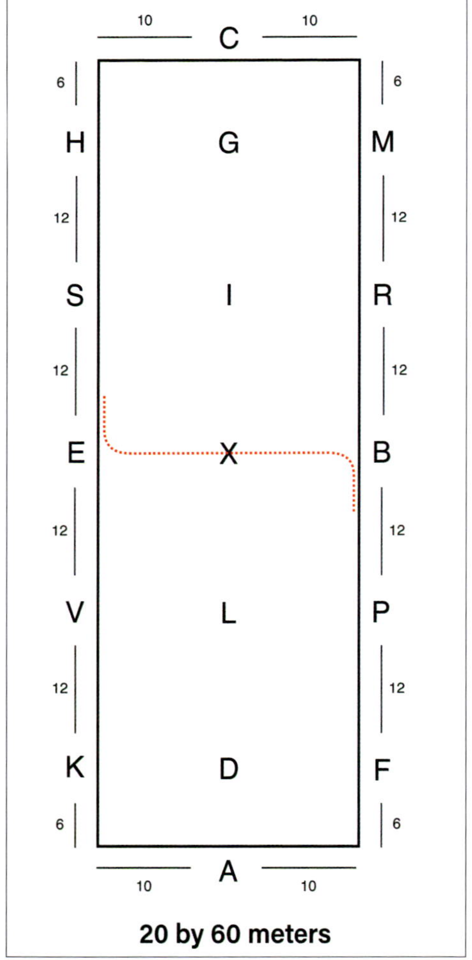

Note: This track is very useful for creating more distance between horses and spreading out evenly in the arena. When used for this purpose, there is *no change of direction* involved.

20-Meter Circles

- **Purpose:** Introduction to riding on bending lines, lateral suppleness, and alignment.

- **Possible tracks:** Circle 20 meters at C; Circle 20 meters at A; Circle 20 meters at B and E.

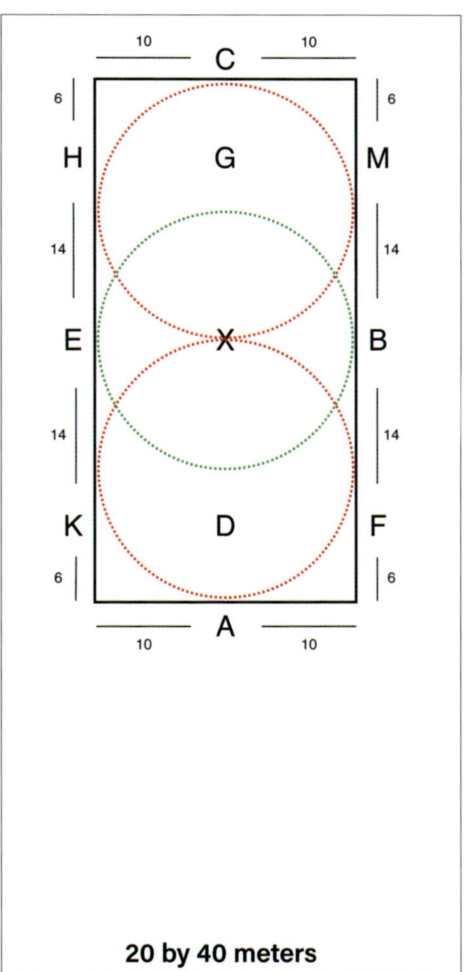

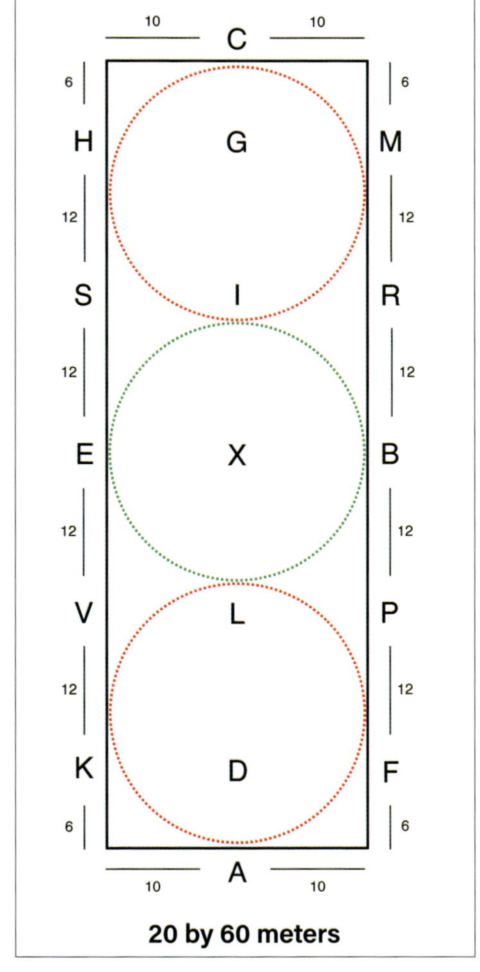

Note: The circle at B and E may also called a "a 20-meter circle in the center."

20-Meter Circles: "Open" and "Closed"

- **Purpose:** Terminology

- **Possible tracks:** Circle 20 meters at A; Circle 20 meters at C.

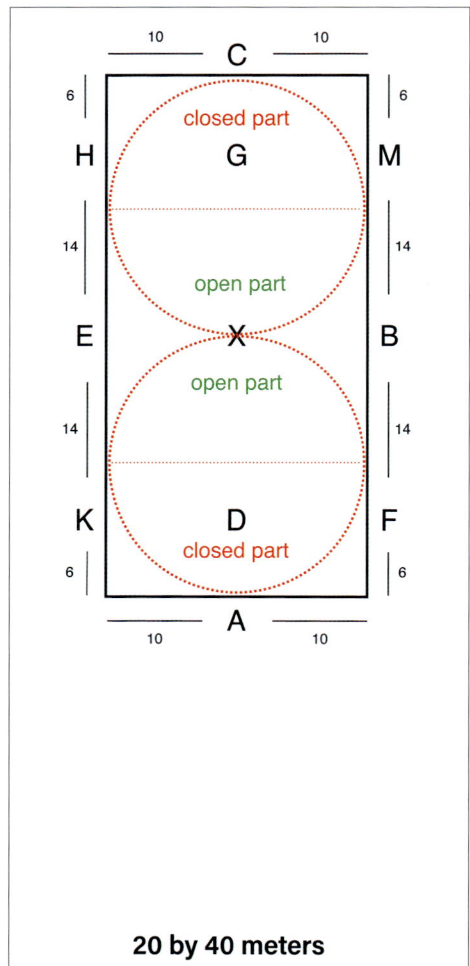

20 by 40 meters

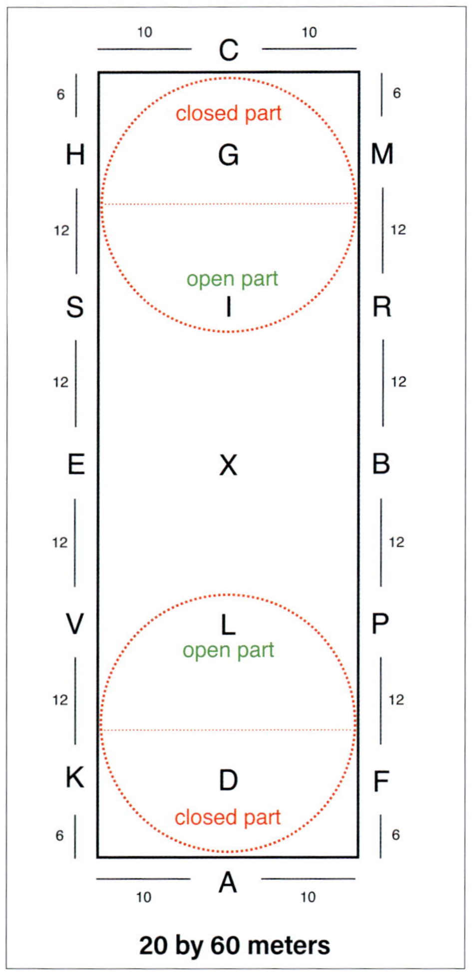

20 by 60 meters

Note: The "open" part of the circle opens to the rest of the arena. The "closed" part is toward the enclosed part of the arena.

Turning Points for Circles

- **Purpose:** To help with orientation and symmetry.

- **Possible tracks:** Examples are for 20-, 15-, and 10-meter circles.

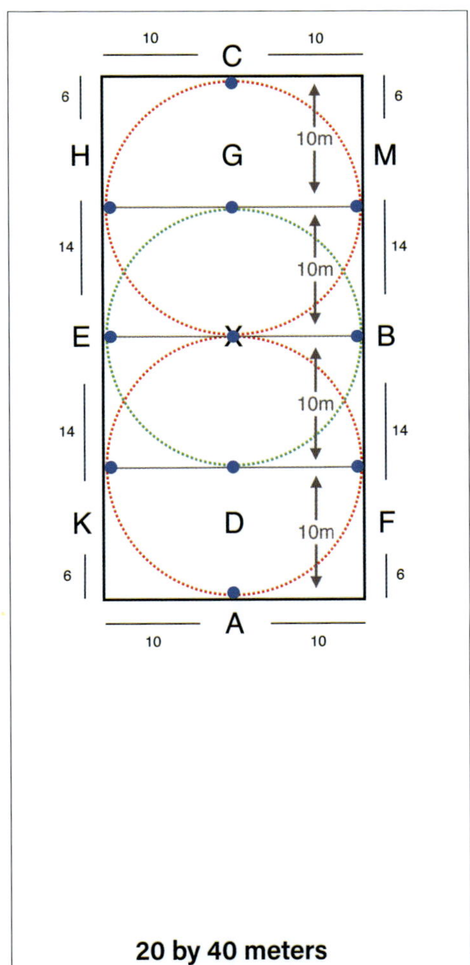

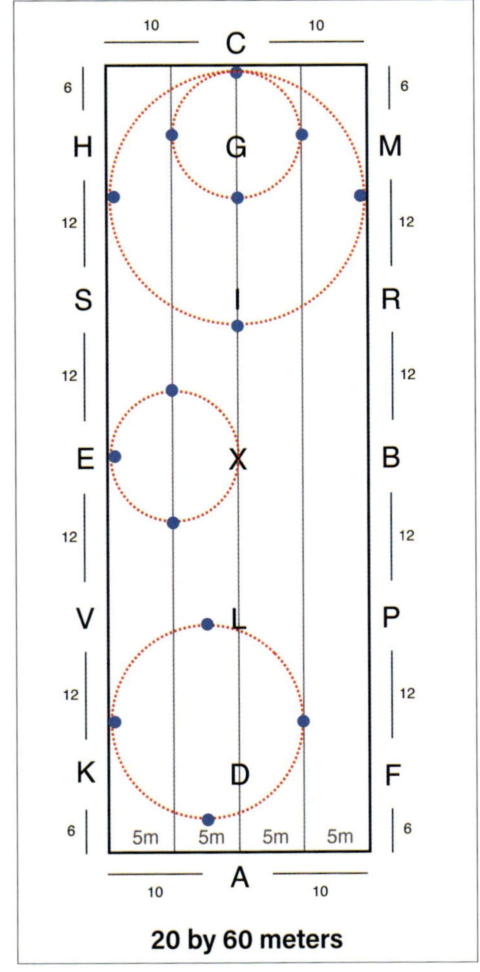

Note: Visual turning points are a great help in keeping circles round and accurate.

Changing Direction Across a Short Diagonal

- **Purpose:** Used to change direction.

- **Possible tracks:** K–B and E–M, M–E and B–K; F–E and B–H, H–B and E–F; P–S and S–P, V–R and R–V.

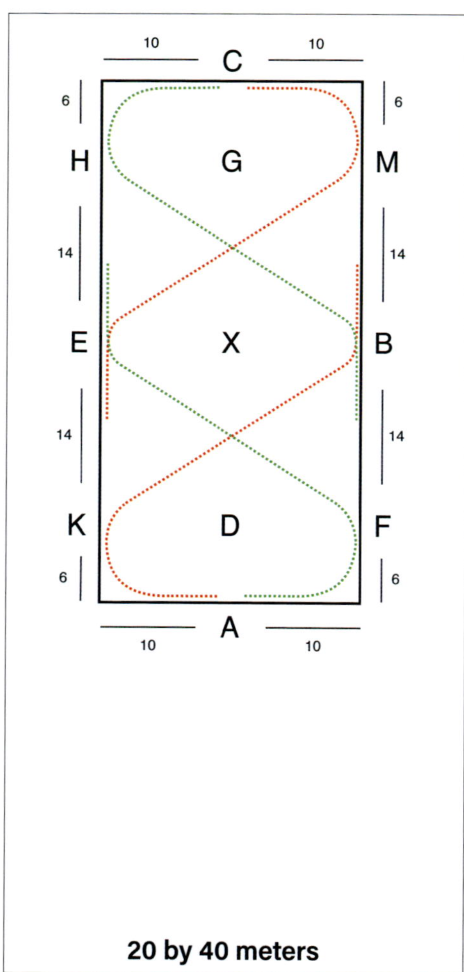

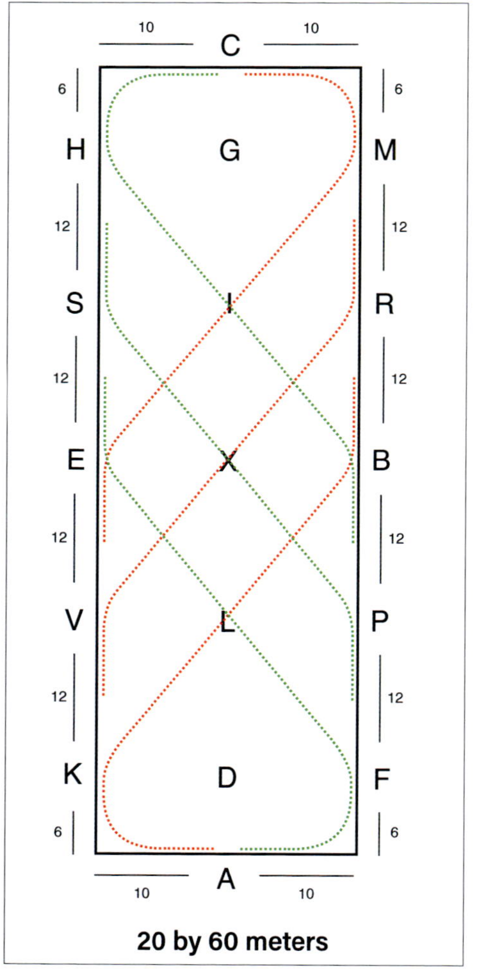

Note: There are many options for changing direction.

Changing Direction Out of the Circle

- **Purpose:** Changing direction while remaining on a 20-meter circle maintaining lateral suppleness and alignment.

- **Possible tracks:** Changing from one 20-meter circle to the next closest 20-meter circle.

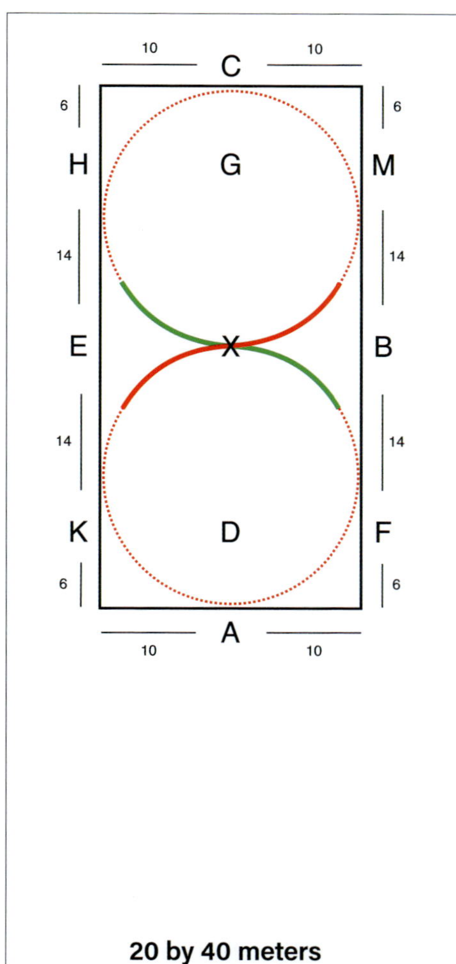

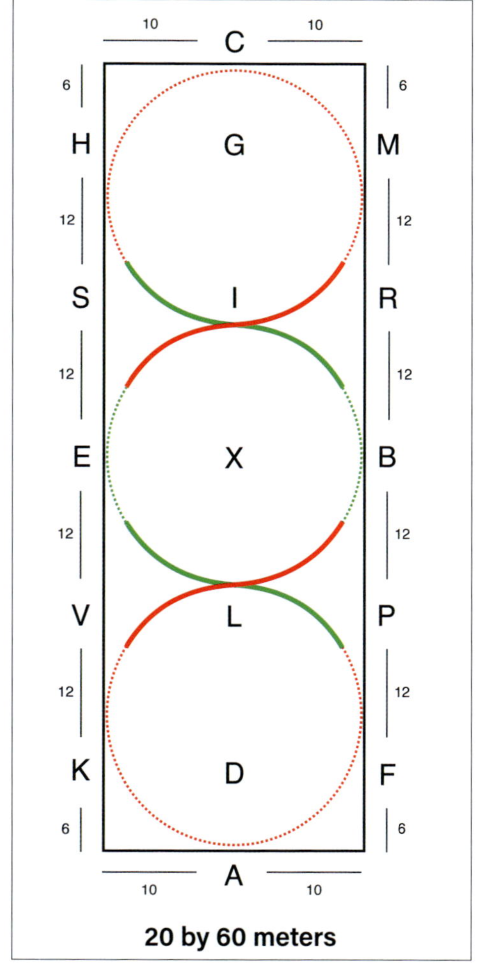

Note: Good control of suppleness and bend.

15-Meter Circles

- **Purpose:** Introducing smaller circles in which the horse has more bend.

- **Possible tracks:** Can be ridden anywhere in the arena.

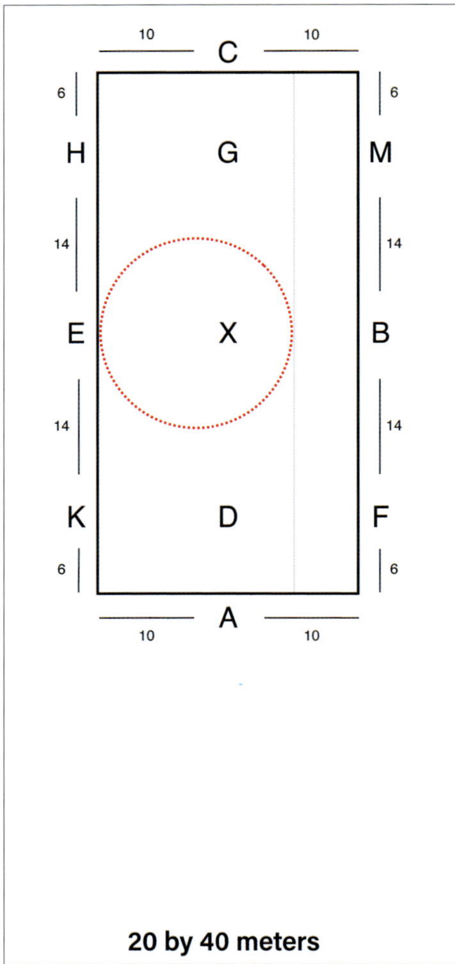

20 by 40 meters

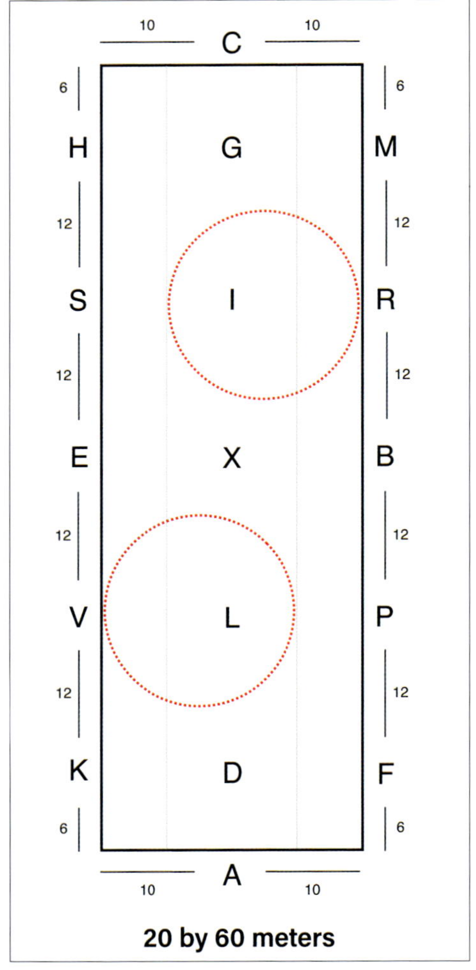

20 by 60 meters

Note: It is helpful to use the quarterline for orientation.

10-Meter Circles

- **Purpose:** Introducing smaller circles in which the horse has more bend.

- **Possible tracks:** Can be ridden anywhere in the arena.

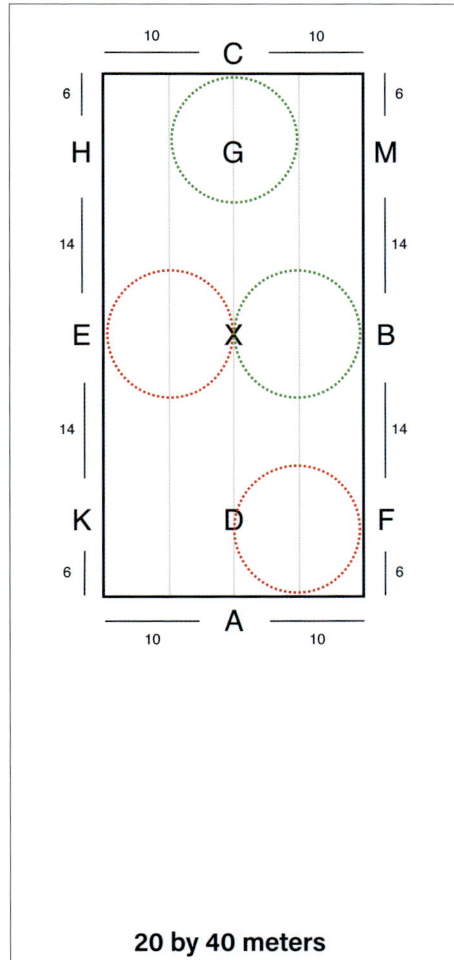

20 by 40 meters

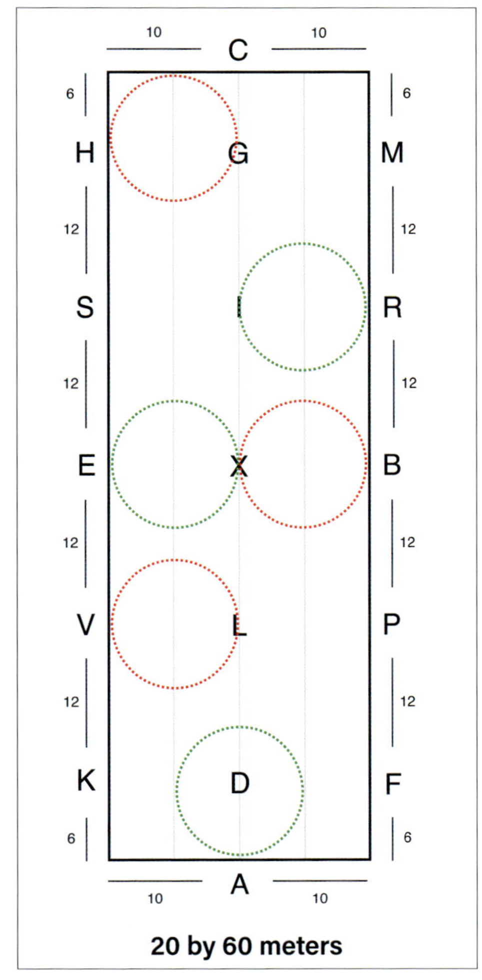

20 by 60 meters

Note: It is helpful to use the centerline or stay in between the quarterlines for orientation.

Single-Loop Serpentine

- **Purpose:** Suppling through the bending line and change of flexion to the turning side.

- **Possible tracks:** From left and right using the quarterline for orientation. If stated in instructions, it can be ridden into X.

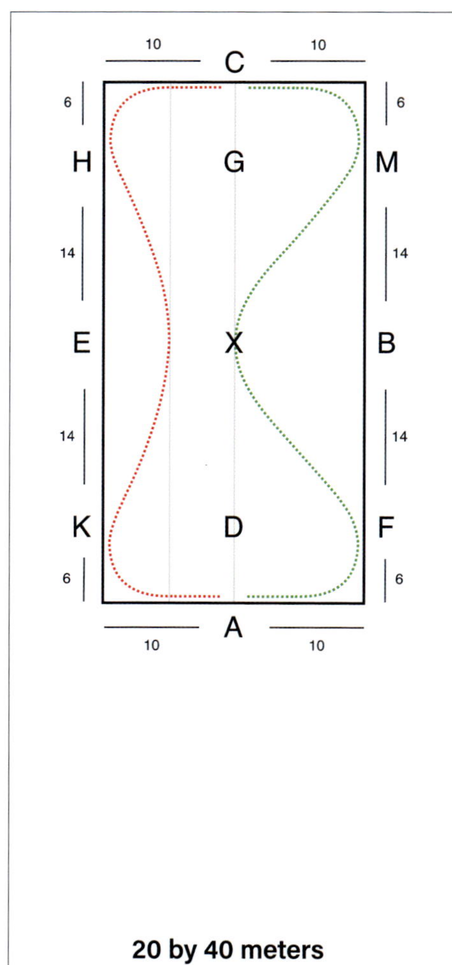

20 by 40 meters

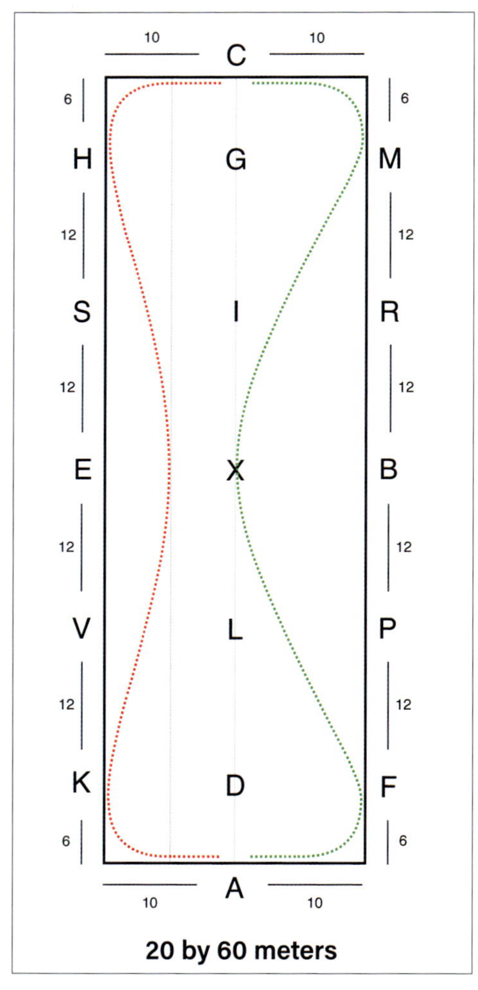

20 by 60 meters

Note: Often used to introduce the feel of counter-canter. When ridden in canter, flexion will (in general) remain to the canter side, which is different in walk and trot where the flexion changes to the turning side. In all United States Dressage Federation (USDF) tests, this track is ridden to X.

Change Direction Through the Circle

- **Purpose:** To change direction within the circle.

- **Possible tracks:** From left and right; from short and long sides.

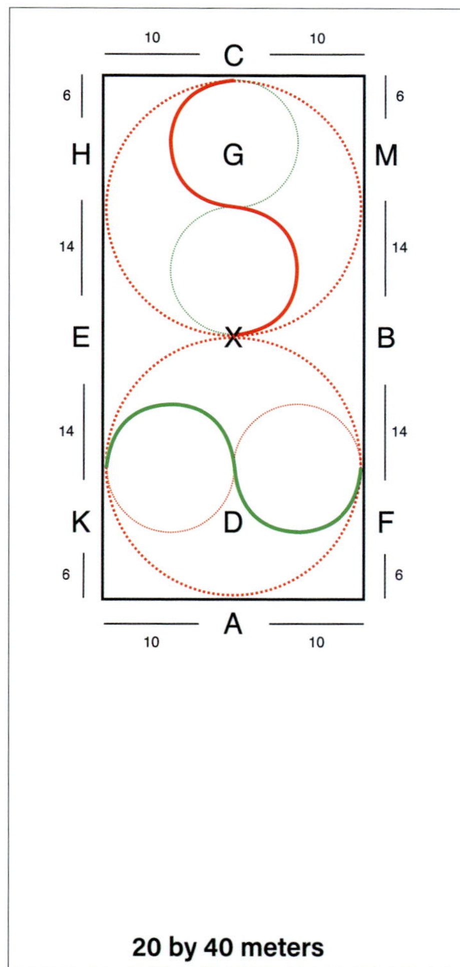

20 by 40 meters

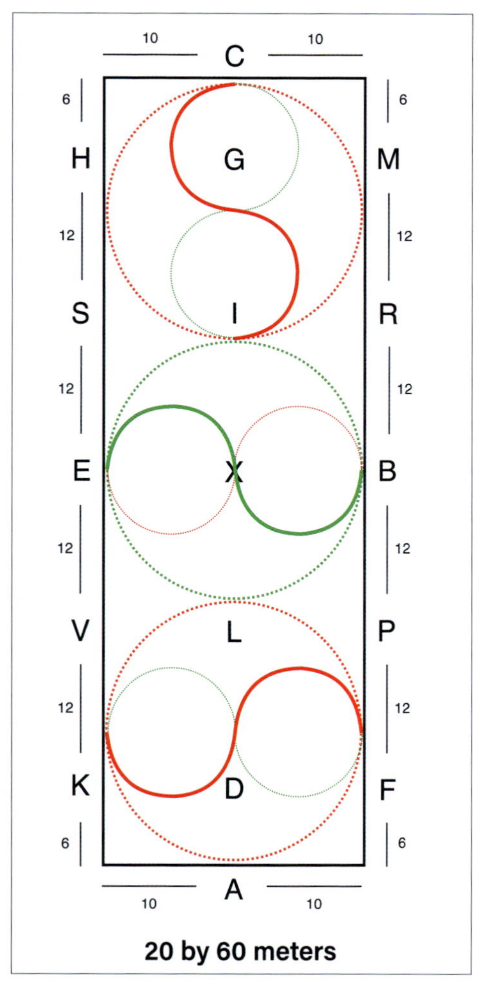

20 by 60 meters

Note: Think of the track as two, half 10-meter circles, using the circle's opposite turning points as start and finish.

Half-Circle Back

- **Purpose:** Used to change direction.

- **Possible tracks:** Usually ridden from middle to end of long sides.

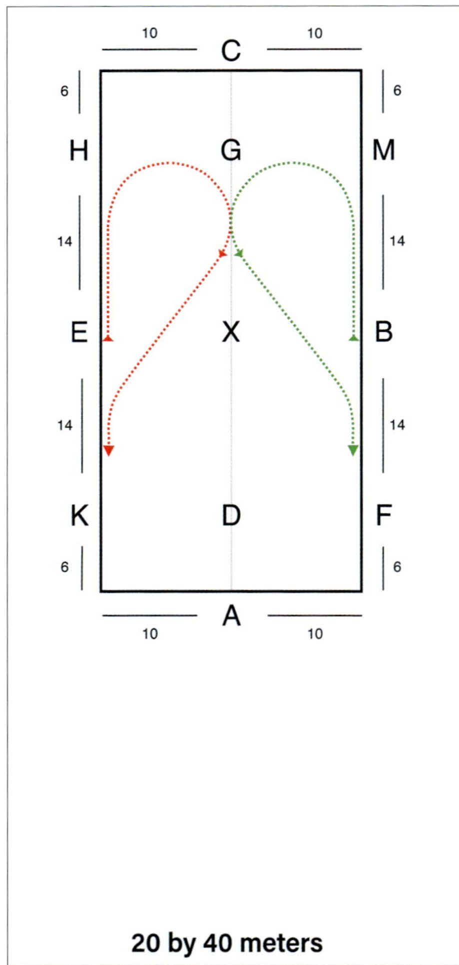

20 by 40 meters

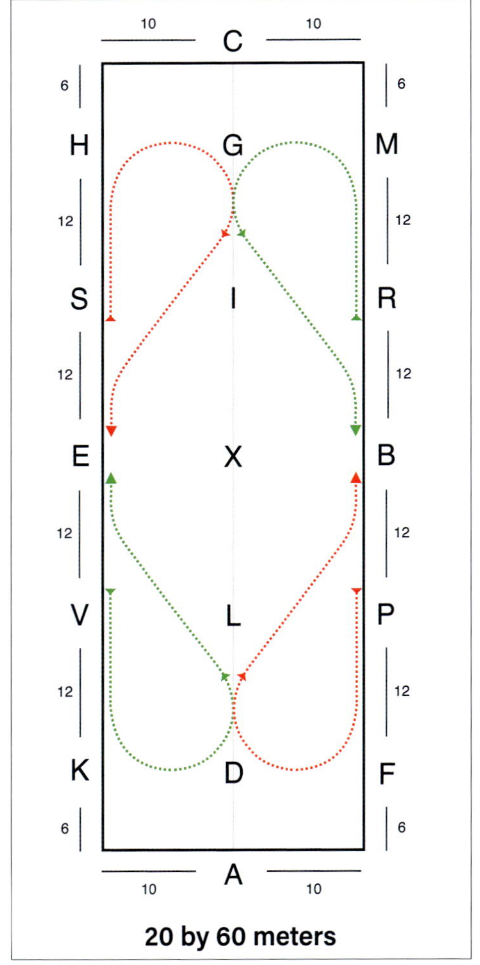

20 by 60 meters

Note: Riding the first part of the track as a half 10-meter circle with the associated turning points can be helpful.

Half-Circle Back in Reverse

- **Purpose:** Used to change direction.

- **Possible tracks:** Usually ridden from the middle to the end of long sides.

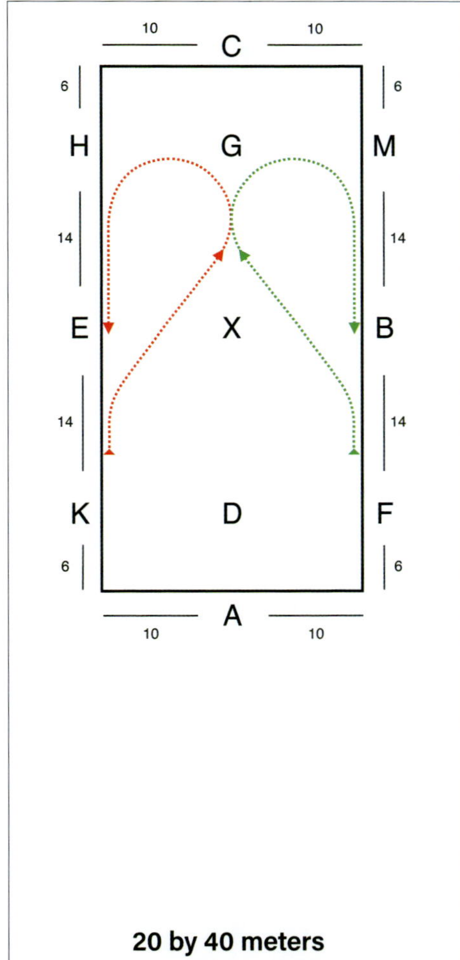

20 by 40 meters

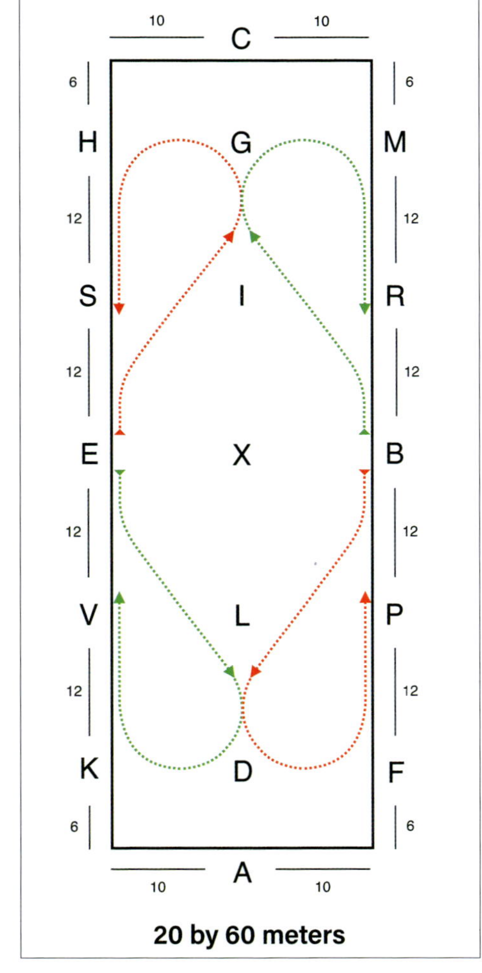

20 by 60 meters

Note: Not as commonly utilized as the *Half-Circle Back* (p. 20).

Three-Loop Serpentine

- **Purpose:** Trains turning, accuracy, and frequent change of bending flexion. It is an excellent suppling exercise.

- **Possible tracks:** Can be ridden from left or right. Serpentines with an even number of loops create a change of direction. Serpentines with an odd number of loops maintain the same direction.

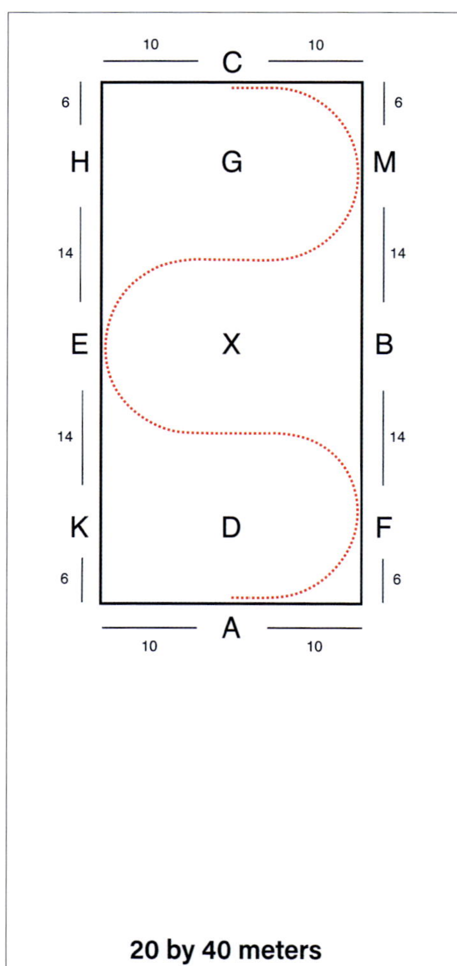

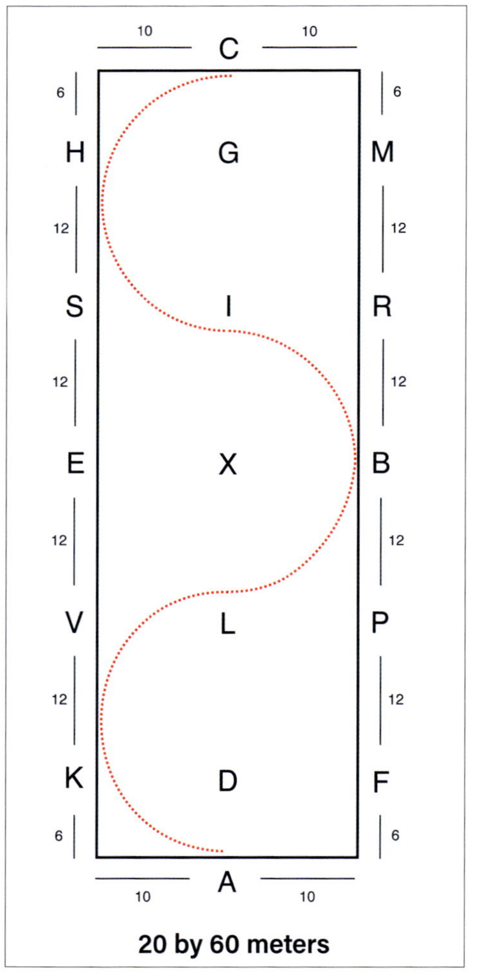

Note: Knowing where the rider wants to be after one-and-a-half loops (at E or B) helps to make the loops even. Count the number of loops while crossing the center-line. Corners are never ridden within the serpentine.

Four-Loop Serpentine

- **Purpose:** Trains turning, accuracy, and frequent change of bending flexion. It is an excellent suppling exercise.

- **Possible tracks:** Can be ridden from left or right. Serpentines with an even number of loops create a change of direction. Serpentines with an odd number of loops maintain the same direction.

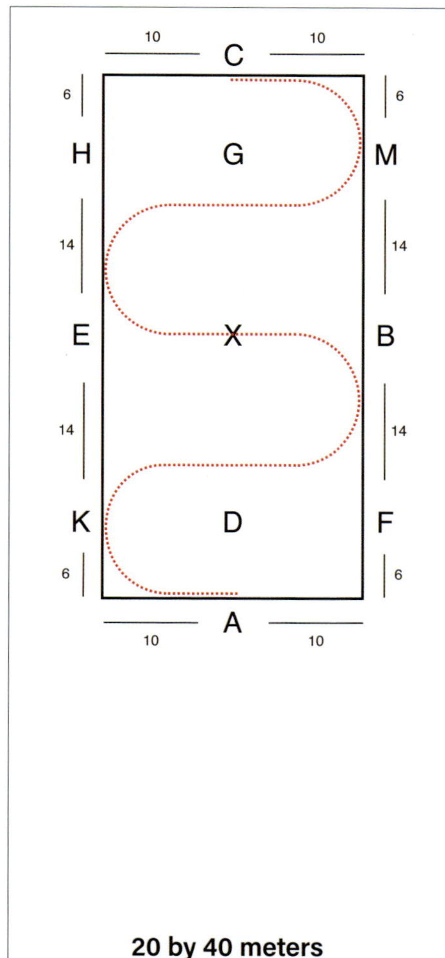

20 by 40 meters

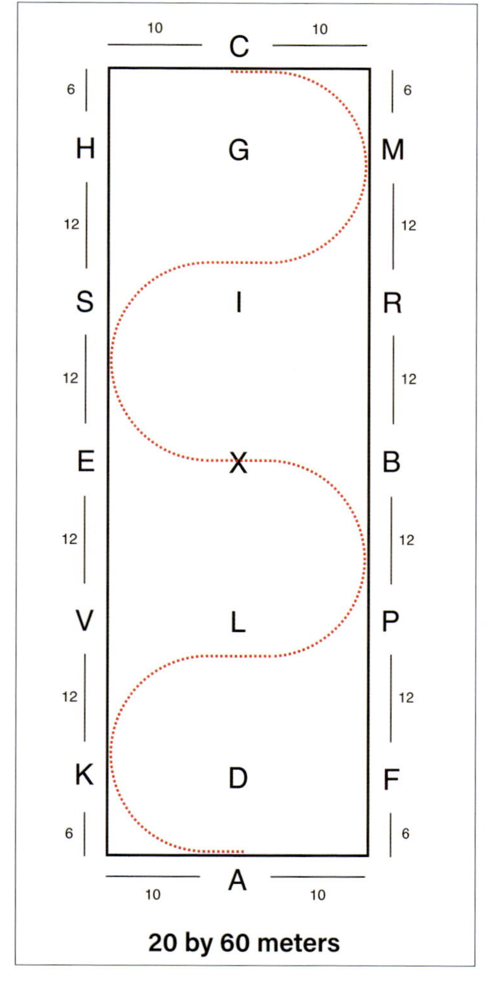

20 by 60 meters

Note: Knowing where the rider wants to be after two loops (at X) helps to make the loops even. Count the number of loops while crossing the centerline. Corners are never ridden within the serpentine.

Five-Loop Serpentine

- **Purpose:** Trains turning, accuracy, and frequent change of bending flexion. It is an excellent suppling exercise.

- **Possible tracks:** Can be ridden from left or right. Serpentines with an even number of loops create a change of direction. Serpentines with an odd number of loops maintain the same direction.

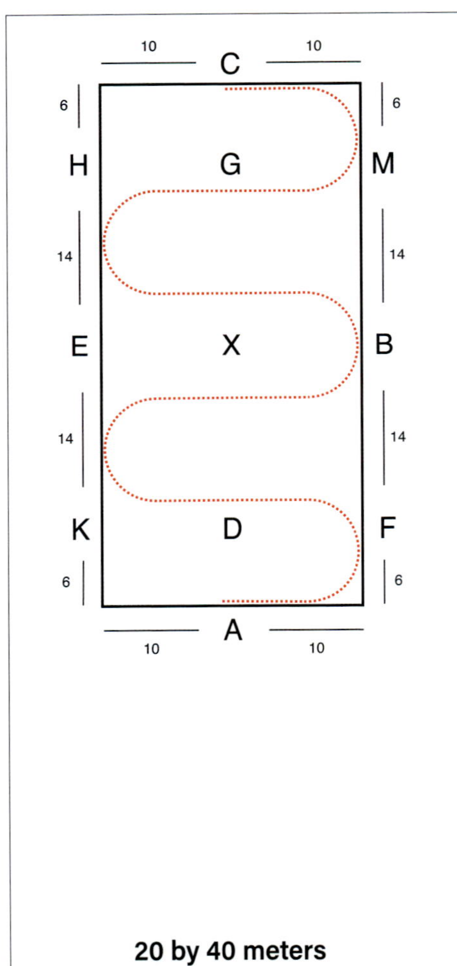

20 by 40 meters

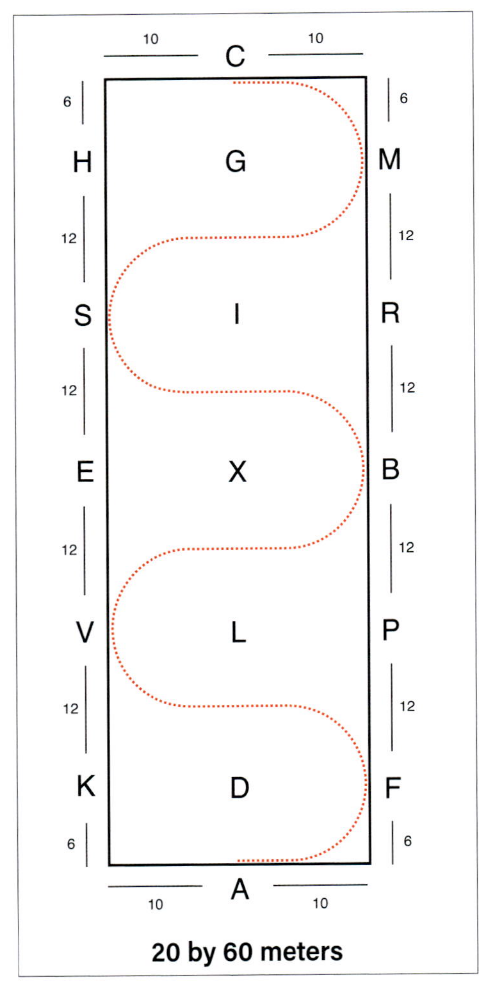

20 by 60 meters

Note: Knowing where the rider wants to be after two-and-a-half loops (at E or B) helps to make the loops even. Count the number of loops while crossing the center-line. Corners are never ridden within the serpentine.

Double-Loop Serpentine

- **Purpose:** Suppling through bending lines and changes of flexion to the turning side when ridden in walk and trot.

- **Possible tracks:** From left and right, using half the distance to the quarterline for orientation (2.5 meters inside the track).

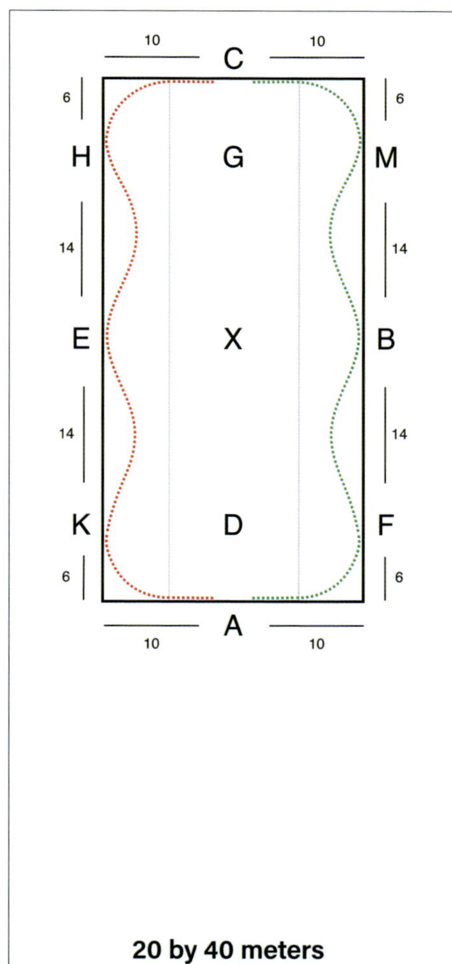

20 by 40 meters

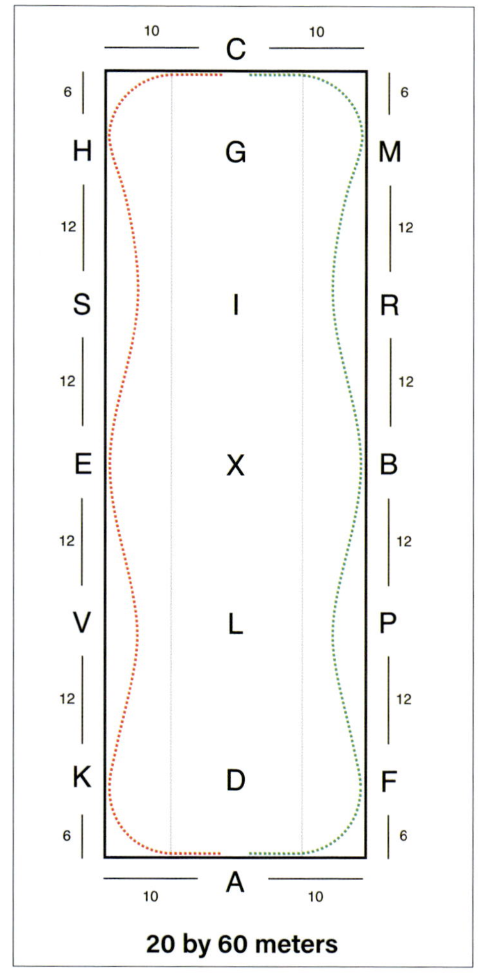

20 by 60 meters

Note: If the track is ridden in canter, the flexion will (in general) remain to the canter side.

Spiral In and Spiral Out

- **Purpose:** Increasing lateral suppleness, engagement, and balance.

- **Possible tracks:** Circle 20 meters at C; Circle 20 meters at A; Circle 20 meters at B and E.

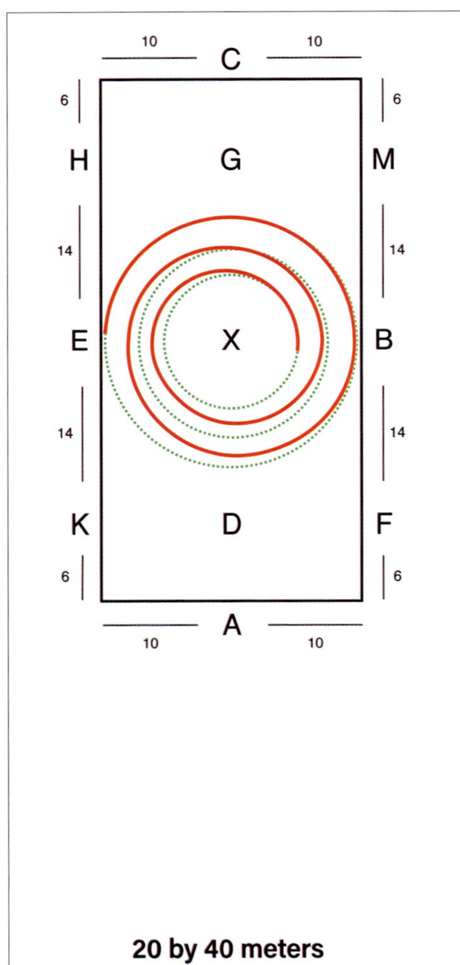

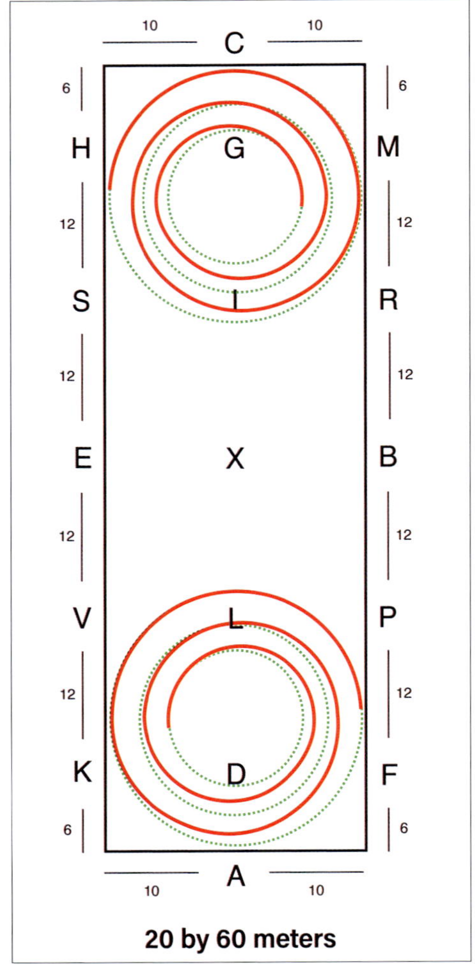

Note: A gradual change in diameter will help maintain harmony. *Spiral In and Out* can also be ridden in differing diameter circles and at different locations in the arena.

PART TWO

GROUND POLE, CAVALLETTI, AND JUMPING EXERCISES

In the present day there is no shortage of information—in fact, in a split second you can find answers on the internet at any time. Access to information is a wonderful thing, *but* it can lead to problems when techniques found through a random search are implemented without already having a solid foundation of knowledge.

The right thing done at the wrong time is, unfortunately, still wrong. The solution to this paradox is *structure*. Having a structure simply helps the riding student know in which order to place the pieces of the puzzle and understand which pieces serve as the foundation for others to be built upon. If a rider is familiar with the important pieces that form the foundation of training the horse (like the tracks used in a dressage arena) it is easy for that rider to implement the knowledge of how to ride these tracks while also training with ground poles, cavalletti, and jumps. In most pole or jumping exercises, you will recognize dressage tracks, or at least a variation thereof.

When the horse and rider are having problems with a certain dressage track, adding a jump to the situation will most likely make it more difficult, and the chances of successfully ending the training session are drastically lowered. Therefore, using the dressage tracks as building blocks while progressing from basic to advanced tracks will likely make the journey for horse and rider more harmonious and effortless.

The structure is a stable part of the training, but the speed in which horse and rider progress can greatly vary, depending on goals, time invested, health, and ability. The reference points that a good structure provides can also be very helpful if horse and rider end up in an overwhelming situation. When a challenge proves too great, the rider can analyze the situation and go back to a previous step in the education before any confidence or trust is lost.

The pole and jumping exercises that are included in this book are divided into sections:

- ***A Formula for Success*** covers the core exercises, which don't offer a huge variety in format but do follow a very direct path to educating horse and rider. These exercises can be used as the backbone of the education and may always be revisited.

- Exercises categorized for ***Suppleness, Rhythm,*** or ***Control*** can be used for variety in training and education but can also be tailored to suit a specific purpose in training—potentially solving a problem discovered while riding another exercise or course.

- ***Grids and Combinations*** can be used as gymnastics, seat exercises, and as an introduction to jumping combinations in courses. These exercises take a lot of thought and understanding to build well as even minor errors in the placement of the obstacles can have a substantial impact on how they will ride. This is mainly due to quickly successive obstacles with fewer strides between for adjustment of stride length, as compared to related distances where the measurement between obstacles is longer.

- ***Courses*** not only highlight how different dressage tracks often can occur in show-jumping courses, but are also included to spark interest and inspiration for riders and trainers to design courses and exercises that support good horsemanship and develop understanding for correct and ethical training. Correct training means the ability to recognize what horse and rider are capable of doing at this point in time and *never* asking the horse to perform in a way that he can't, or that goes against his nature.

Specific terminology is important for both theoretical understanding and for practical communication with students when working with poles, cavalletti, and jumps.

Ground Pole

Single or multiple poles can be used to prepare horse and rider for jumping. They can be utilized in gymnastic exercises, also as a ground line in front of the obstacle.

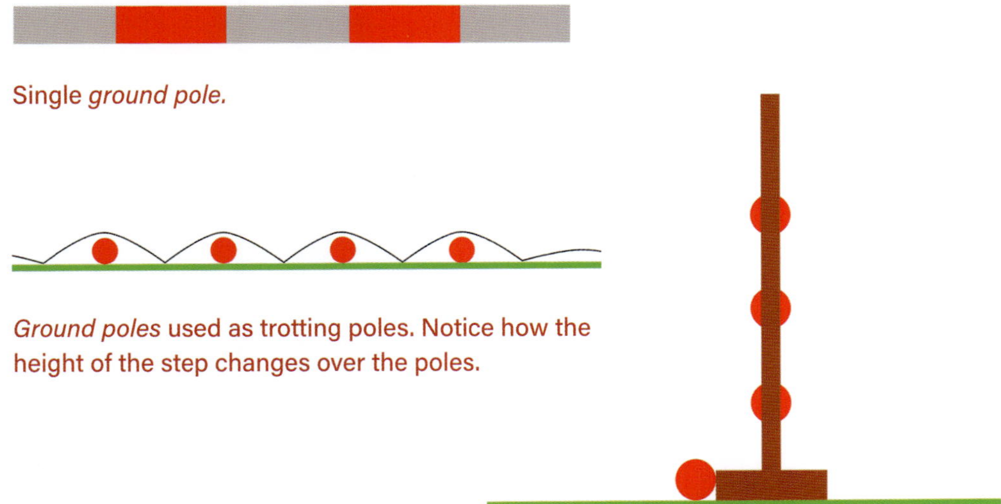

Single *ground pole.*

Ground poles used as trotting poles. Notice how the height of the step changes over the poles.

Vertical with *ground pole* on the takeoff side.

Cavalletti

Typically, a pole raised slightly above the ground—single or multiple cavalletti can be used for gymnastic, balance, and control exercises, also in preparation for jumping.

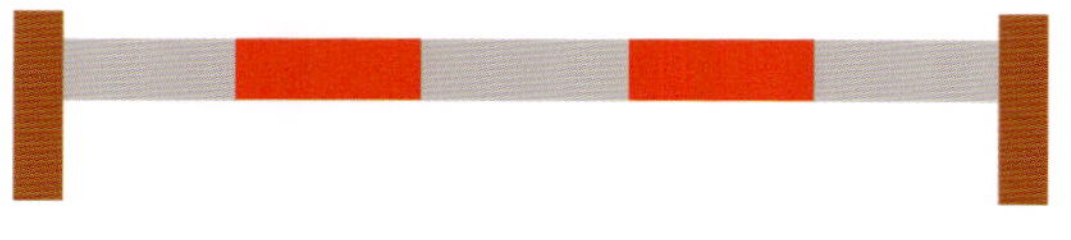

A single *cavalletti.*

Traditional *cavalletti* are often set to different heights. Rotating the *cavalletti* changes the obstacle to three different height settings.

Cavalletti set as bounces. The horse jumps in and immediately takes off for the next. *Note:* The bounces are often incorporated into gymnastic grids for the horse and can be built with a variety of obstacle types.

Cross-Rail (Cross-Pole)

A useful obstacle type that encourages horse and rider to jump in the center. The cross-rail should be used with caution for very young or inexperienced horses due to the horse's visual perception (he sees the higher sides of the cross-rail while jumping, and this interpretation of height can lead to the horse jumping too high and becoming insecure).

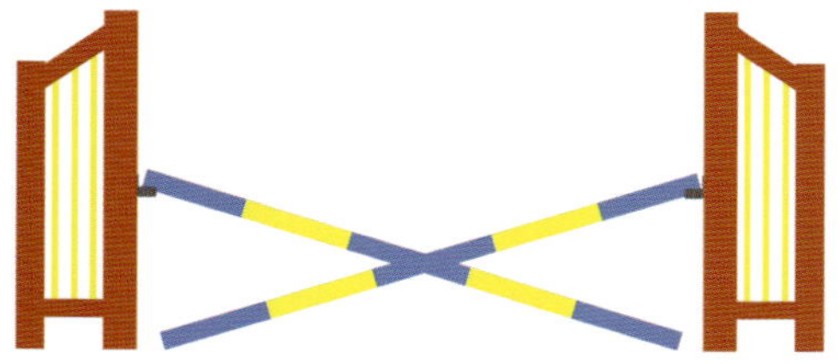

A *cross-rail* with wing standards.

Vertical

An obstacle commonly seen with fillers such as poles, planks, gates, flowers, placed underneath the top element.

A *vertical* with a plank as the bottom element.
Note: The plank is placed on flat cups.

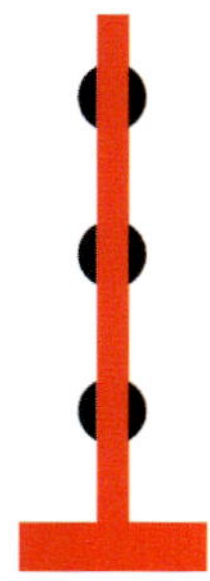

A *vertical's* side view.

Oxer

A spread obstacle that requires the horse to jump up and forward. It is often seen with fillers similar to the vertical under the front element. The oxer can be built square or ramped. When ramped, the horse can see the back pole more easily, making it suitable for young or inexperienced horses, but it is also frequently used when training specifics of the horse's jumping technique.

Note: During competition the back pole will, in general, be placed in safety cups; these cups allow the pole to fall straight down to avoid injuries and falls. If available, these safety cups are very beneficial for training as well.

A *ramped oxer. Note:* The back pole is slightly higher than the front pole.

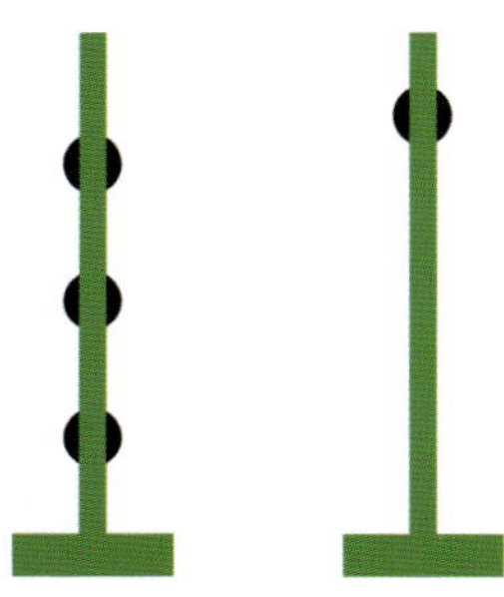

A *ramped oxer's* side view.

A *square oxer. Note:* The front and back pole are the same height.

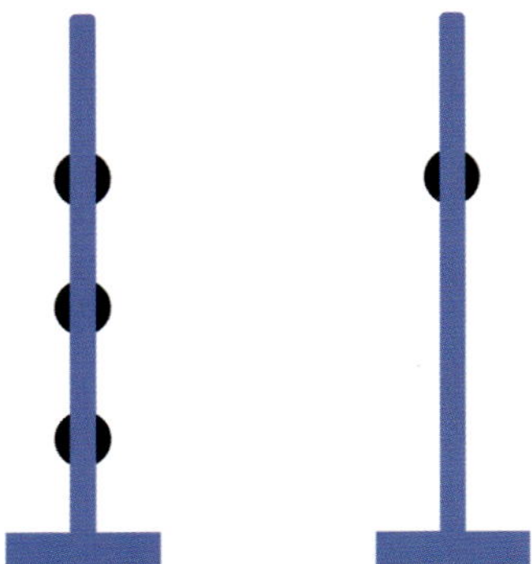

A *square oxer's* side view. *Note:* The true square oxer has the same spread as height.

Triple Bar

This is a spread obstacle consisting of three elements; it generally has a greater spread than the obstacle height. Usually, the front pole is about half the height of the back pole, which creates a slow rising curve over the obstacle. As long as the takeoff spot is suitable to the *triple bar*, it is not a technically difficult obstacle for the horse to jump. During competition the back and middle poles are placed in safety cups that allow the pole to fall straight down for avoiding injuries and falls.

A *triple bar. Note:* The front pole is about half the height of the back pole.

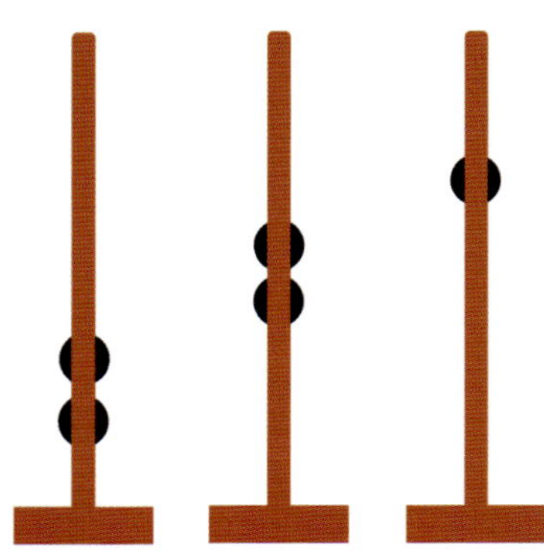

A triple bar's side view. *Note:* The spread is greater than the height.

Liverpool

A *Liverpool* is a water-tray obstacle intended to imitate water. Usually constructed of a resilient vinyl material and edges filled with soft foam, it comes in various sizes and is generally placed under *verticals* and *oxers*.

A *Liverpool* placed under a *vertical* filled with planks.

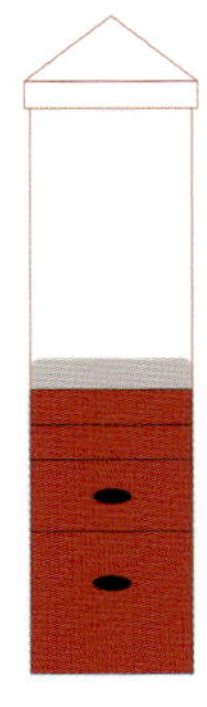

A *Liverpool* placed under the center of the *vertical.* Placement of the *Liverpool* can vary, impacting the difficulty of the obstacle.

Wall

A *wall* is a very solid obstacle. It is often made to look like stone or brick and can be jumped by itself or used as a filler for *verticals* and *oxers* during training and in competition. Traditionally the *brick wall* is always used in *Puissance* classes.

A solid wall made to look like bricks, traditionally built out of different-sized wooden boxes.

Wall from the side. *Note:* The wooden boxes are larger toward the bottom with smaller pieces toward the top, the top pieces having rounded edges.

Water Jump

The *water jump* is typically dug into the ground and filled with water. A smaller takeoff element is generally placed on the takeoff side.

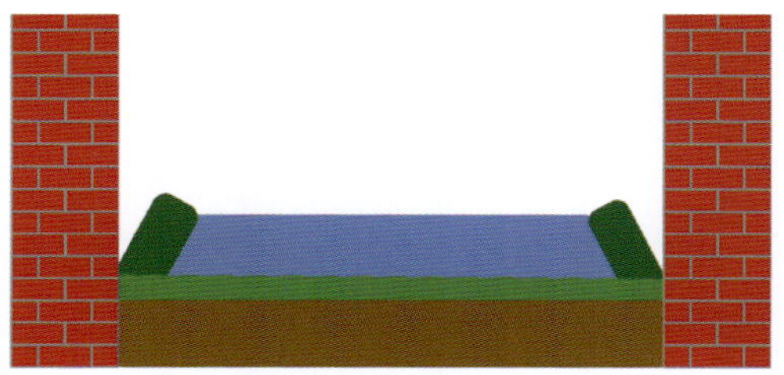

A *water jump* with takeoff element and framed in with wall standards and plants on the sides.

A *water jump* from the side with the takeoff element in front.

Combination

The *combination* is a group of typically two or three obstacles, called a *double* or *triple combination.* The distance in between the obstacles is set for one or two strides. In competition, there are regulations on minimum and maximum distance in between the obstacles.

Double combination with one stride between *oxer* and *vertical.*

Double combination, oxer to vertical.

Related Distance

A *related distance* means that an obstacle is affected by how the horse lands after the previous obstacle. If the related distance is measured to a certain number of strides in a regular rhythm and the horse lands in a regular stride after a normal takeoff, no change to the stride length should be needed. The landing spot is the result of the takeoff: a short takeoff leads to a short landing spot and a long take-off leads to a long landing spot.

Other common factors that have a large influence over how the related distance will ride are footing, whether terrain is uphill or downhill, the type of obstacle, stride length of the horse, speed, track, and rhythm.

In general, the fewer strides there are in between the obstacles, the less time there is for reaction—when the horse lands short after the obstacle leading in to a seven-stride related distance, he has seven strides available for adjustments. The same situation in a three-stride related distance means there are only three strides available for adjusting stride length.

This *vertical* illustrates how the takeoff affects the landing. The black line illustrates a normal takeoff and landing. The red line illustrates how a short takeoff leads to a shorter landing. The blue line illustrates how a long takeoff leads to a long landing.

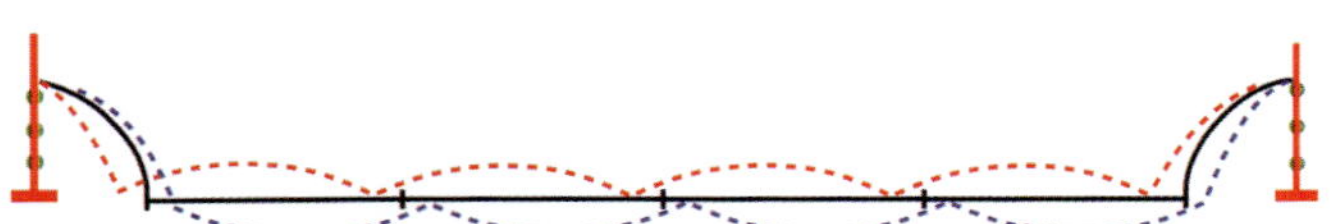

A *related distance* set to be ridden in four even strides. The black line illustrates how a normal landing leads to four normal strides, and a normal takeoff spot. The red line illustrates how a short landing makes for a long takeoff spot at the second obstacle. The blue line illustrates how a long landing makes for a short takeoff spot.

Direction of Jump

An obstacle without a ground line, or with a ground line that is centered under the obstacle, can be jumped from both directions. When the ground line is placed more toward one side, the obstacle should only be jumped from the side where the ground line is; otherwise, it is considered a *false ground line*.

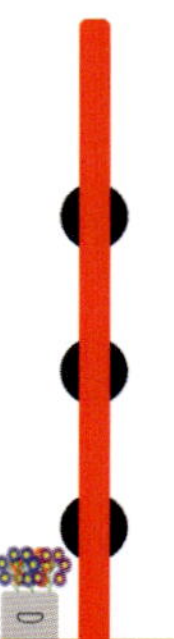

A *vertical* with a flower box as a ground line.
Note: It should only be jumped from the side where flower box is placed.

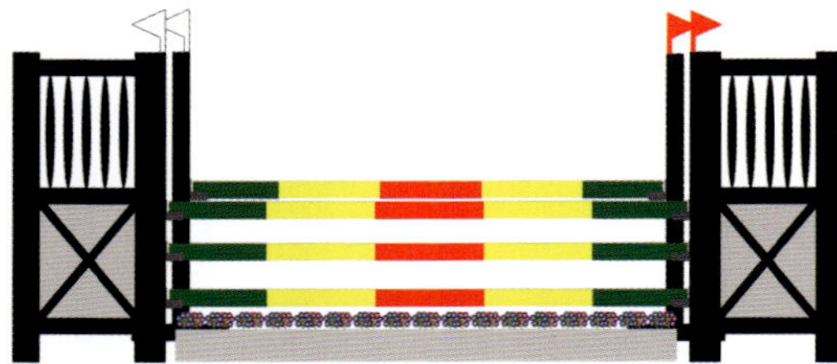

An *oxer* with a flower box used as filler and ground line. Notice the flags on top of the standards indicating in which direction the obstacle should be jumped. The flags used in most competition formats have red flags on the right and white flags on the left.

Rhythm

Rhythm as referred to in jumping is the regularity of the strides in between the obstacles. A rhythm that is drastically changing between the obstacles makes it more difficult for the horse to mentally and physically relax, and perform his best.

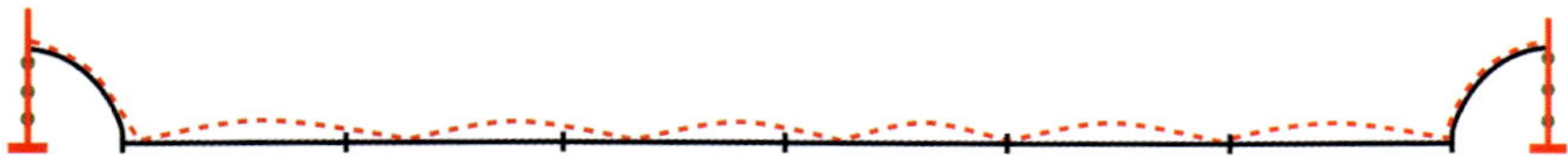

A *related distance* with six strides in between. The black line illustrates six regular strides in a steady rhythm. The red line illustrates a horse jumping in fast with a long stride, then shortened too much, which leads to the rider having to lengthen the stride again. Both scenarios are counting six strides: black with ideal rhythm, and red with poor rhythm.

Track

The *track* in jumping is the continual line from approach to the first obstacle to landing from the last obstacle within the course or exercise. The track should follow harmonious lines to support a free, forward-moving gait. Each individual obstacle has an approach line that leads to the center of the obstacle in a 90-degree angle. When horse and rider can follow the ideal track, it is easier to modify it to a shorter track and even allow for jumping out of different angles (as is frequently done when riding against the clock).

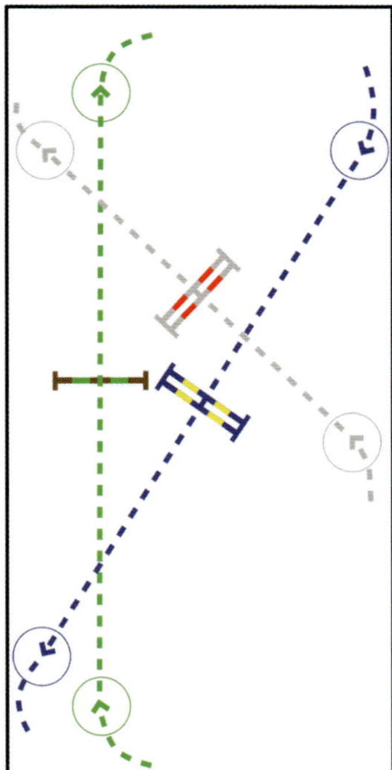

Approach lines marked at a 90-degree angle from the center of the obstacle. See how the lines also continue straight afterward and how they closely relate to dressage tracks.

Common situations that make jumping more challenging. The green line approach illustrates an early turn where the horse gets straight very late in front of the obstacle. The blue line shows a turn that is late. Because of this late turn, the horse has to turn twice to get on to the straight approach line (this situation often causes a wiggling approach). The gray line illustrates a late turn as well but the horse is kept straight, which results in him jumping the obstacle too far to the right.

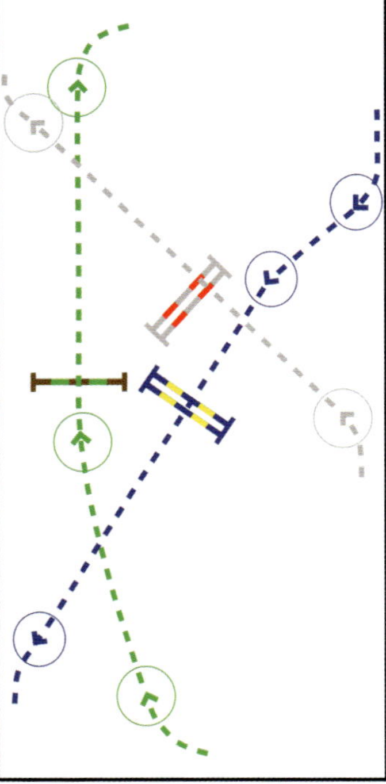

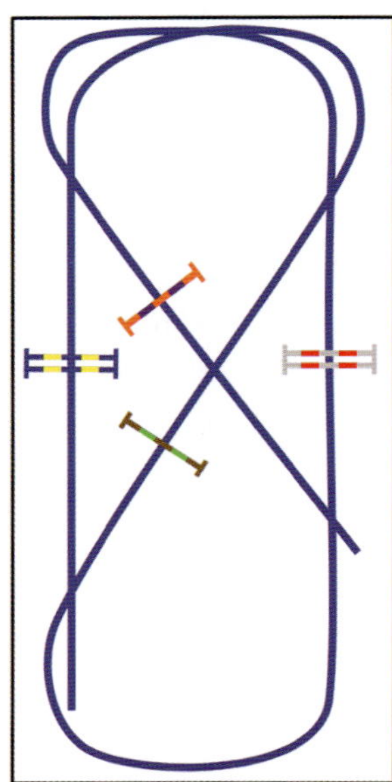

An example of a *basic track* with obstacles placed on it. The track plays a major role in the level of difficulty of the exercises or courses.

Variation of Distances in Combinations and Related Distances

Because of the many different variables, setting suitable distances between obstacles is a very complex topic. There are many factors and combinations of factors that determine how a distance will ride. Although determining which measured distance to use is based on math, the end result is always associated with a lot of experience and feeling for any given situation.

VARIATION EXAMPLES IN DISTANCES FOR HORSES
Normal training distances in meters

Number of strides	Small arena 20 x 40 m Pure sand footing Cross pole obstacles	Large arena 40 x 80 m Pure sand footing Verticals 50-90cm	Large arena 40 x 80 m Modern fiber & sand footing Verticals 90-120cm
1	6.50	7.00	7.50
2	10.00	10.50	11.00
3	13.00	14.00	14.50
4	16.50	17.50	18.00
5	20.00	21.00	21.50
6	(23.50)	24.50	25.00
7	(27.00)	28.00	29.50

FACTORS AFFECTING THE DISTANCE

Makes the distance feel long	Makes the distance feel short
· deep and slippery footing · away from the in-gate · bending lines · ground sloping uphill · small arena or out of turn slow speed · oxer obstacle, -25 cm per oxer in a line · triple bar, -50 cm per triple bar in a line · for ponies and shorter-strided horses	· grippy and springy footing · toward the in-gate · ground sloping downhill · after big spread obstacles requiring higher speed · large arena · higher speed · between B & C in a treble combination · long-strided horses · related distance following the last obstacle in a combination

The purpose of this chart is to bring awareness to the fact that there are a variety of distances that will work for the same number of strides and that depending on the circumstances, the measured distance can vary.

Dressage Tracks and Different Levels of Difficulty for Jumping

Different tracks create different sets of circumstances and challenges while working with ground poles or obstacles (from most basic level, to intermediate level, to most advanced level). Speed is also a factor that changes the difficulty level of a track. The difficulty levels illustrated here are based on the horse being ridden in a dressage arena 20 by 40 meters, and they assume that the is horse moving in trot or canter since these are the gaits mainly used for jumping. A course designed for competition or training is often a combination of different dressage tracks or variations, thereof.

    Note: The arena size is a key factor in determining the difficulty level of a track.

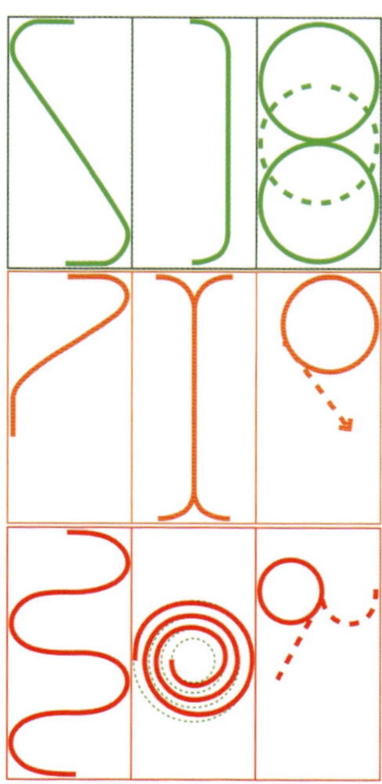

These tracks illustrate the general difficulty level with a *basic track* shown in green, *intermediate* shown in orange, and *advanced* shown in red. The level of difficulty should be suitable to the skills of the rider as well as the level of education and strength of the horse.

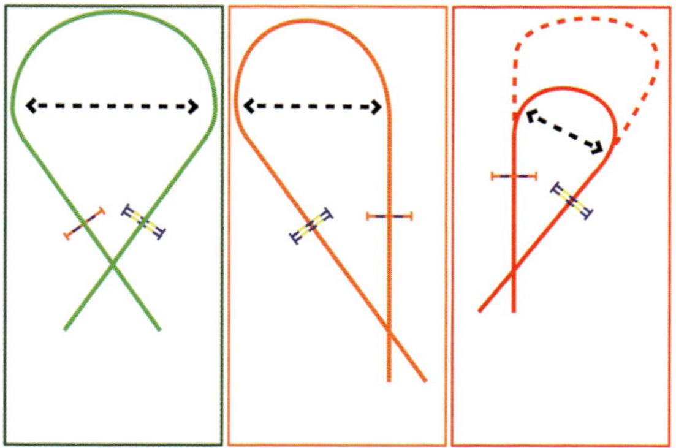

The green track illustrates a *basic level track* with a diameter of about 20 meters. The orange track is *intermediate* level due to the diameter of the turn being roughly 15 meters. The red track is the most advanced of the illustrated examples with a diameter of roughly 10 meters, and will most likely be seen in competitions against the clock or in similar situations.

The illustrated arena size for the Pole Exercises is 30 by 50 meters. The exercises and courses with a green track indicate basic level exercises; orange tracks indicate intermediate level; red tracks indicate advanced level. Pole exercises can be used for horse and rider in preparation for jumping as well as for variation in any training plan.

A Formula for Success—Poles

These are core exercises that are meant to help horse and rider through a structured development. This basic knowledge helps both rider and trainer know which step to take next when sufficient skills are achieved, but also which previous step to go back to when difficulties are experienced.

The Beginning

Single pole and trot poles on a straight line, the single pole is the most basic exercise in the education toward jumping and is generally approached at the walk and trot during the beginning phase. The trot poles are the next step following the single pole, wherein the rider will feel the horse taking higher steps with more suspension. The trot poles should ideally be set to a regular length of step. For most horses this will be 1.2 to 1.4 meters, but the rider and trainer should be open to changing the distance to accommodate different types of horses and give the best possible experience for each.

▪ **Purpose:** The rider learns about steering to poles on the ground, gains an understanding about the approach line to an obstacle, and practices balance in regards to the rider position—including how and when to transition to half-seat and incorporate a long release (the rider slides the hands about halfway up the horse's crest, allowing the horse freedom to use his body over the pole or jump). The horse learns to step over poles on the ground with the goal being to maintain relaxation and a steady rhythm throughout.

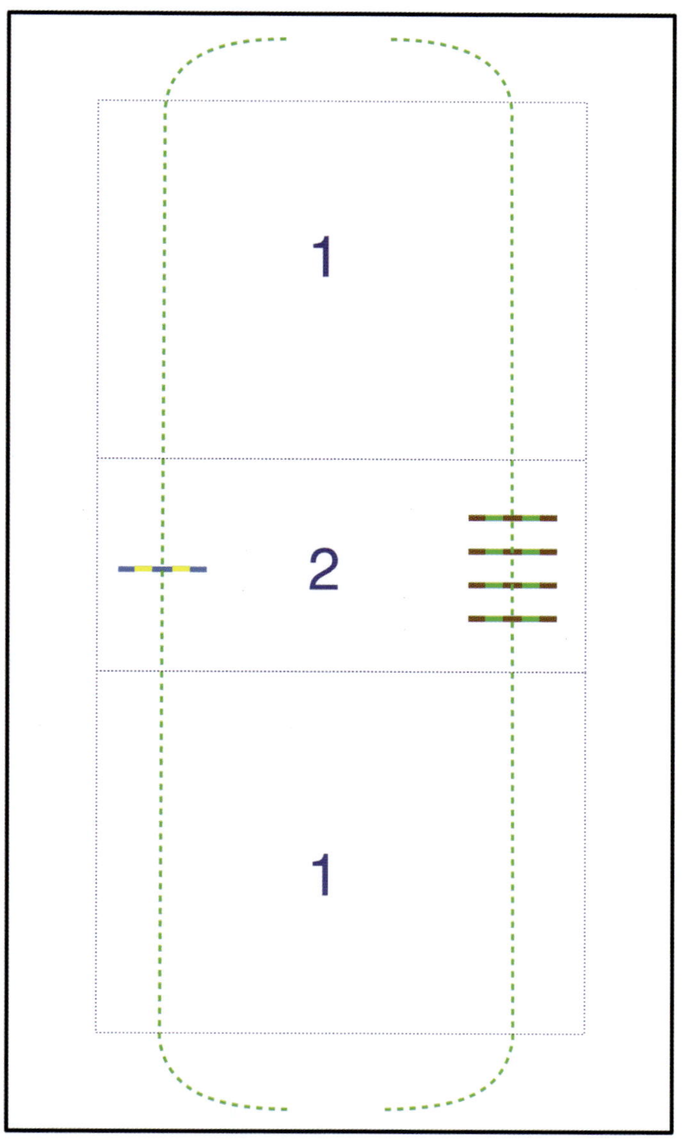

Single pole and trot poles. In Zone 1, the rider is in half-seat; in Zone 2 the rider gives a long release with a grab in the mane, and after the long release, the rider remains in half-seat to ensure correct balance with soft hands through Zone 1. Upon exiting Zone 1 after the pole exercise, the rider changes back to another position, either rising or sitting trot for the upcoming long side.

Note: The exercises can be ridden in both directions, but for the most basic level, should not be ridden consecutively—this provides the rider with time to analyze and adjust rhythm and positioning in the saddle as necessary.

Symmetry and Rhythm

A single pole on a circle in trot and canter to school rhythm and symmetry of the track. The circle is a valuable tool since the pole reoccurs on every round ridden and allows for quick improvements. Poor symmetry of the circle makes it more challenging to maintain a steady rhythm, therefore, the quality of the exercise stems from the understanding of the tracks and rhythm ridden in dressage. Being able to relate to the turning points while riding circles of different sizes is a great help in understanding and maintaining symmetry (to review turning points, see p. 13).

▪ **Purpose:** The rider learns about the importance of the track and rhythm over a single pole, together with the importance of how weight aids and rein aids should communicate the same instruction to the horse. A frequently occurring problem is when the rein aid tells the horse to turn as the weight aids (unintentionally) tell the horse *not* to turn. When this happens, communication with the horse becomes only about which aid is stronger and overriding the other. In this situation, the horse must choose which of the rider's aids to follow, but in the long term many horses will start to ignore the rider's weight aids altogether. In this basic level exercise, the horse is learning to go over a pole on the circle in a relaxed manner without any unintentional changes in speed and rhythm.

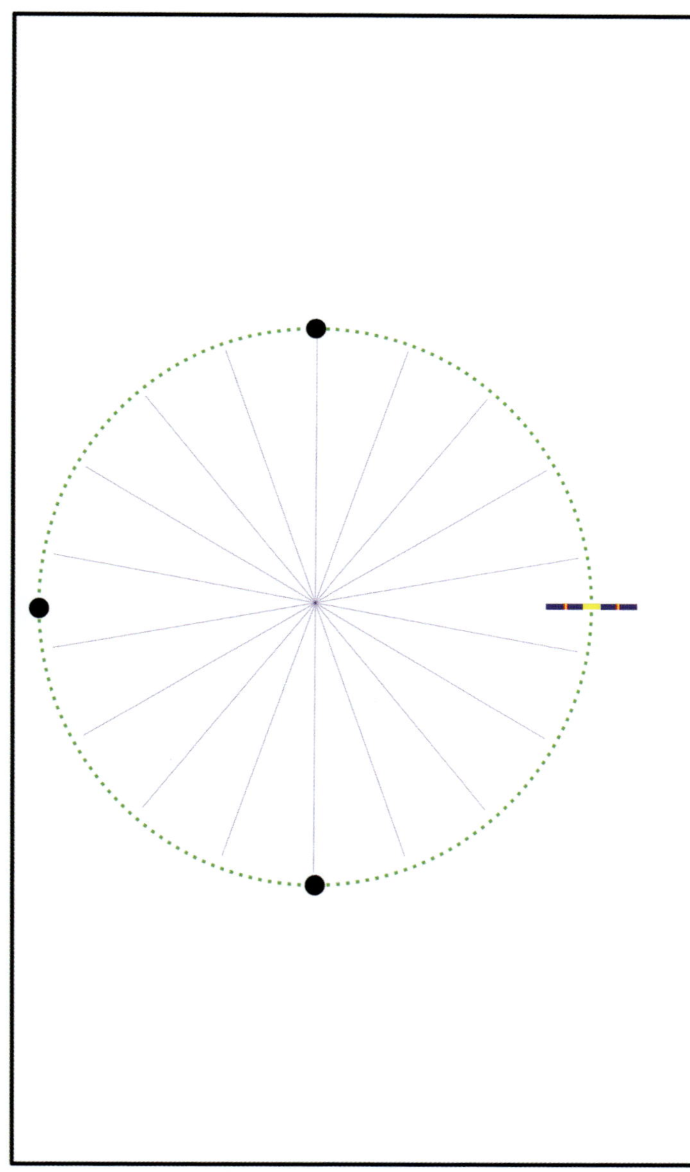

A single pole on the circle.

Note: Observe the turning points on the circle and how the fourth turning point is in the center of the pole. The blue lines illustrate the importance of maintaining regular speed and stride length.

Rhythm Straight Ahead

A single pole on a straight line in canter. This basic level exercise is used to school the ability to maintain a regular rhythm with a good track. Although it is not technically a difficult exercise, it is not easy to ride a precise track in a regular rhythm. The straight line in canter generally requires a bit more skill and feel from the rider than the same task ridden on the circle.

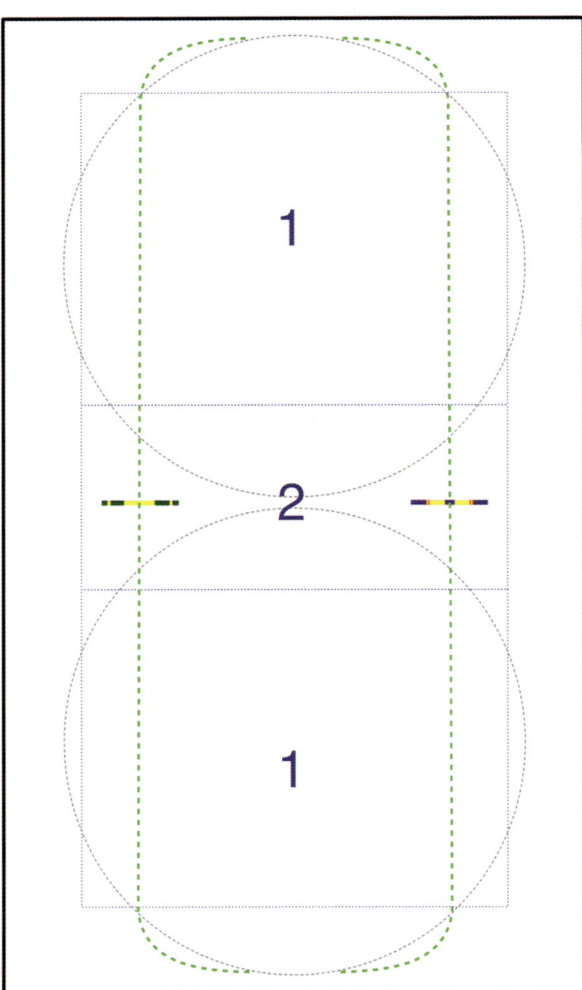

When rhythm and track are well maintained, half-seat and long release over the pole can be incorporated as preparation for jumping. The rider will be in half-seat in Zone 1 and demonstrate a long release with a grab of the mane in Zone 2. The better the timing and coordination becomes, the later the rider changes to half-seat before the pole, and eventually, at an advanced level, the change occurs in sync with the horse taking off to clear the pole.

▪ **Purpose:** The rider uses the skills taught in canter over the single pole on the circle to ride a straight line in regular rhythm and stride length.

A single pole on the straight line. Placing one pole on each long side simply provides more options, and a circle on the short side can be used as a help to reestablish rhythm and balance if needed.

Change Direction

Change Direction out of the circle ridden over a single pole in canter can be used to teach the rider to change from one direction to another with synchronized weight and rein aids. The pole encourages a flying-lead change, but for the horse that cannot perform a flying change at this point, a simple-lead change is ridden after the pole.

▪ **Purpose:** The rider must coordinate aids and balance so the horse does not receive signals contradicting each other for the turn. Practicing a long release with the outside hand in combination with a grab in the mane can be very beneficial for future jumping exercises.

A single pole on the center line. The riding of correct circles with good understanding of the turning points (as illustrated) *before* attempting to ride the change of direction will support better control and balance within this progressive exercise (compared to riding the figure eight immediately at the onset of the exercise).

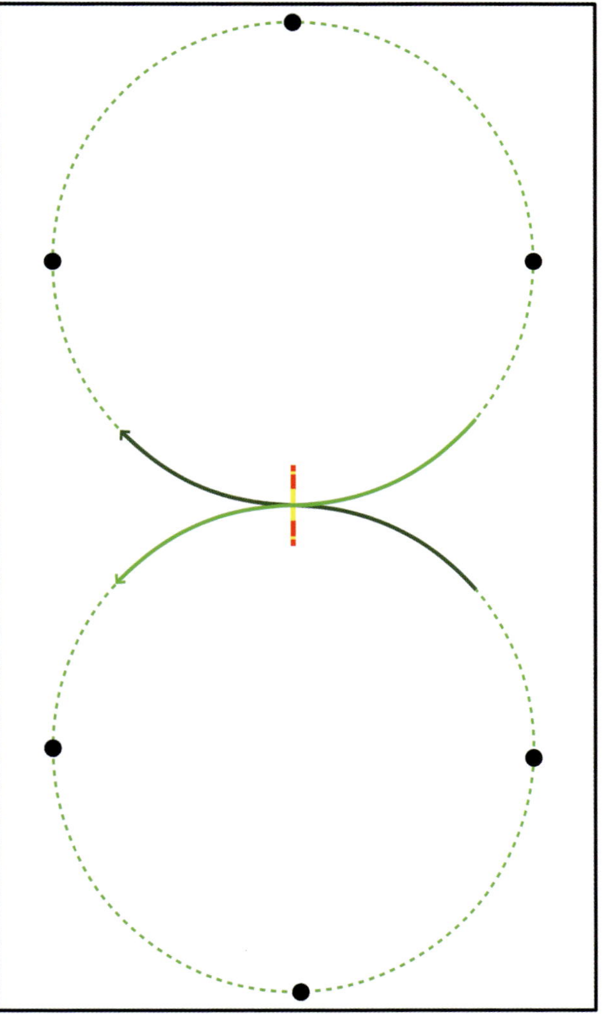

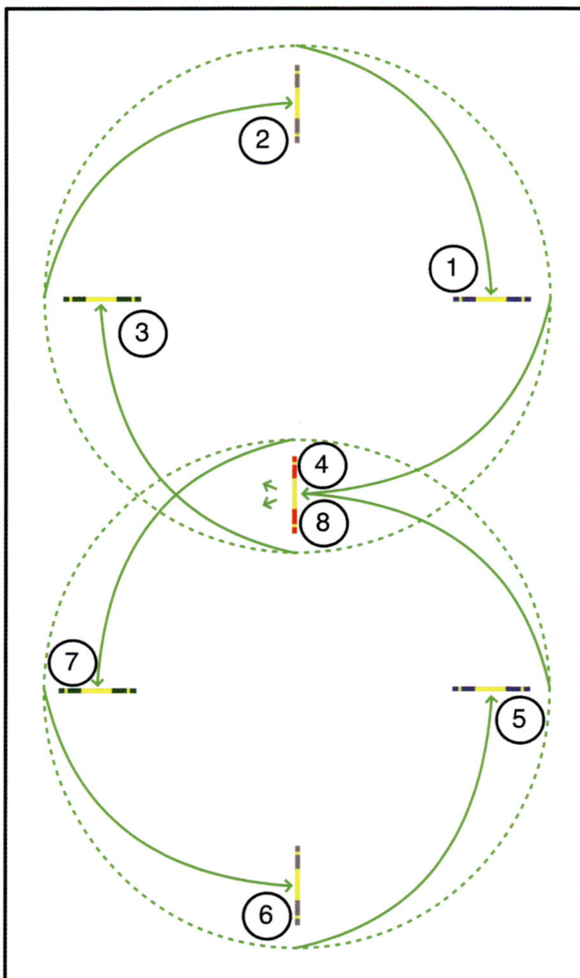

The Circle is a versatile exercise that can be used in a wide range of arenas by simply altering the dimensions of the circles. Notice how different colored poles are used to simplify the process of learning and explaining the exercise.

The Circle

The Circle is an exercise that introduces horse and rider to a longer exercise in canter, by riding the circle as a familiar track with an incorporated change of direction out of the circle. If a mistake happens in these types of exercises, the setup allows for repetition with very little disruption to the continuation of the exercise.

Note: Riding the exercise in trot can on a basic level be very helpful for gaining confidence in riding with good rhythm, track, balance, and relaxation.

- **Purpose:** To demonstrate that track, rhythm, balance, and relaxation can be maintained but also regained in the case of temporary loss in a longer exercise over a series of poles while repeatedly practicing the same type of arena track.

Long and Short Approaches

This exercise teaches the horse and rider to be comfortable with three different types of approaches—the numbers in the round circles illustrate *long approaches* while the numbers in the squares illustrate *short approaches* (with the exception of Obstacle 3, which is ridden out of the circle).

Once the separate exercises are demonstrated to a satisfactory level, they can be combined: after Obstacle 5 (round) the rider continues to Obstacle 1 (square) and finishes the exercise.

Note: The poles are of different colors to support easier memorization and explanation.

- **Purpose:** To demonstrate that track, rhythm, balance, and relaxation can be maintained, but also regained in case of temporary loss in a longer exercise including different types of approaches.

The *Long and Short Approaches* exercise can be used in a wide variety of arena sizes and provides horse and rider with the feeling of riding a course.

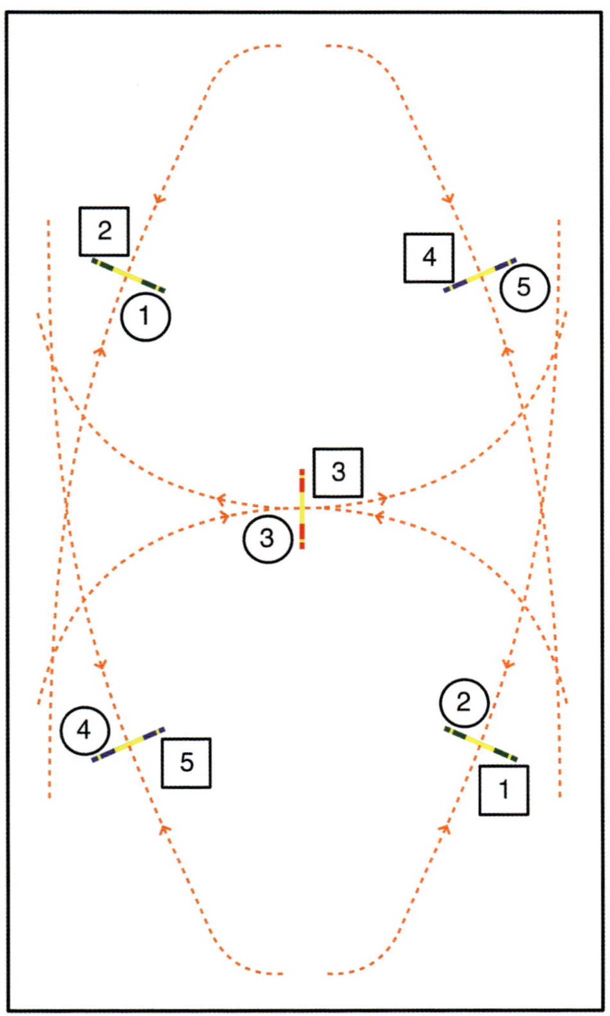

Related Distances and Awareness of Stride Length

Related distances are an important part of riding courses, but this exercise also serves as an excellent one for any horse and rider practicing the *awareness of stride length,* especially in canter. A good starting point is to set the related distances for a normal stride length (which for rider and horse is easily achievable, assuming the basic work with rhythm and track does not create any problems).

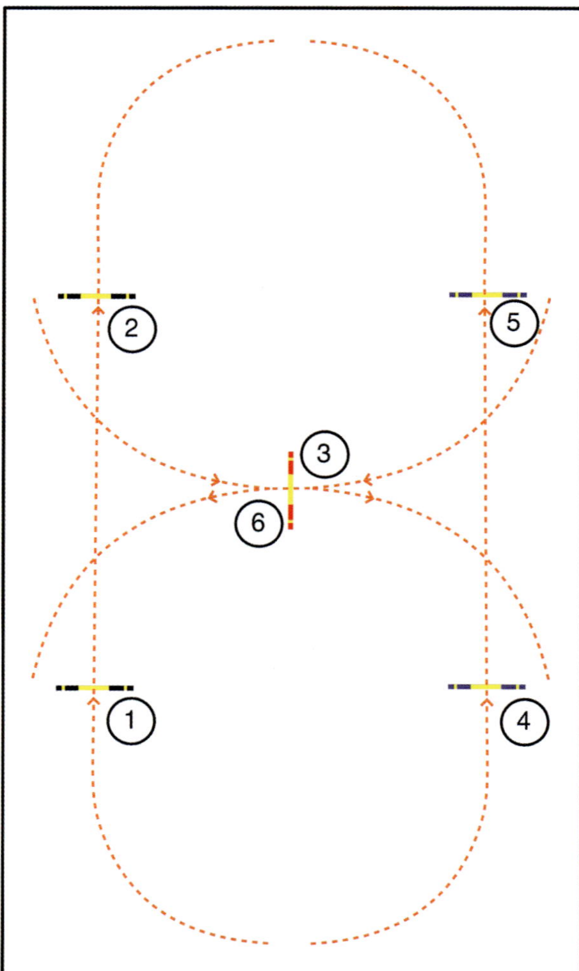

Once rider and horse are able to repeat the distances with control that results in the same number of canter strides, the next progression of the exercise is to ride one extra stride in the distances (assuming the horse is strong enough for the required stride length). Since the last obstacle on the centerline puts horse and rider on track to the first obstacle again, it is easy to repeat the exercise, this time with a different number of

This exercise can be altered to suit most arenas. In the illustrated arena the distance is set on 18.50 meters (60.7 feet) and will ride in five strides or six short strides—the latter will require that the horse and rider are able to shorten the canter strides.

Note: Footing and arena size will have a significant impact on how the related distance rides.

strides for demonstrating awareness of how many strides are ridden between the poles at all times.

▪ **Purpose:** For the rider to create awareness of the canter stride and to be able to adjust how many canter strides are ridden between the poles set in a related distance.

Canter Poles

Canter Poles combines work over poles in left and right lead canter. The single poles and series of poles can serve to train the skills of riding and maintaining a certain length of stride suitable to the distance between the poles. The canter poles provide the rider with immediate feedback about the canter stride length in relation to the measured distance between

The canter poles can be set in most arenas; however, the arena size, types of horses, and desired outcome for the exercise will determine the measured distance between the poles. In the illustration here, the poles are set for horses with a normal stride length—measured distance between each pole here is 3.20 meters (10.5 feet).

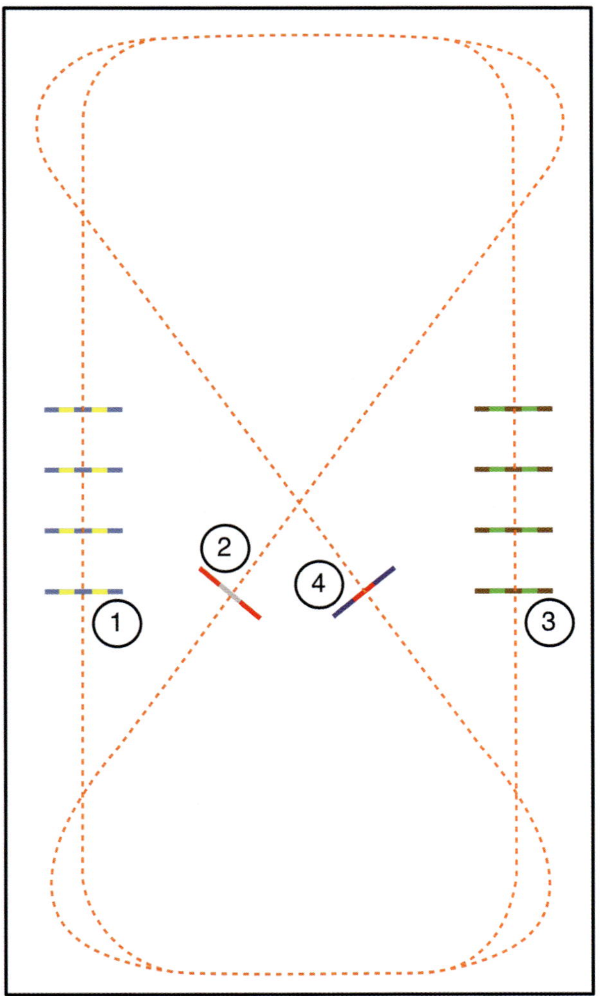

the poles. Speed and stride length are variables with significant importance in the outcome of the canter poles—when they feel short, the horse most likely is approaching in a fast or long canter stride; when they feel long, the horse most likely is approaching in a short or slow canter stride.

Notice the single poles on the diagonals. These allow the rider more time to process the feedback received over the canter poles and make the necessary adjustments instead of being faced with another set of canter poles again. The short sides of the arena also allow enough space to ride a circle, should this be necessary to regain the control of rhythm within the exercise.

▪ **Purpose:** To train the awareness of riding and maintaining a specific stride length.

Trot Poles with Adjustment of Step Length

The adjustability of step length and the smooth change between different lengths of steps with a balanced, relaxed horse is of significant importance to the well-schooled horse.

This exercise can be ridden in both directions. In general, riding in the direction of short steps to long steps will be the easier option during initial introduction to the exercise. The poles serve as a feedback source for the length of step, telling the rider if the trot was adjusted to a correct length suitable to the individual sets of poles.

▪ **Purpose:** To maintain a relaxed and balanced horse while transitioning between different step lengths.

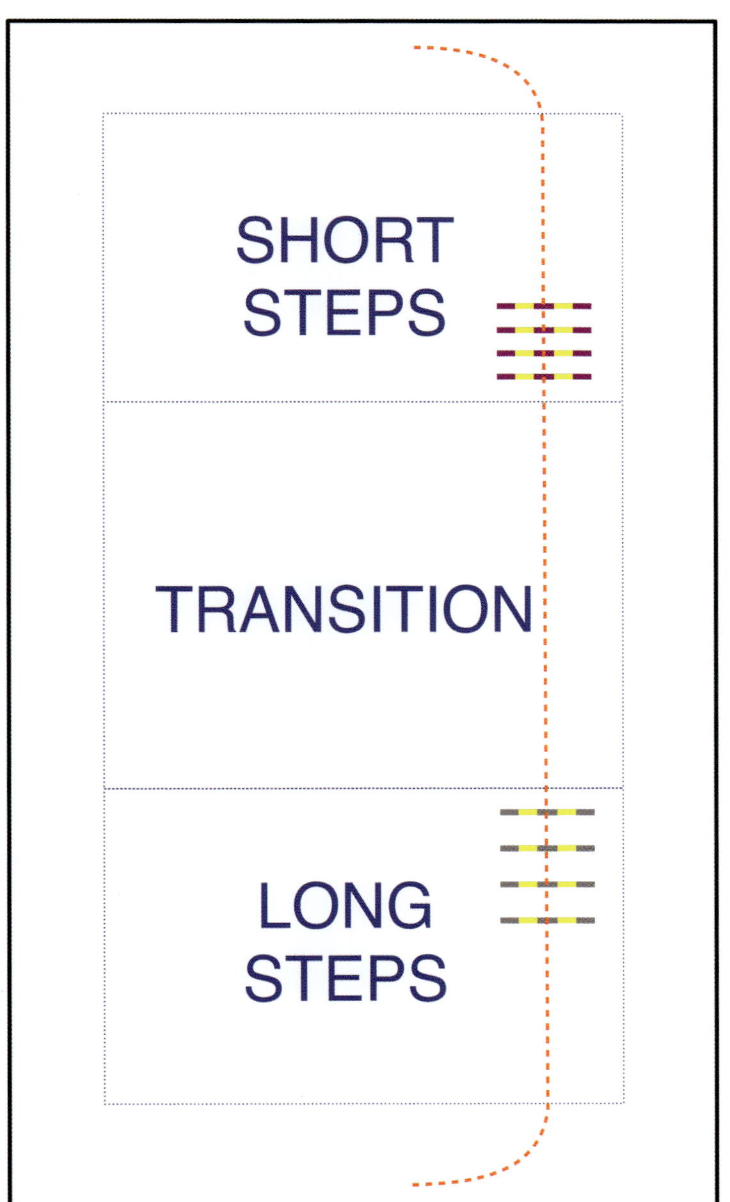

An exercise that can be set in most arenas, this particular one shows poles set with 1.05 meters (3.5 feet) between the short trot poles and 1.35 meter (4.5 feet) between the long trot poles. These measurements can be adjusted in order to make the exercise more or less advanced.

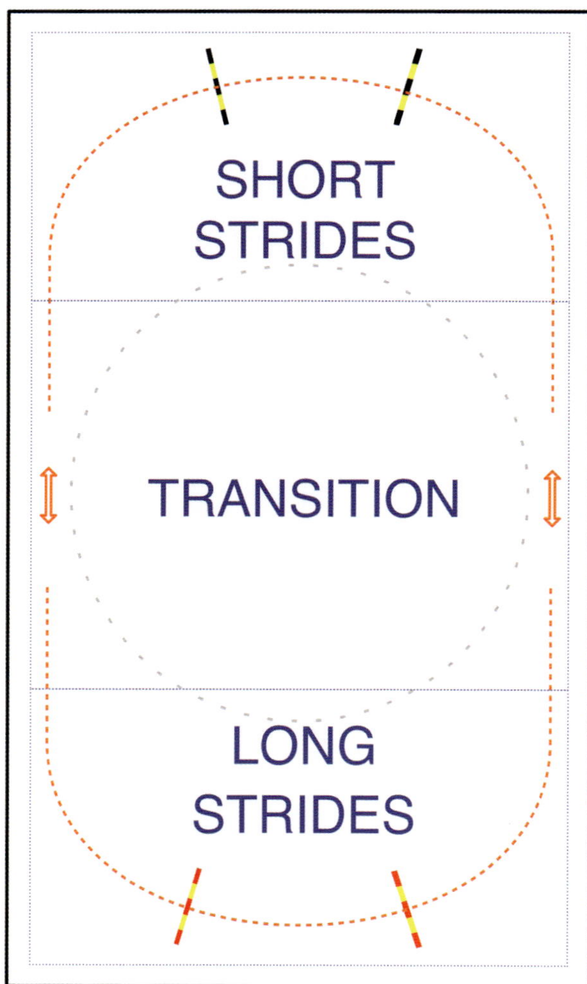

Canter Adjustability Between Poles

Canter Adjustability Between Poles focuses on changing stride length at the canter. The horse and rider alternate between riding three short strides and three long strides on a curved line with a long side in between. Should the horse and rider need more time for the change of stride length, there is an option to use the circle in the center.

- **Purpose:** Change stride length with precision for the exact number of strides desired while maintaining a relaxed and balanced horse.

An exercise that can be set in most arenas, this one shows the distance between the poles for the three short strides set at 9 meters (30 feet) and the distance between the poles for the three long strides set at 11 meters (36 feet). These distances can be adjusted to suit different arena sizes and types of horses.

Canter Poles with Adjustment of Stride Length

This exercise requires an immediate change in length of stride on a bending line. The rider will either ride into the long canter poles and shorten the strides to suit the shorter poles, or vice versa. Should the rider not be able to bring the horse to the suitable stride between the two sets of poles, there is the option to use the circle in the center to help in gaining more time and space to reach the suitable stride length for the next set of canter poles.

▪ **Purpose:** Immediate change between different lengths of stride while maintaining a relaxed and balanced horse.

An exercise that can be set in most arenas, the distance and the track between the two sets of poles will have a significant impact on the difficulty level. The distance between the poles set for the short strides is 2.80 meters (9 feet) and the distance between the poles set for the long strides is 3.50 meters (11.5 feet). This distance can be adjusted to accommodate different types of horses but also to change the level of difficulty of the exercise as a whole.

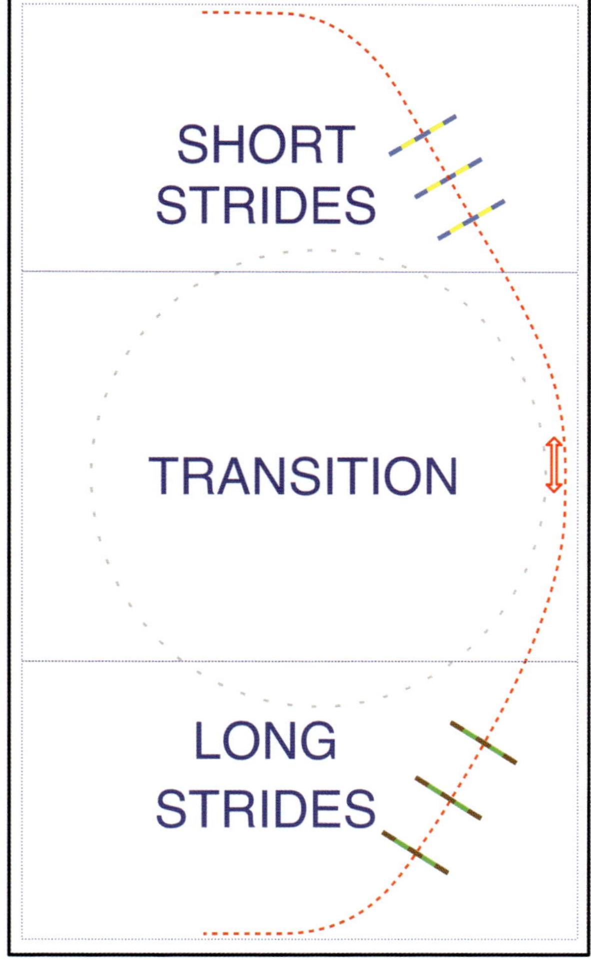

11 Meters

This is an exercise requiring increased ability and strength for the horse to shorten his canter stride while remaining relaxed and balanced. The rider adjusts the canter stride to a suitable stride length in order to fit three or four strides between the poles. If the rider needs more time to adjust the canter stride length, there is the option of riding a circle on the short sides before proceeding to the next set of poles.

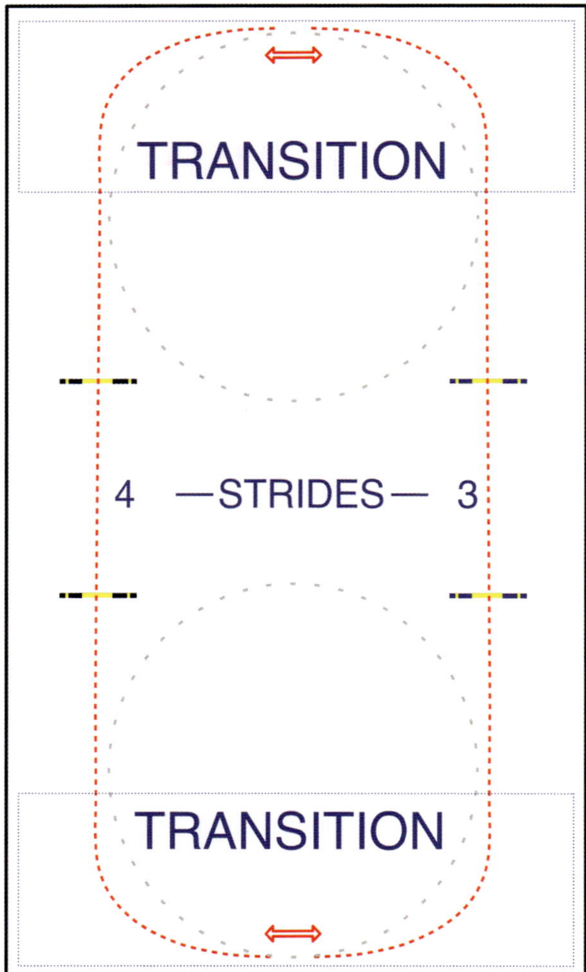

- **Purpose:** A good indicator of the horse's strength is whether or not he can fit three and four relaxed and balanced strides between the two sets of poles (which are both set at the same distance). For the rider, it is also valuable training for adjusting the canter to the specific stride length necessary for a variable number of strides in the same measured distance.

An exercise that can be set in most arenas, the distance between both sets of poles is set at 11 meters (36 feet).

Double 11 Meters

This is an exercise that requires a good feel for rhythm and the ability to instantly change stride length in the canter while still maintaining relaxation and balance.

Riding 3 to 3 schools the ability to maintain rhythm over poles.

Riding 4 to 4 tests and schools rhythm and the strength of the horse due to the required shortening of the canter stride.

Riding 4 to 3 tests and schools the ability to lengthen the canter stride instantly and smoothly without compromising balance.

Riding 3 to 4 is the most challenging combination of canter

An exercise that can be set in most arenas, the distances from green to red pole and from red to green pole are identical, both measuring 11 meters (36 feet). The stride combinations illustrate a general guideline for order of progression to obtain the best results with most horses.

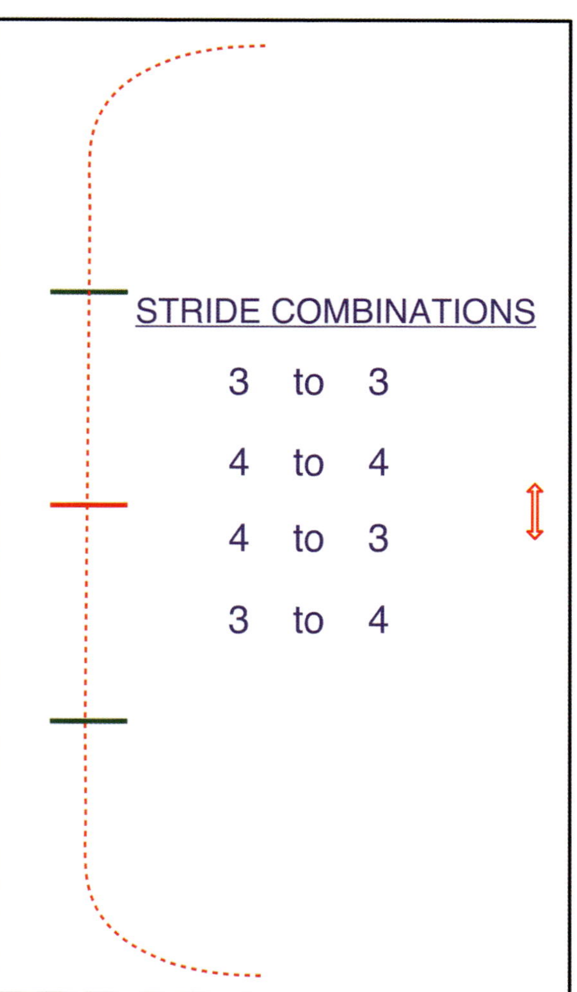

Note: Setting the exercise in the center of the long side provides rider and horse with exactly the same approach from both left and right. Maintaining this variable in approach allows focus on the main purpose of the exercise.

strides, as coming from a longer stride and instantly changing to shorter strides in a harmonious way is testing the horse's ability to shorten the stride together with the rider's awareness of stride length.

Note: Not all combinations of striding must be practiced within one session— sometimes focusing solely on riding 3 to 3 steady strides followed by practice with 4 to 4 steady strides is enough of a challenge for horse and rider in one session.

▪ **Purpose:** High-level schooling of rhythm, rideability, awareness, and control of stride length in canter. It is essential that relaxation and balance are maintained in the different combinations of strides in order for this exercise to serve its purpose.

Suppleness—Pole Exercises

These exercises are meant to serve as useful exercises on their own while also providing options for variety in the training. In these exercises, the horse is increasing the engagement of his body due to the fact that the legs must be lifted higher from the ground. The physics of these exercises have a suppling effect on the horse. The poles can also be used to simulate jumps and as a help to encourage flying-lead changes. A helpful hint for maintaining the integrity of pole exercises as they should be set, is to place cones at the ends of the poles that will help in repositioning the poles if they are moved or knocked out of place during a session.

Poles and Circles

Poles and Circles focuses on circles as helpful basic level tracks to supple the horse. There are many different options to vary the track— the tracks illustrated here are straight ahead, circle 20 meters, circle 15 meters, and change direction out of the circle. The size of the circles can be adjusted, which will have a significant impact on the level of difficulty.

- **Purpose:** Incorporate trot poles on the circle track to increase the suppling effect on the horse's body.

An exercise that can be set in most arenas. Common distances between the trot poles are 1.20 to 1.40 meters (4 to 4.6 feet) measured in the center of the poles following the bending line. The distance can be adjusted for different types of horses and varying stride lengths.

Trot Poles Serpentine

Trot Poles Serpentine is an exercise that combines the frequent changes of flexion and bend ridden on the serpentine track with the suppling effect of poles. Note how circles can be ridden within the serpentine to help with preparation for the next set of poles. These circles can be a useful tool for improving rhythm, balance, and track within the loops.

▪ **Purpose:** Combine the frequent changes of bend and flexion required by the serpentine track with trot poles for an increased suppling effect. The important aspects of rhythm, track, balance, and relaxation will be greatly affected by the correctness of the rider's aids, and ultimately by the feeling of the rider for coordinating subtle changes of aids to smoothly guide the horse through the exercise.

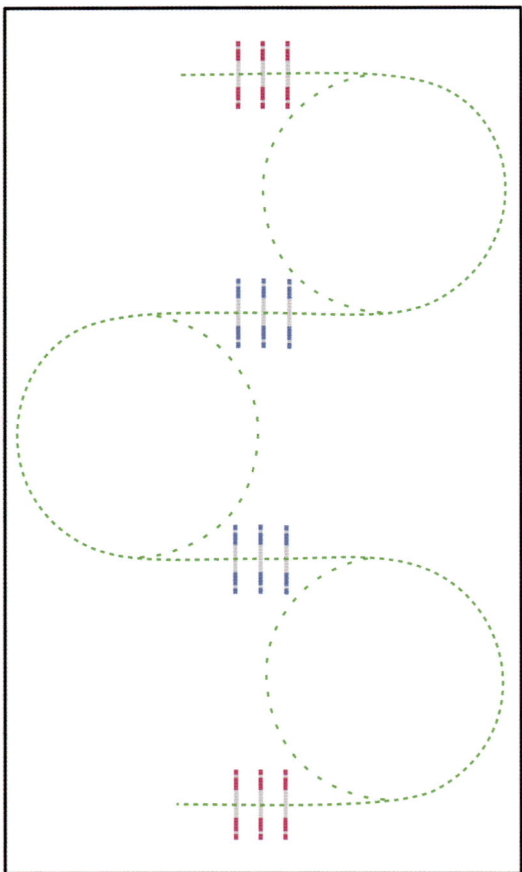

A basic level exercise that can be set in most arenas. For setting in different-sized arenas, the number of loops can be adjusted to accommodate more or less space and ensure a suitable diameter of the optional circles. Common distances between the trot poles are 1.20 to 1.40 meters (4 to 4.6 feet) measured in the center of the poles. The distance can be adjusted for different types of horses and stride lengths.

Trot Poles Quarterline

This is an exercise that combines quarterlines and trot poles in different ways. The black poles are partially raised and set on a long approach, and the red poles are set on the quarterline but ridden as a single-loop serpentine, which includes changes of bend and flexion. On an advanced level, the single-loop serpentine can be combined with lateral work, which will add an enhanced suppling effect to the exercise when executed correctly.

▪ **Purpose:** Suppling and strength building for the horse due to the increased lifting of the legs as a result of the raised black poles. Maintenance of rhythm and relaxation within the changes of flexion and bend over the red poles.

An exercise that can be set in most arenas, when introducing the raised black poles, it can be helpful to raise only one side at the time—for example, the second black pole on the left and the fourth black pole on the right. Common distances between the trot poles are 1.20 to 1.40 meters (4 to 4.6 feet) measured in the center of the poles. The distance can be adjusted for different types of horses and stride lengths.

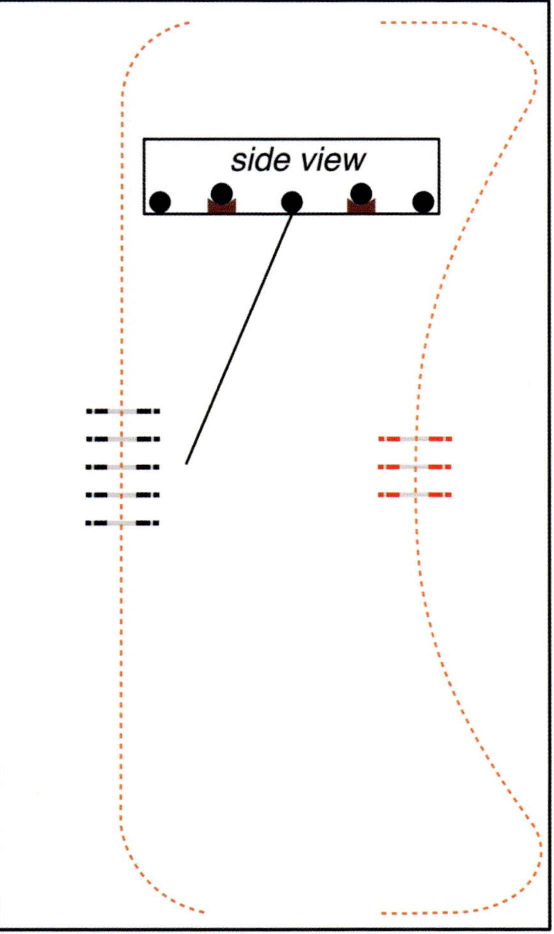

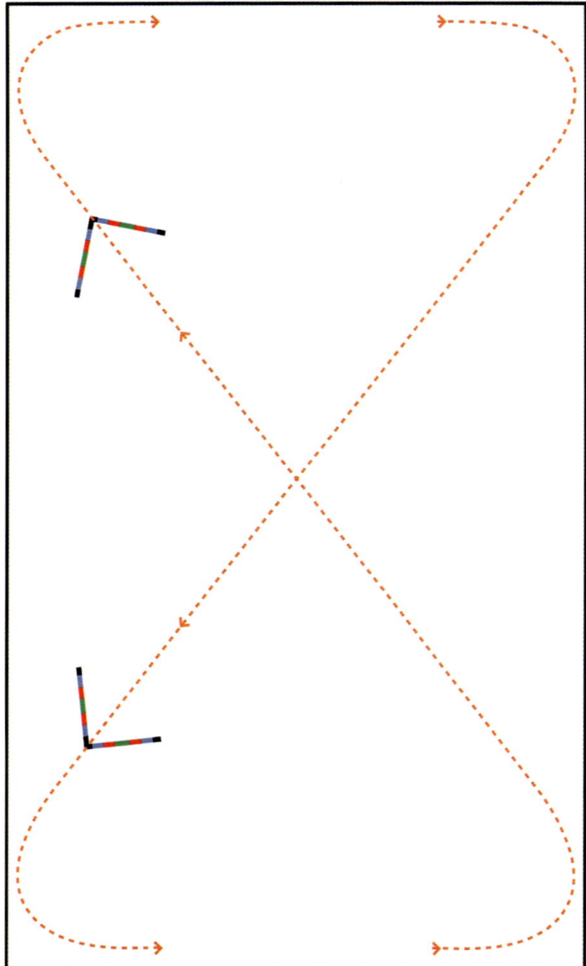

Introducing the V

This pole exercise will create a more elevated stride when riding through the center of the two poles positioned as a V. The elevated stride is suppling for the horse, and for the rider it gives a similar feeling to jumping. Additionally, it encourages the horse to do a flying lead change. Should the horse not jump enough to encourage a flying lead change, the V-shaped poles can be adjusted to a narrower opening. This will encourage the horse to jump higher as long as it is approached in the center.

- **Purpose:** For the horse to be encouraged to make flying lead changes and for the rider to practice long approaches with a feeling of jumping over the poles.

This exercise can be set in most arenas. Here, the poles are set relatively close to the corner. This way, the long side will encourage the horse to land in the new canter lead.

Canter Poles Serpentine

Canter Poles Serpentine combines canter poles with change of direction and requires the rider to be very precise regarding maintenance of rhythm, suitable canter stride length, and good track. The circles within the loops can be beneficial if the rider needs to reestablish balance, rhythm, or ride a simple lead change.

- **Purpose:** Maintain a suitable stride length for the canter poles while riding a correct track. Canter poles encourage the flying lead change.

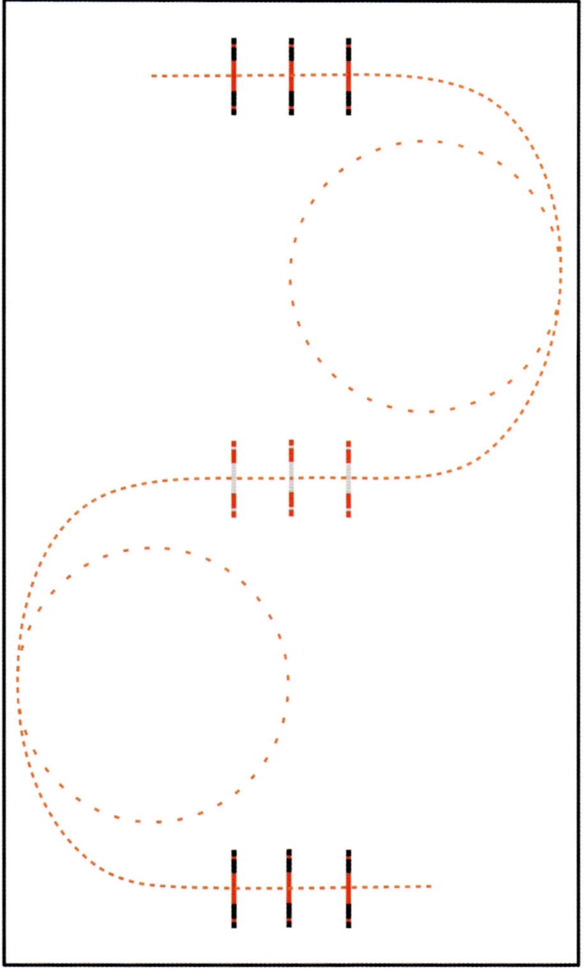

This exercise can be set in most arenas. Common distances between the canter poles are 3.00 to 3.25 meters (9.8 to 10.6 feet). This distance can be adjusted to accommodate different types of horses and stride lengths.

Note: The exercise also can be ridden as a continual exercise.

Centerline V

Centerline V combines change of canter lead with different stride lengths and approaches. The first group of poles on the centerline is set for a regular stride length and the V, in this case, is placed in a way that leads into the turn, which will encourage the horse to do a flying lead change. The V can also be opened and simply used as a marker for horse and rider to pass through without having to step over, and with the option of riding a simple lead change through walk or trot.

The third group of poles is ridden from the left or right canter lead (depending on which direction is chosen after the V). The distance in both third groups of poles are set for a longer canter stride out of a forward canter. After the longer stride length, the stride is shortened for the fourth group of poles that are set for a regular stride but ridden out of a half-circle back, in which the size of the turn will affect how the canter poles ride. The fourth set of poles will feel very different compared to the first set of poles, even though they are exactly the same (only ridden in the opposite direction and out of the turn).

In summary, the three main challenges in this exercise are: the V because they require a balanced and coordinated rider; the third set of poles because it requires a longer canter stride; and the fourth set of poles because they are approached out of a turn.

▪ **Purpose:** Schooling different stride lengths that are pre-determined by the different distances set between the canter poles and understanding how a shorter approach affects how distances will ride. The V on the centerline requires good preparation for the turn and, when correctly ridden, the V supports a flying lead change.

An exercise that can be set in most arenas. Common distances between the poles in the first and fourth set of canter poles are 3.00 to 3.25 meters (9.8 to 10.6 feet) and in between the poles in both third sets of poles, the distance is 3.60 meters (11.8 feet). The distance can be adjusted to accommodate different types of horses and stride lengths, but also to change the level of difficulty. The V is in this situation is set 6.00 meters (19.6 feet) from the short side.

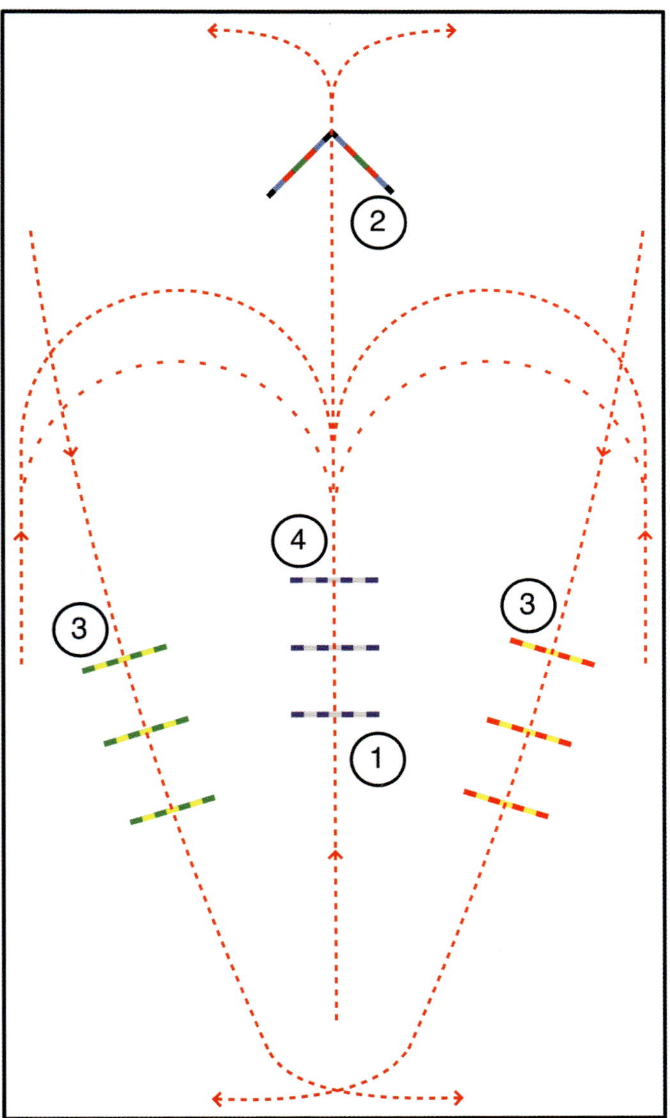

Canter Poles Reverse Half-Circle Back

This exercise will lead horse and rider into a smaller diameter turn, wherein the rider must be very certain and confident about the track the horse must follow, otherwise it often leads to the horse misunderstanding in which direction to continue. The canter poles together with the turn, and the corner that limits the size of the turn, will also encourage a flying lead change.

It is important the rider allows the horse to flex and bend in the turning direction—insecure or less-than-committed riders often hold the reins too tightly in an exercise they are unsure of. Especially when the outside rein is held too tightly, it restricts the horse from making the necessary inside flexion for the size of the turn and will create difficulty for the horse to maintain his balance in the turn. (In some situations, it can be helpful to ride a turn with the horse straight or even lightly flexed to the outside, but these situations are unique and will, in general, not be helpful in introducing the rider and horse to smaller sized turns.)

The trot poles ridden on the same track can be very helpful in preparing horse and rider for the canter poles—minor difficulties felt in the trot will increase and become more significant in canter. Eliminating any misunderstandings between horse and rider in trot will set them up for more success with the exercise in canter over the poles.

▪ **Purpose:** To school a smaller diameter turn after a straight line and feel the importance of a soft outside rein, which allows for correct flexion and bend in the horse.

An exercise that can be set in most arenas. Common distances between canter poles are 3.00 to 3.25 meters (9.8 to 10.6 feet) and between the trot poles the distance is 1.20 to 1.40 meters (4 to 4.6 feet). The distance can be adjusted to accommodate different types of horses and stride lengths but also to change the level of difficulty. The number of poles used as trot or canter poles can be varied. Using one ground pole only offers more flexibility in regards to the stride length used in the approach, while several poles placed as trot and canter poles determine more exactly which stride length to use for the approach.

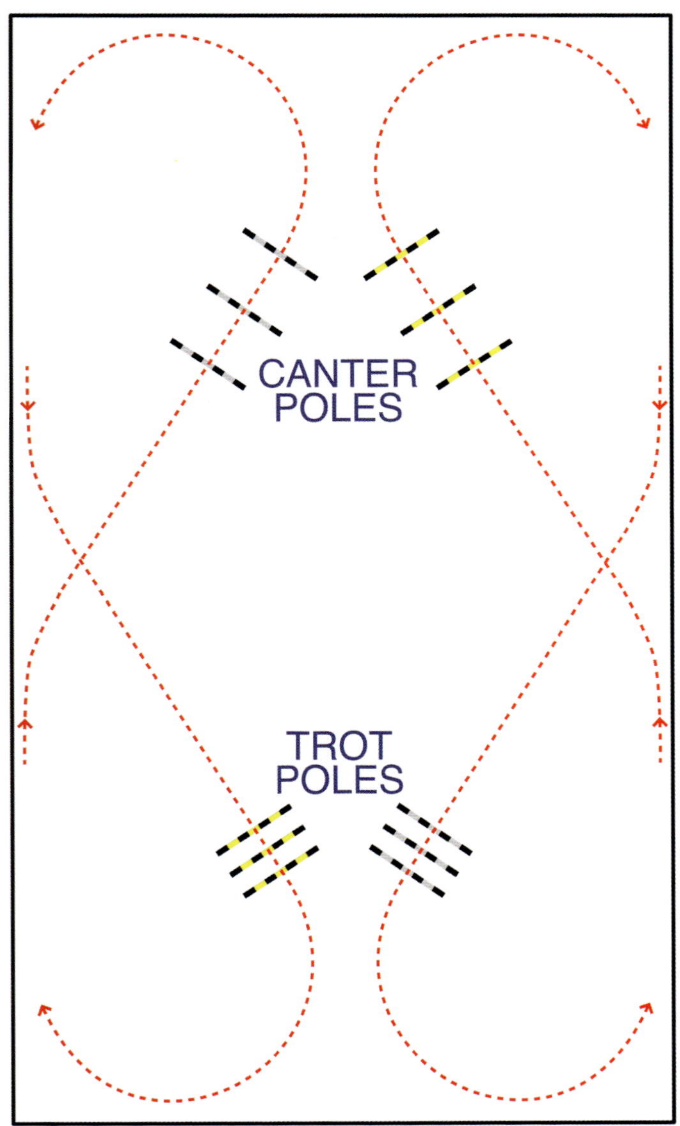

Pole Courses

These courses are alternatives for riders not wishing to jump, young horses, or dressage riders looking for variety in their work. The *pole courses* can serve as a great tool to practice the skill of riding courses with good balance, rhythm, and precision without the horse having to jump. For the rider, this means that more repetitions can be achieved without the wear and tear created by jumping too many obstacles. For the school horse, it means that more riders can be taught about riding courses without having to jump an excessive amount with any one horse.

The number of poles used as trot or canter poles can be varied—using one ground pole offers more flexibility in regard to stride length used in the approach, while several poles placed as trot and canter poles determine more exactly which stride length to use for the approach.

Basic Rhythm and Track Course

This basic course includes the tracks straight ahead and diagonals that are two of the most basic fundamental tracks (see pp. 5 and 7). Using tracks on a basic level allows the rider to devote most of the attention to riding with good rhythm and track. Understanding these fundamentals sets up a rider for a better chance of success when more difficult tasks arise. This tactic of pursuing excellence in the basics supports optimal learning for both horse and rider.

▪ **Purpose:** To teach and test the understanding of suitable canter rhythm while maintaining a good track.

A basic level exercise that can be set in most arenas. Common distance between canter poles is 3.00 to 3.25 meters (9.8 to 10.6 feet). The distance can be adjusted to accommodate different types of horses and stride lengths, but also to change the level of difficulty.

Note: By using the tracks illustrated here, the course can be started anywhere with the additional option of reversing the direction that the poles are ridden.

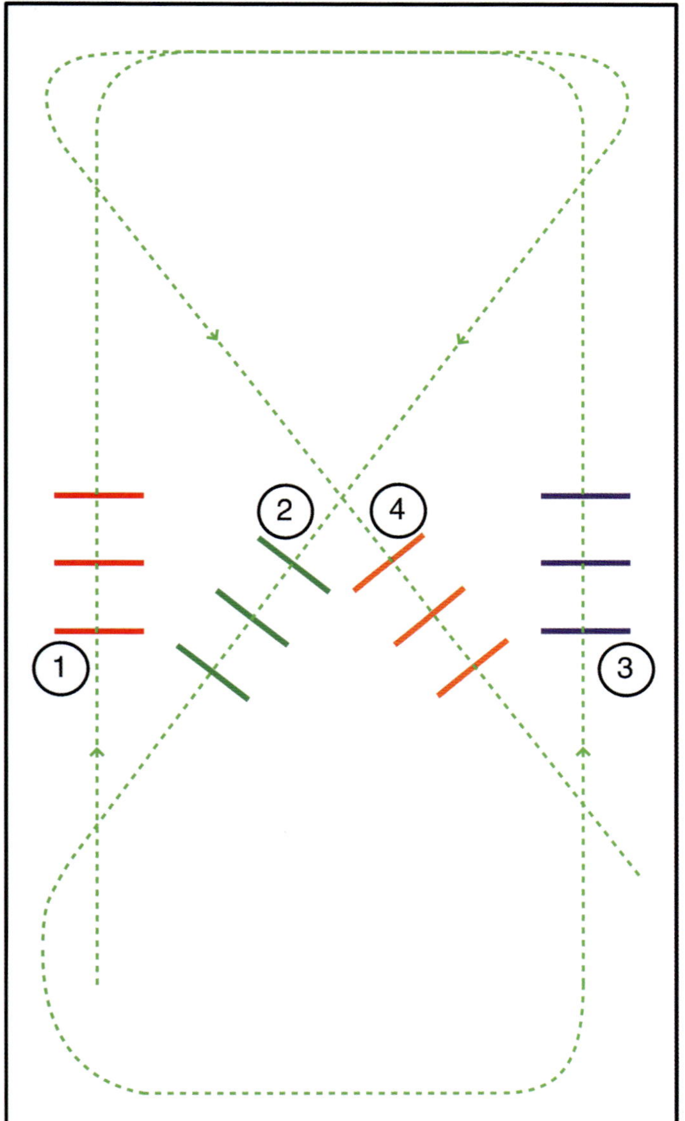

Basic Rhythm and Track Course Incorporating Circles

This basic course includes the tracks straight ahead, diagonals, and circles—all three of which are basic tracks (see pp. 5, 7, and 11). Keeping the variation of tracks minimal allows the rider to focus on essential skills such as a good rhythm and a track ridden with a relaxed and balanced horse.

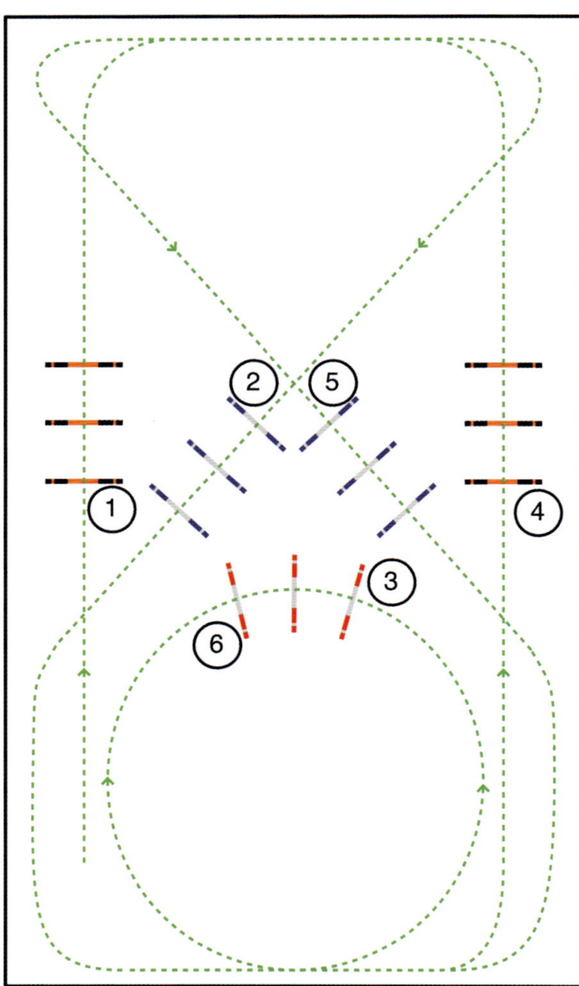

- **Purpose:** To maintain good canter rhythm and track while riding straight ahead, circles, and diagonals.

An exercise that can be set in most arenas, with more poles added to the canter poles in a larger arena and singles poles used in a smaller arena. Common distances used between canter poles are 3.00 to 3.25 meters (9.8 to 10.6 feet), which can be adjusted to accommodate different types of horses and stride lengths, but also to change the level of difficulty of the course.

Note: By using the tracks illustrated here, there are several options where the course can be started with the additional option of reversing the direction that the poles are ridden, as well. By reversing the course, the approaches change from longer to slightly shorter on the straight lines.

Longer Basic Rhythm and Track Course

This basic course includes some variation and modification of the basic tracks used in the arena. The slightly longer length of course and the fact that the track is not mirrored from left to right is an additional challenge for the rider. Maintaining a relaxed and balanced horse ridden in good rhythm on a good track are fundamentals that will remain important regardless of the level of horse and rider, from most basic to most advanced.

▪ **Purpose:** To maintain good rhythm and track while riding a variation of the basic tracks.

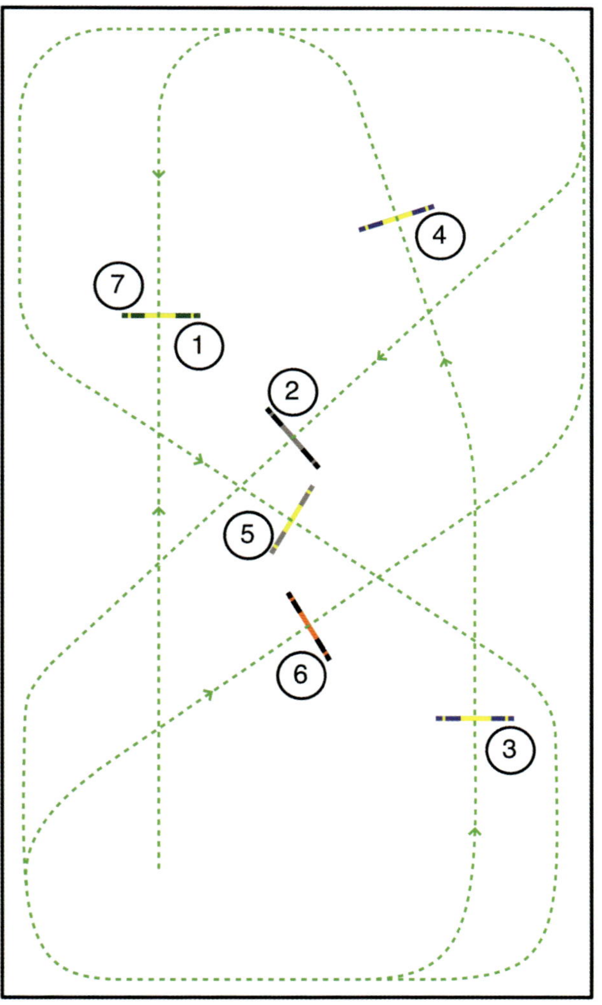

An exercise that can be set in many different sizes of arenas, however, if the course is set in a narrower arena, caution must be taken that the turns do not get too small in diameter, as this creates a very different level of difficulty than intended. The rider and trainer have many options in adding length to the course through the use of the poles in two directions, as done here with pole numbers 1 and 7.

Basic Course Incorporating Related Distance

This setup brings a related distance into the course, and obstacle number 2 (the canter poles) helps the rider determine if the length of the canter stride is suitable for the distance (which, in this illustration is set for five normal strides). To understand and ride a related distance with the intended number of strides is a major milestone in understanding the canter stride of the horse in between obstacles.

- **Purpose:** To introduce a related distance and be able to ride the intended number of strides with canter poles, guiding the rider toward suitable stride length for the related distance. Good track and rhythm are key skills that should be maintained throughout the course.

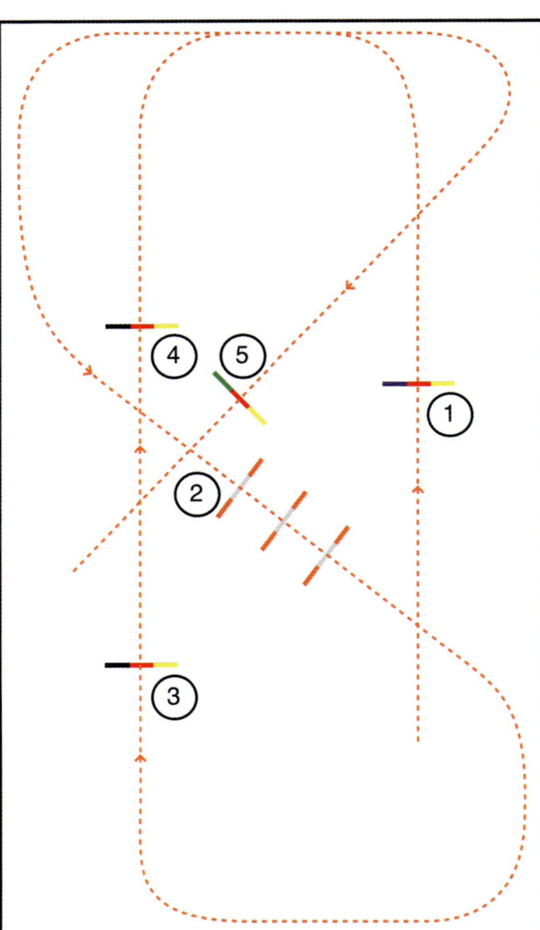

An exercise that can be set in many different sizes of arenas. In this course, the canter poles (obstacle number 2) are set with 3.00 to 3.25 meters (9.8 to 10.6 feet) in between, which for most horses and riders will ride normally. The canter poles set up the horse and rider for five normal strides in the related distance (pole numbers 3 and 4), which has the measured distance of 18.50 meters (60.6 feet). Note how after pole number 5, the rider can continue to number 1 and repeat the course. The distances in the canter poles and the related distance can be adjusted to suit different types of horses and stride lengths.

Longer Basic Course Incorporating Related Distance

A longer course with 12 efforts using only six poles, which can be jumped from either direction. The longer course is very useful in practicing the steadiness of rhythm, track, and balance. Mastering the skill of staying disciplined with track and rhythm from the beginning of the course to the end, together with the ability to analyze and make necessary adjustments of stride length and balance is another important milestone in the education of the rider.

- **Purpose:** Awareness of suitable stride length for the related distance while maintaining good track and rhythm throughout the longer course.

An exercise that can be adjusted to suit many different sizes of arenas. Pole numbers 3 to 4, and pole numbers 7 to 8, both have a measured distance of 18.50 meters (60.6 feet—which will be a normal five strides for most horses). The distance can be adjusted to suit different types of horses and stride lengths. Pole numbers 10 to 11 are set on a bending line for more than seven strides without a measured distance.

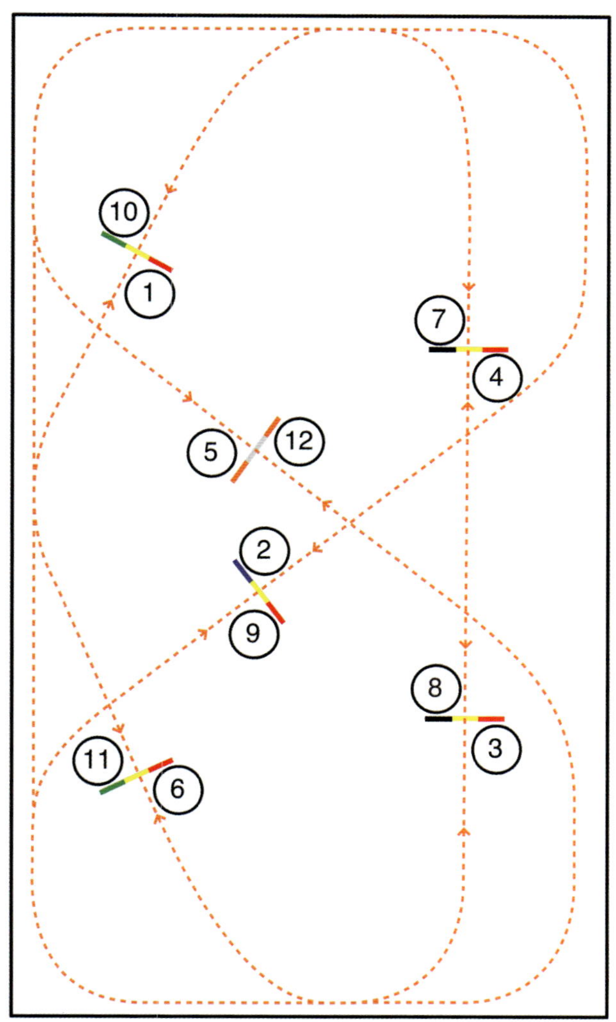

Basic Course Incorporating Related Distance and Combination

A short course that includes a related distance and a combination, with the related distance giving the rider more time to correct the canter stride length (if an adjustment is necessary), compared to the combination that requires the rider to be even more precise in selecting the canter stride length due to the shorter distance between the poles. With only one to two strides in the combination, there is less time for a major change of stride length (a major change in stride is never desired since it could disturb the horse's balance or surprise him and cause a loss of focus on the pole).

- **Purpose:** To demonstrate understanding of suitable canter stride length and rhythm throughout this short course containing both a related distance and a combination.

This is an exercise that can be adjusted to suit many different size arenas. The course begins with a related distance, which can be helpful for the rider to gauge the horse's rhythm. Pole number 1 to 2 has a measured distance of 18.50 meters (60.6 feet), which will ride in a normal five strides for most horses. The distance between 4a and 4b, is 9.00 meters (29.5 feet), which for most horses will ride in two strides. The distances can be adjusted to suit different types of horses and stride lengths.

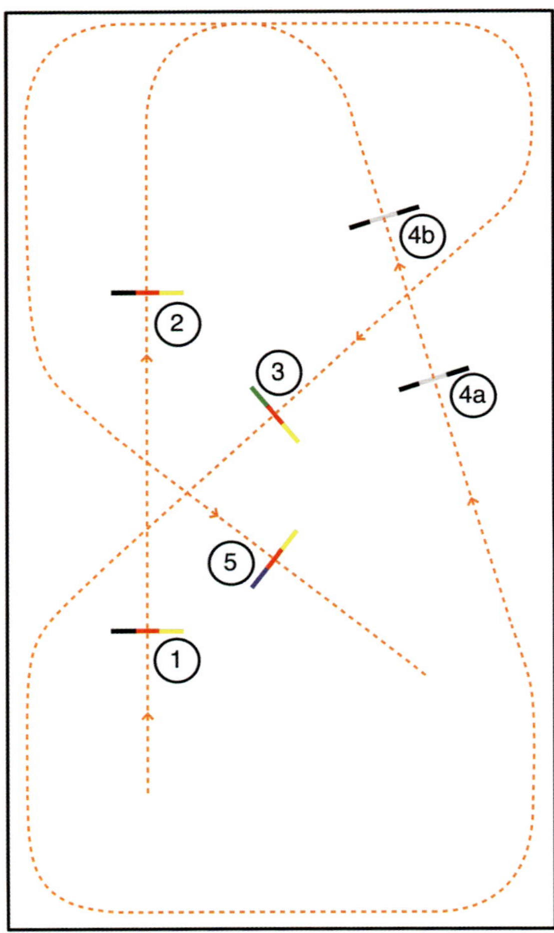

Longer Basic Course Incorporating Related Distance and Combination

A longer course that includes a related distance and introduces a one-stride combination. The one-stride combination requires more precision in regard to the length of canter stride due to minimal time for adjustment in between pole "a" and pole "b." The location of the combination also introduces the rider to the difference in feeling in a shorter approach versus a longer approach.

- **Purpose:** To maintain a suitable length of canter stride throughout the longer course using the related distance and combination as a gauge of success.

This exercise can be adjusted to suit many different sizes of arenas. The longer course with repetition of the related distance and the combination from both directions is a good gauge for rhythm, balance, and track throughout the course. Pole numbers 2 to 3 have a measured distance of 18.50 meters (60.6 feet), which for many horses will be suitable for five strides, and the distance between 5a and 5b is 5.50 meters (18 feet), which for most horses will ride in one stride. The distances can be adjusted to suit different types of horse types and stride lengths.

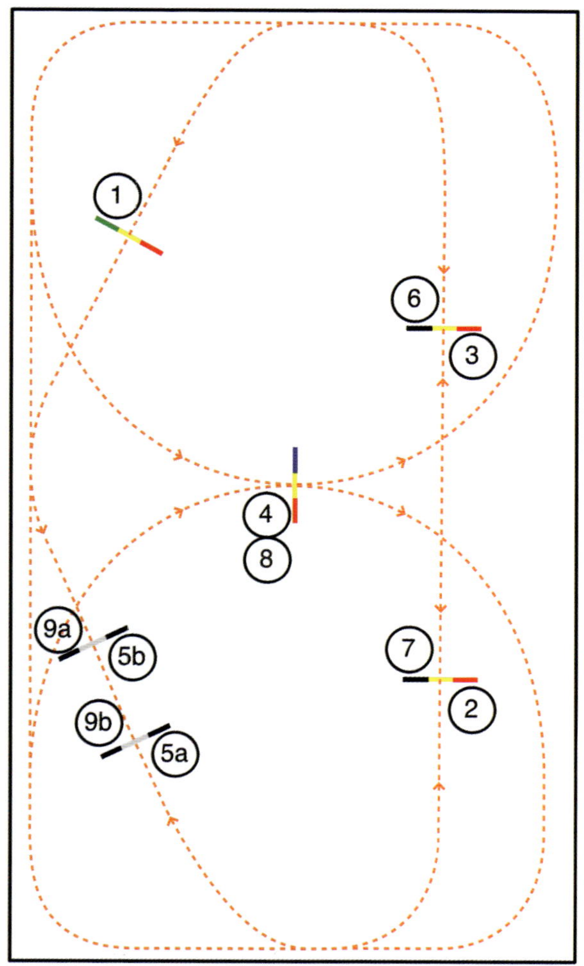

Adjusting the Canter Stride

This course schools a high level of awareness regarding speed and stride length in the canter. The canter poles give the rider immediate and clear feedback about the chosen canter stride length without putting horse and rider in a troublesome situation in the event of choosing the incorrect stride length. The feedback from the poles can then immediately be analyzed and acted upon by the rider as a learning experience to optimize progression.

The course starts with number 1 (canter poles set for a normal stride), continues to

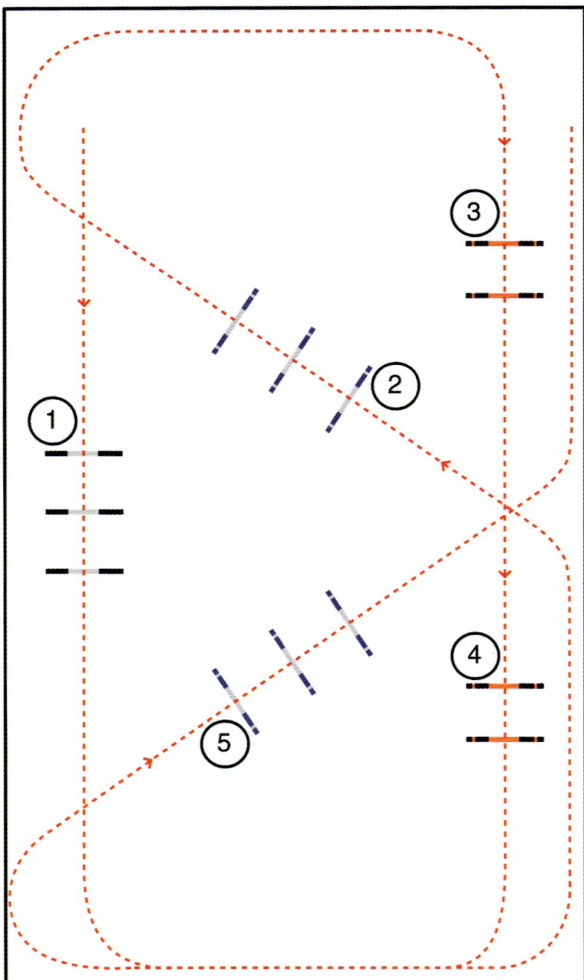

This exercise can be adjusted to suit many different sizes of arenas. Due to the symmetrical setup of the course, the poles can also be ridden in both directions for variety. Number 1 poles are set for a normal stride with a measured distance of 3.10 meters (10.2 feet) between poles. Number 2 and number 5 poles are set for a longer stride with a distance of 3.40 meters (11.2 feet) between poles. Number 3 and number 4 poles are set for a shorter stride with a distance of 2.80 meters (9.2 feet) between poles. The distance from poles 3 to 4 is 18.50 meters (60.6 feet) and rides in six short strides. The distances can be adjusted to suit different types of horses and stride lengths, but also to change the courses' level of difficulty.

number 2 (canter poles set for a longer stride), then on to the long side over 3 and 4 (canter poles set for a short stride). Numbers 3 and 4 are set as a related distance as well and ride in six short strides. The course ends over number 5 (canter poles set for a longer stride).

Note: After number 5, the rider is on track to start the course again from number 1 if it is determined that immediate repetition would be beneficial.

- **Purpose:** To recognize and ride suitable stride length over the canter poles that are set for short, normal, and long strides.

Related Distances with Poles

This course combines training to improve the rider's feeling for suitable rhythm as well as counting strides between poles. The number of strides gives the rider an indication of how their track quality and rhythm maintenance are progressing. The track has a large impact on the number of strides between the poles especially in bending lines, therefore, the track should always be considered when analyzing

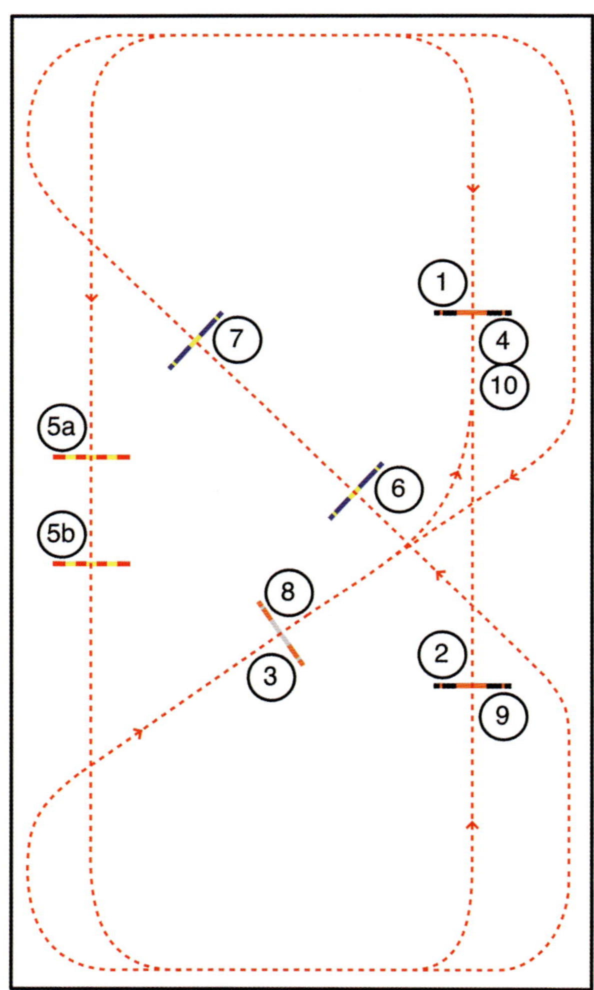

This course can be built in most arenas. In a narrower arena, the distance between pole numbers 6 and 7 could be set for one stride less. The course can be ridden in many different variations and combinations of the existing tracks. Pole numbers 1 to 2 are set for five normal strides and has a measured distance of 18.50 meters (60.6 feet); pole numbers 3 to 4 is set for six strides with a distance of 22.00 meters (72 feet); poles 5a to 5b are set for one stride with the distance of 5.50 meters (18 feet) between; poles 6 to 7 is set for four strides with a measured distance of 15.00 meters (49.2 feet). The distances can be adjusted to suit different types of horses and stride lengths, but also to change the level of difficulty.

Note: The distances depend significantly on arena size and footing and should, therefore be adjusted for each arena specifically.

and making changes to the stride length. This course starts with a related distance set for five strides, which encourages the rider to start in a good rhythm. The course then continues to numbers 3 and 4, which are a related distance set on a bending line— for most, this distance will ride in six strides (in addition to the stride length now the track also has a large impact on how the related distance will ride).

Numbers 5a and 5b is a one-stride combination on the long side, after which the rider changes direction across the diagonal over numbers 6 and 7, which are set as a related distance with four strides in between. The course finishes over the single pole number 8, which is set on the short diagonal.

▪ **Purpose:** To maintain suitable stride length in canter before, between, and after the poles while maintaining an overview of how many strides should be ridden in the given related distances and combination under normal circumstances.

Turns—Awareness of Turning Technique

This exercise combines larger turns with smaller turns, which can both be practiced separately before combining. Pole numbers 1, 2, and 3 can be ridden as a continual exercise (whereafter pole 3, the rider may continue to 2 and then to 1, and so on. Pole numbers 4 and 5 can also be ridden as a continual exercise. By doing so, any tension or other issues can be corrected before combining the two sections into one course.

- **Purpose:** To remain in good rhythm, relaxation, and control of the track while practicing shorter approaches out of the turn.

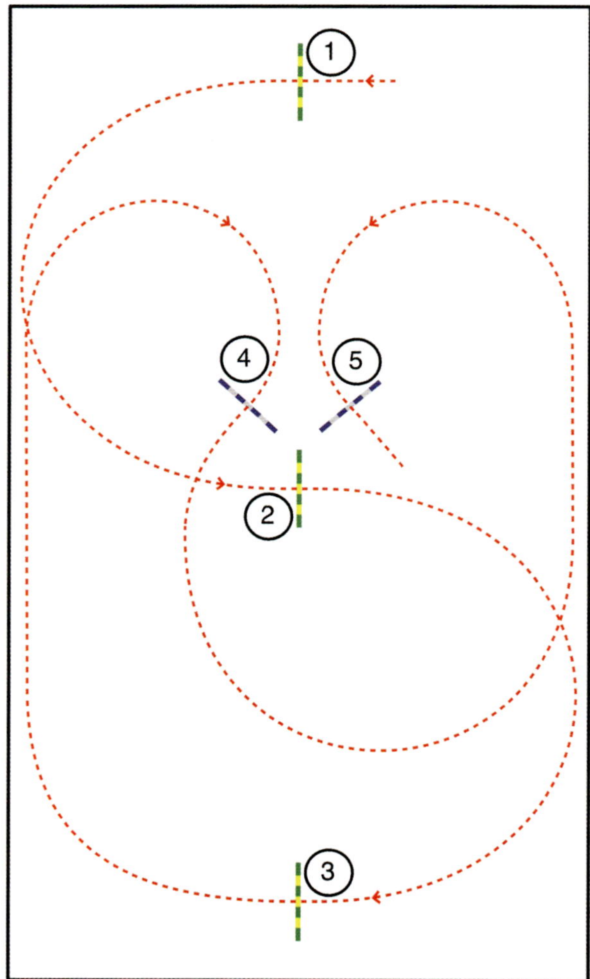

This course can be built in most arenas, and in a longer arena a fourth pole could be added to the centerline. A few words of advice when setting the exercise: keep even distances between the poles on the centerline. The diameter from the center of pole 2 to the center of poles 1 and 3 should be of a size that the horse can easily maintain the canter (a minimum diameter of 20 meters suits most horses).

Course Including Adjustment of Stride, Related Distances, and Turns

This course combines several tasks. From the beginning, the rider must decide whether to adjust for a longer or shorter canter stride as pole numbers 1 to 2 are measured to ride just between five and six strides.

Number 2 is set on the short diagonal, which gives the rider time to analyze the canter stride after the first related distance and determine if a change in the canter stride should be made. Pole numbers 4 to 5a and 5b are set as a related distance on a bending line into a combination, which is set for five normal strides with one stride in the combination. The choice of track in the bending line is of significant importance: riding an inside track will shorten the measured distance, while riding an outside track will lengthen the measured distance from pole numbers 4 to 5a.

Understanding the consequences of how the track impacts the related distance and how the combination will ride is very important when choosing the track to ride. For example, riding fast on the outside track leads to the combination riding short. Conversely, riding slowly on the inside track leads to the combination riding long.

The two single poles, numbers 6 and 7, are each set on diagonal lines to give the rider time to evaluate the canter and make changes if needed in preparation for the related distance from numbers 8 to 9 (exactly the same as the initial line in the course, as it is numbers 1 and 2 ridden in reverse), which may ride shorter due to the flow of momentum gained through the course.

The adjustment of stride length and turns onto the diagonals and short diagonals, together with repeated checks of stride length for the related distances, makes this a good "milestone course." Satisfactory completion ensures the rider's understanding of rhythm, track, and relaxation on course.

▪ **Purpose:** To expose horse and rider to a variety of different situations (varying approaches, adjustment of strides, related distances, and a combination ridden out of a related distance).

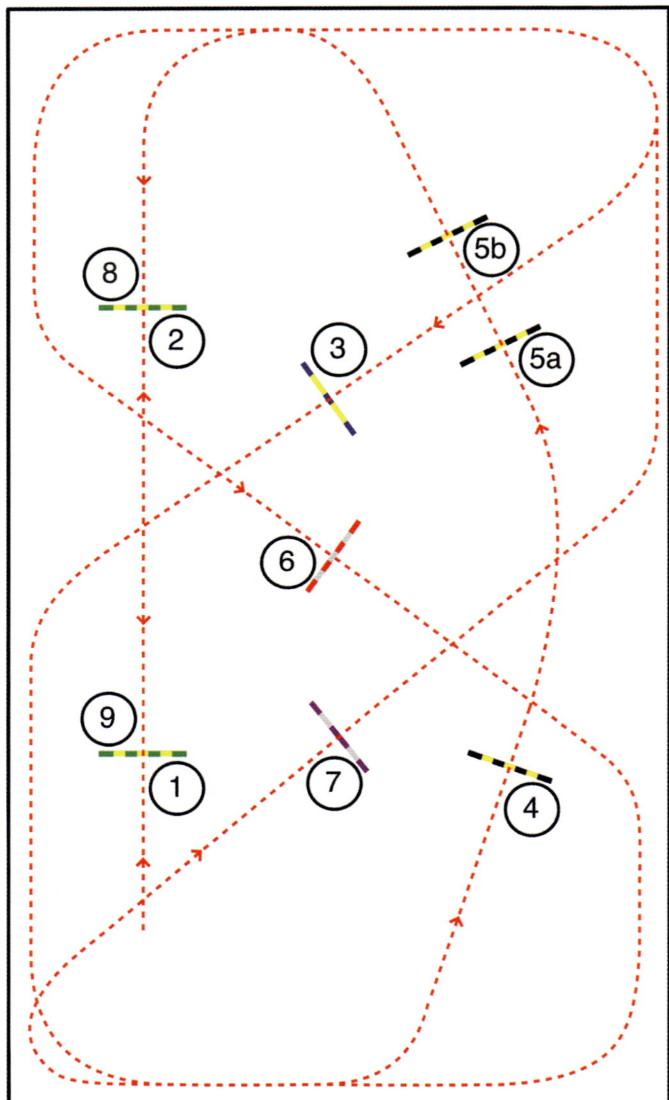

This course can be built in most arenas, with distances adjusted for different arena sizes and footing types in order to achieve the desired teaching effect of the course. The measured distance from pole numbers 1 to 2, is 20 meters (65.6 feet), and will require the rider to ride with a slightly longer stride in five strides, or with a slightly shorter stride in six strides (this should be done according to a plan determined before starting the course). Pole numbers 4 to 5a are set with 18.5 meters (60.6 feet) between, which for most horses will be five normal strides. The measured distance between 5a and 5b is 5.5 meters (18 feet) and rides in one normal stride for most horses. Riding this as a jumpoff course could be of value for the horse and rider that master this course in an elegant way. The poles for the jumpoff are: 1, 2, 3, 5a & b, 6, 7, 9.

The illustrated arena size for the jumping exercises included here is 30 by 50 meters. The green track indicates basic level exercises, the orange track indicates intermediate level, and the red track indicates advanced level.

These jumping exercises all have their foundation in dressage. Having an understanding of dressage tracks and how dressage training serves to shape a strong and healthy horse well into an old age, cannot help but make better riders, and therefore, happier, more highly performing horses. Most solutions to common problems that occur in jumping can be found within the basic dressage work. Jumping exercises often highlight both strengths and weaknesses in the overall training of horse and rider, and the true understanding of dressage allows the rider to go back and improve the training where improvement is needed.

A Formula for Success—Jumping

These are the core jumping exercises that are meant to help horse and rider through a structured development—*together*. The knowledge contained within these building-block basics help both rider and trainer know not only which step to take next when sufficient skills are achieved, but also to which previous step to return if difficulties are encountered.

The Beginning of Jumping

Jumping out of trot can be very beneficial at the beginning of the jumping training due to the fact that trot is a slower gait than canter, often making the track easier to manage, and the takeoff spot at the obstacle is easier to predict (with the additional help of a trot pole in front of the obstacle). This basic level exercise lays the foundation for the position of the rider over fences. In the initial phase, the rider approaches in a light seat and demonstrates a long release and hold of the mane over the fence (thus ensuring that the rider's hands do not disturb the horse's mouth). In this beginning phase, it is very helpful *not* to transition into a light seat right at the trot obstacle while simultaneously giving the long release because the rider often becomes overwhelmed, frequently leading to missing some of the key points for which this exercise is intended—for example, track, position, and release. Executing each skill separately in the beginning as illustrated supports learning, understanding, and further advancement.

In this exercise, it is important to remember that the track *after* the obstacle is equally important as the track *prior* to the obstacle. Jumping courses means jumping several obstacles in succession, and in this regard, the point of landing after one obstacle is simultaneously the track before the next obstacle. Emphasis must be made, when teaching beginning jumping skills, that each part of the track is equally important and requires attention from the rider.

In this most basic exercise, the rider has ample time after the obstacle to reestablish contact with the reins, check which canter lead the horse is on, and, if needed, ride a simple lead change through trot just before the turn, then use a large circle to establish a rhythmic and relaxed working canter.

As the rider advances, the movement over the obstacle will become less mechanical and more automatic, with the obstacle becoming a smooth part of the track.

▪ **Purpose:** For the rider to feel the motion of the horse jumping, and practice key skills such as track, position, and release.

This exercise can be built in most arenas, and to avoid favoring one particular side, it is helpful to utilize this setup of obstacles so that the approach can be ridden from the left and right. The obstacles can be built as lower verticals or cross-rails (the advantage of the cross-rail is that it supports the approach to the center of the obstacle). The pole on the ground in front of the obstacle will support a good takeoff spot, with the distance between the pole and the obsta-cle for an approach out of trot being 2.20 to 2.40 meters (7.2 to 7.9 feet). This distance should be adjusted for horses with smaller or larger strides, as well as for different types of footing.

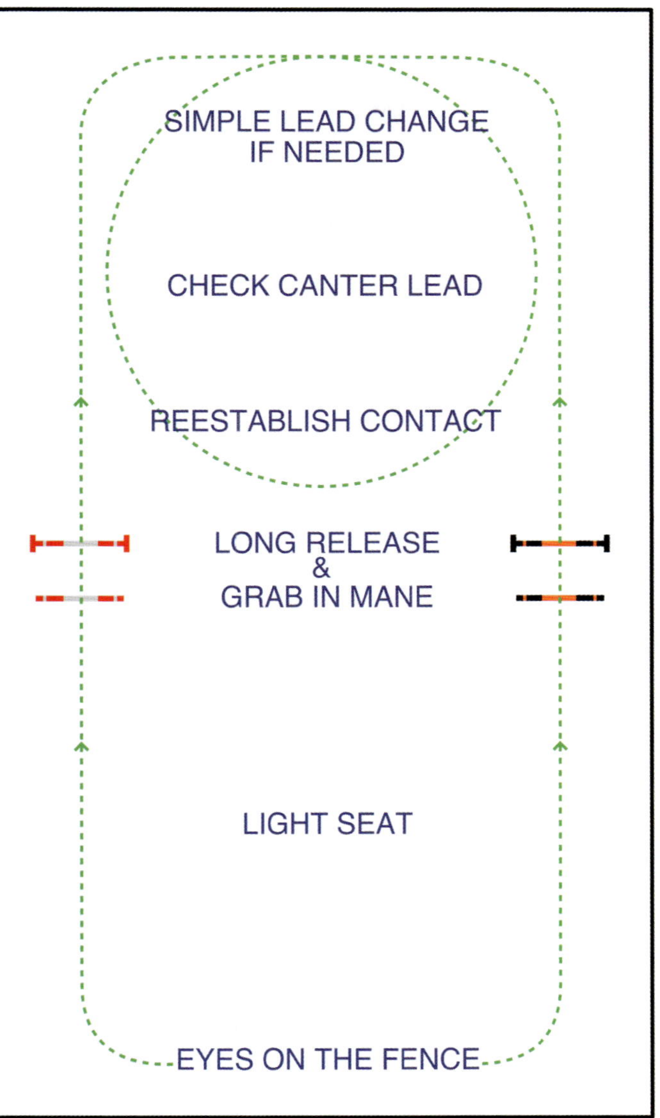

Obstacle on the Circle

This basic level exercise is introduced with a low obstacle or simply a pole on the ground, with the circle being an excellent way of keeping the speed under strict control compared to a long straight line in which there are several possibilities for situations, leading to drastic changes in speed that should certainly be avoided.

To support positive learning, the obstacles should be adjusted to a height where the rider remains calm and confident—this supports the rider's focus on riding a steady rhythm with a good track. To help the rider follow a good circle track,

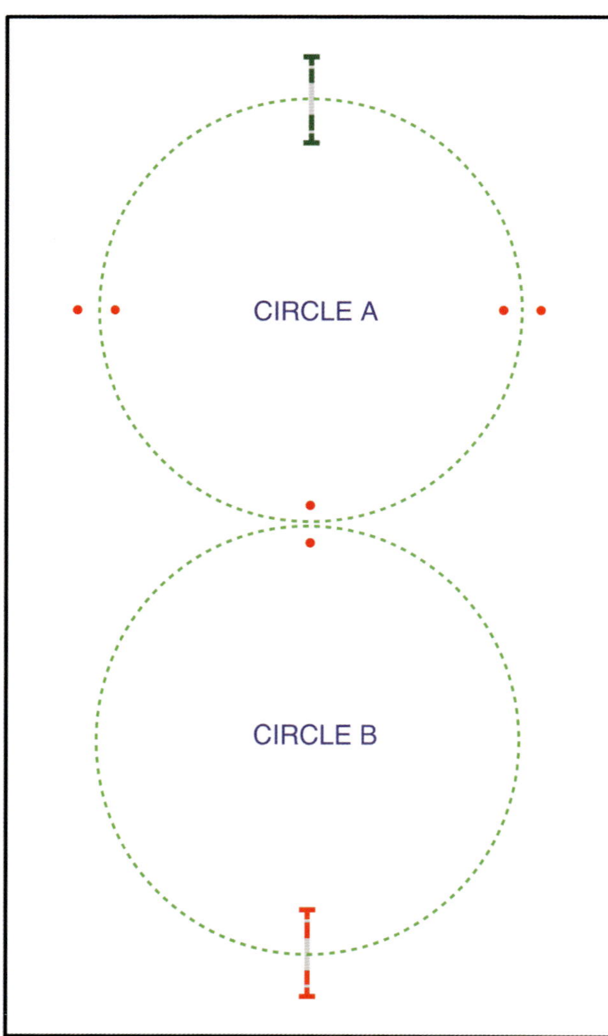

This exercise can be built in most arenas, and building the obstacles on the short ends eliminates the factor of the horse misunderstanding the aids and turning the opposite direction of what the rider intends upon landing (this can more easily occur when the obstacle on the circle is placed at X). Note how the two circles are identical, which will encourage the rider to ride the same shaped circle track with a very similar feeling in both situations.

cones can be placed on either side of the turning points on the circle as a channel to ride through. In the beginning, these cones can be very helpful for the rider to feel the symmetry of the circle. Good symmetry on the circle will make it easier to maintain a good rhythm to the obstacle, as compared to squared-off turns with a straight line ridden over the obstacle. While the rider often does this in an attempt to help the horse, more often it creates a "yo-yo effect" on the rhythm.

The position of the rider should remain balanced before, over, and after the obstacle. In the initial phase, it can be very helpful for the rider to think of a long release with a grab of the mane with the outside hand—the purpose being to avoid miscommunication between horse and rider caused by an overly tight or pulling outside rein. The inside hand gently supports the turning weight aids to remain on the correct circle track.

Circle A shows a supportive start in this exercise for the most novice rider by utilizing the cones as clear directives for a symmetric track.

Circle B is a good gauge for how much the rider has automatized riding a symmetric track in steady rhythm while remaining focused, even if the takeoff spots at the obstacle vary slightly between short, normal, and long. Frequently, the slight differences in takeoff spot disturb the concentration of the rider, which then often affects the track after the obstacle.

The repetition of the obstacle with priority remaining on rhythm and track will help the rider build a solid foundation and strong confidence in jumping out of canter.

▪ **Purpose:** To ride continuously in canter on a circle over an obstacle with steady rhythm and good track.

Obstacle Straight Ahead

This basic level exercise is designed as a continuation from jumping on the circle. Maintaining a good track with a steady rhythm requires a high level of attention from the rider and, when mastered, lays a good foundation for jumping obstacles on straight lines. It is important to understand that the obstacle is part of a track with one part before and one part afterward—thinking of jumping this way will help the rider to understand the value of riding an equally good track before and after the obstacle.

Cones can additionally be used to guide the rider to an ideal track. Placing an obstacle on the long side without the cones before and after can then be used as a check to ensure that the rider is not depending on support from the cones to maintain a good track. In the event that the rhythm changes after the jump, circles on the short ends can be a great help to reestablish a suitable rhythm again.

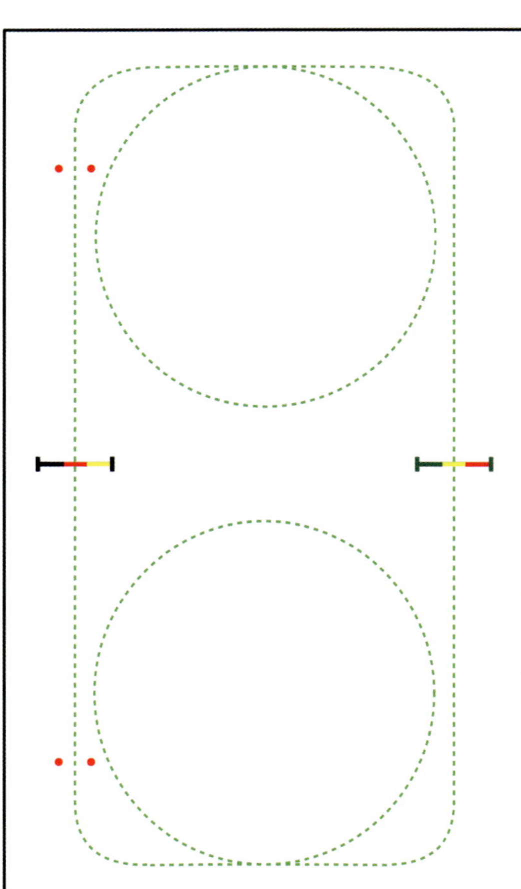

- **Purpose:** To ride a straight line in canter over an obstacle with a steady rhythm and good track.

This exercise can be built in most arenas, with the obstacles placed in the middle of the long sides to provide the rider with the same feeling in the approach from left and right (with and without cones).

Note: The circles can be used after the obstacle to reestablish rhythm and relaxation, if needed. Also, note how the track after the obstacle is completed before beginning the circle track.

Introduction to Changing Rein Over an Obstacle

This basic level exercise introduces changing rein over an obstacle in a smooth way. The placement of the obstacles in conjunction with the arena wall and the corner of the arena makes the change of rein and landing in the new canter lead very natural for the horse.

Starting with each diagonal ridden as a single exercise helps to break the exercise down in the beginning, and as horse and rider become comfortable with each single change of rein, the two obstacles can be ridden immediately after each other with the option of riding them as a continuous exercise as well. The long approach on the diagonal gives the rider plenty of time to be well prepared with a good track, steady rhythm, and a relaxed horse.

The position of the rider is also very important for a harmonious change of direction—to prepare for the exercise on a basic level, it can be very helpful to start with jumping out of trot to ensure a balanced position with correctly applied aids.

The cones are placed so they are helping the rider only with portions of the track. In the approach

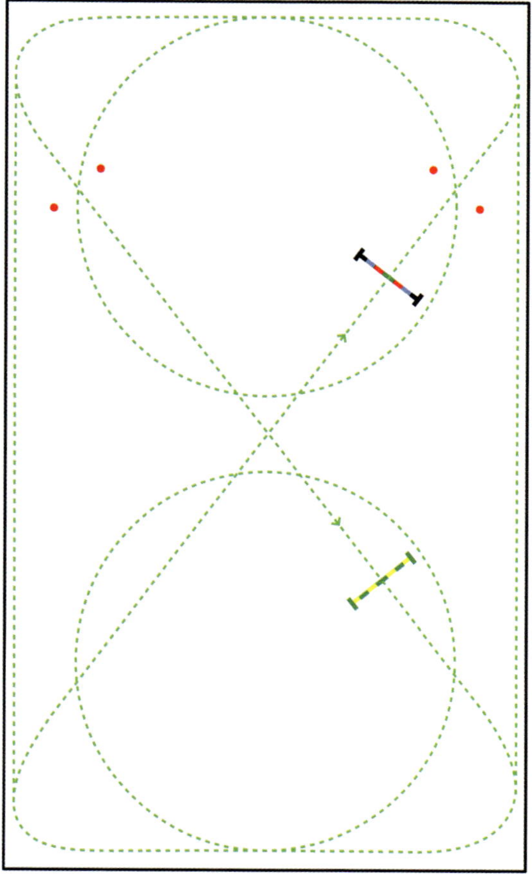

from the left, the rider has help with the approach to the obstacle; in the approach from right, the rider has help with the track after the landing. Placing the cones in this way helps to determine the rider's level of awareness for maintaining a good track.

- **Purpose:** Introduction to change of rein over an obstacle and understanding the importance of rhythm, balance, and track for a smooth change of direction while jumping.

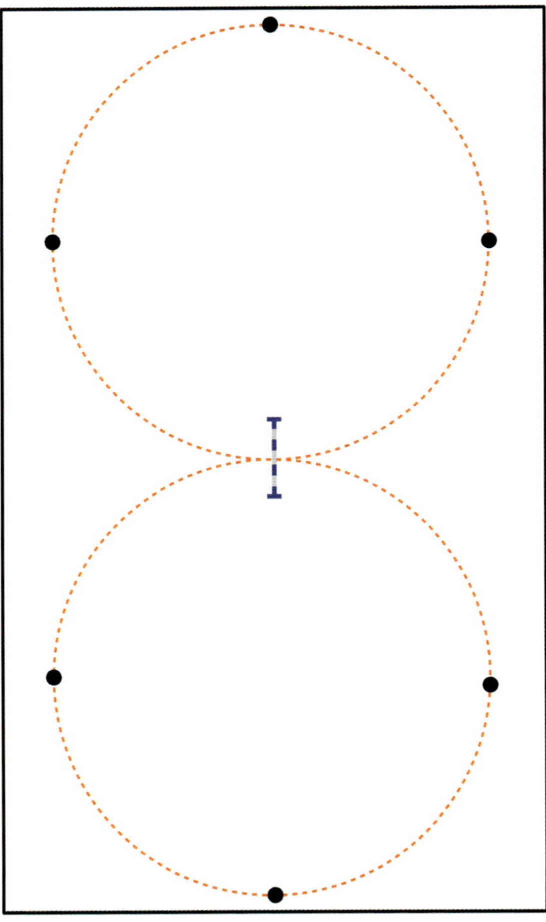

Changing Direction Out of the Circle Over an Obstacle

This type of direction change over an obstacle is more complex than a regular diagonal. For the horse, it is not as obvious in which direction to continue after jumping, since both turning left and right are equal possibilities. This situation requires the aids and signals that the rider is giving the horse (both voluntarily and involuntarily) be fair and clear.

This exercise can be built in most arenas. Note the marked turning points for the circle that underline the importance of riding a correct track. Following a correct track is crucial for mastering this exercise with balance and harmony.

To prepare for the change of direction, the horse and rider should be comfortable staying in one direction before changing direction out of the circle. When riding the exercise, it is very helpful to stay on the same circle for about three rounds or until horse and rider are relaxed and following a good track before changing direction.

The understanding of the arena tracks (see Part One—p. 3) is very important in this exercise because if not ridden precisely, this track often turns into a more challenging diagonal-like track (which also can be a good exercise but with a very different purpose behind it). It is of great importance that the weight aids and rein aids of the rider are matching; when not well coordinated, the horse tends to be confused in the landing and doesn't understand in which direction to continue.

It can be very helpful to approach the obstacle in trot to establish the feeling needed for a safe and harmonious change of direction at first.

▪ **Purpose:** Changing direction out of the circle over an obstacle and understanding the importance of rhythm, balance, track, and timing with the turning aids.

The Circle

This exercise offers the opportunity to canter many obstacles in succession, even in a smaller arena. The minimal amount of variation in track allows for the rider to focus on the practice of rhythm, balance, and relaxation while turning. Through the repetition of similar turns throughout the exercise, there is less chance of horse and rider becoming overwhelmed as compared to riding a varied track where the rider has to handle many different situations without the benefit of repetition.

A track with less variety is often helpful for rider and horse on a basic level for maintaining calmness of mind—with a calm mind there is more potential for horse and rider to grow in a positive direction through good experiences. The structure of the training is very important (literally crucial) in orchestrating calmness in the training. The progress at which horse and rider advance is very different from individual to individual, but calmness and relaxation should always be a priority in all training exercises. If calmness cannot be maintained, it is often an indication that previous work or exercises need to be revisited.

To prepare horse and rider for the complete consecutive exercise, it can be helpful to divide it into two sections: Obstacles 1 through 5, and Obstacles 6 through 10 executed separately, with a break for analyzing in between the two sections of the exercise.

Two factors that have a huge impact on the level of difficulty of this exercise are speed and obstacle height. As poles on the ground in trot, it is a very basic exercise suitable for most horses and riders; when the jumps are raised to Grand Prix height with higher speed, the nature and difficulty of the same exercise become very different.

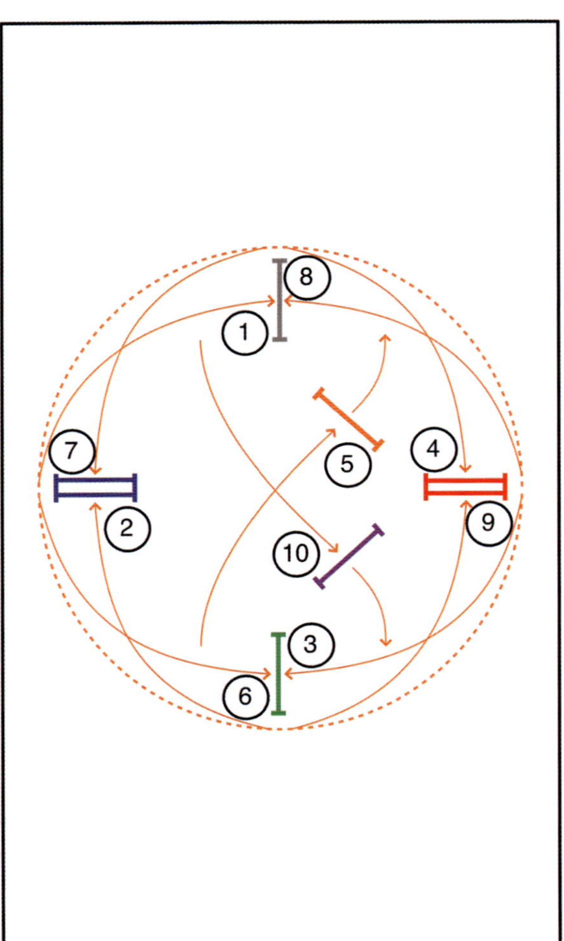

- **Purpose:** To canter several obstacles in succession while maintaining good rhythm, balance, track, and relaxation.

This exercise can be built in very small arenas and still transmit the feeling of riding a longer exercise by encouraging lots of canter. When built in a larger arena, it is beneficial to place cones outside Obstacles 1 through 4 to help maintain the integrity of the circle. The distance from the center of the circle to the obstacles on the circle should be equal to maintain symmetry.

Introduction to the First Course

This course connects a selection of previously described jumping exercises into an actual course that gives the rider a sense of familiarity when realizing this milestone in their training. The task of remembering the order of obstacles in a course adds an additional challenge for the rider along with the constant tasks of maintaining good position, rhythm, tracks, relaxation, and balance while jumping. When the horse and rider are learning new skills, it is helpful not to introduce several new tasks at once in order to support the best possible learning experience for both.

This exercise can serve as a gauge to see how well the skills of the rider are applied throughout different sections of

This exercise can be built in most arenas. Note how the various tracks within the course relate to previously illustrated exercises in this book and how these tracks stem from the classical dressage tracks in Part One. The orange line that represents the track is smooth and harmonious to ensure none of the tracks are taking the horse and rider steeply into a corner or creating other situations too difficult to be handled by the level of horse and rider.

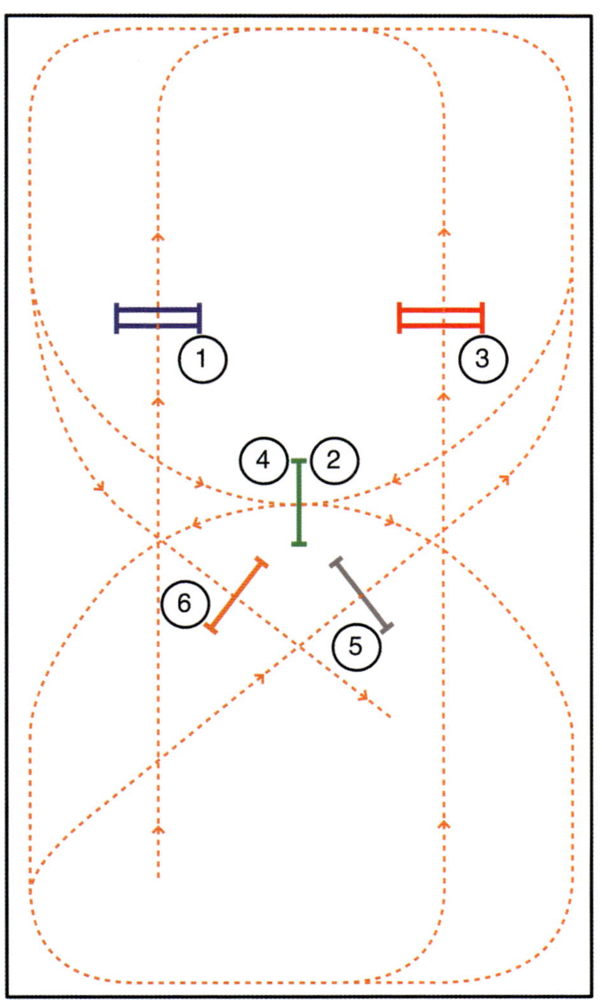

the course, then if the necessity arises, certain segments can be revisited in the training through practicing tracks like *straight ahead, changing direction across the diagonal,* and *changing direction out of the circle,* with or without poles or obstacles (pp. 5, 7, and 15).

▪ **Purpose:** To connect familiar tracks in a continual course with the emphasis remaining on maintenance of good position, rhythm, balance, tracks, balance, and relaxation.

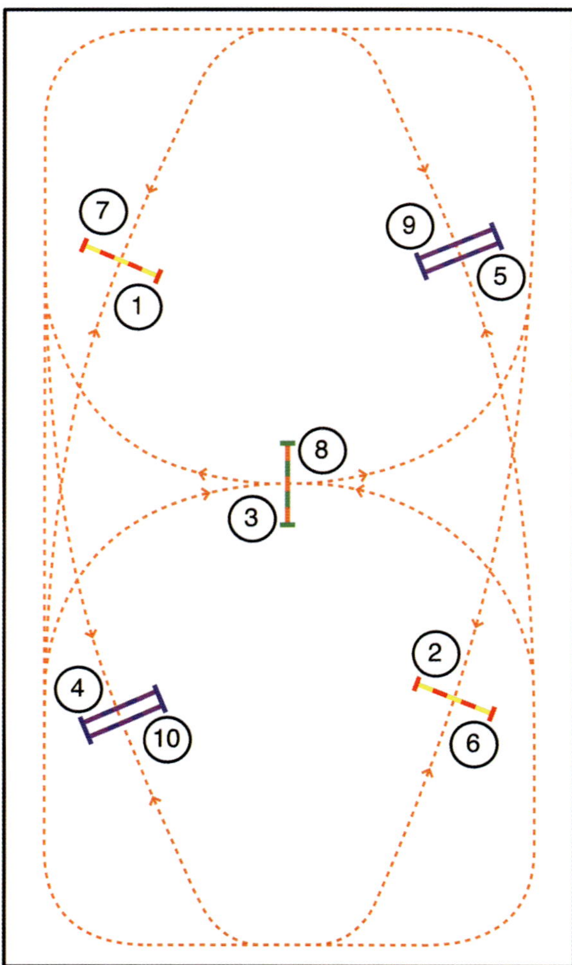

Longer Course with Long and Short Approaches

This course introduces the rider to a longer course of 10 obstacles. Obstacles 1 to 5 involve mainly long approaches, and Obstacles 6 to 10, mainly short approaches. The symmetry of the exercise together with minimal variation of track supports a very focused

In this illustrated exercise, the distances between the obstacles on the long sides are 20 meters (about 65.6 feet, measured on a bending line). This design is suitable for smaller arenas (20 by 40, 30 by 50 meters). If the course is used in a larger arena, it should be scaled symmetrically in order to maintain the integrity of the exercise.

training for maintaining rhythm, relaxation, and precision in the track.

The different types of approaches such as *long approach to vertical*, *long approach to oxer*, *short approach to vertical* and *short approach to oxer*, provide the rider and trainer with a clear overview of strengths *and* areas in need of improvement. Once identified, the areas that are in need of improvement can then be revisited and improved.

The antithesis is a course with many different types of approaches and situations, which is not wrong to create, but for educational purposes for riders on a more basic level, can be challenging to assess given the many variables and the complexity of determining exactly the strengths and weaknesses. Exact determination of these is crucial for a systematic education with the best possible progression.

- **Purpose:** Maintaining rhythm and relaxation during a longer course combining various approaches.

Introduction to Related Distances

This exercise introduces the importance of speed, stride length, rhythm, counting strides, and teaches the rider the correct reaction for the short, long, or normal takeoff spots at the obstacle leading into the related distance.

Speed is generally correlated with stride length—slower speed usually results in a shorter stride while higher speed generally results in a longer stride.

Stride length is also largely affected by the size and type of horse, but within the different sizes and types of horses and ponies there is also a large variety in stride lengths due to the various quality of the gaits.

The *rhythm* is another important factor in riding related distances—when a horse lands after the obstacle leading into a related distance, in a perfectly suited stride length for the given situation and that rhythm is maintained, the chance of having a good jump over the following obstacle is drastically *increased*. An irregular rhythm will conversely drastically *decrease* the chance of having a good jump over the second obstacle.

Counting strides between the obstacles in a related distance is another skill of significant importance, as it provides the rider with immediate feedback about the ridden stride length. Based on this feedback, the rider can then analyze if the stride is suitable, too short, or too long and then make the necessary changes if an adjustment of stride length is needed. Counting the strides is very important for training the rider's awareness of speed and stride length. (For example, in a related distance measured for five normal strides, on the first attempt, the rider counts six strides, which means the strides need to be longer. The opposite situation occurs if the rider counts four strides, then realizes that the strides need to be shorter). Such a basic explanation of counting strides is a good introduction to the general principles of riding related distances.

The reaction from the rider following the takeoff spot at the obstacle leading into the related

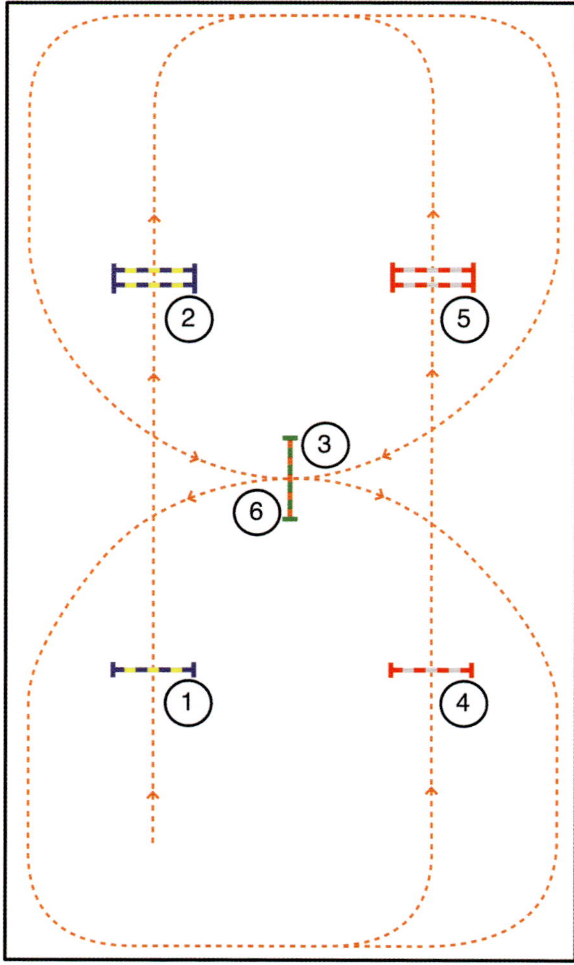

In this exercise, the distances between the obstacles on the long sides are set for five strides and measure 20 meters (about 65.6 feet—suitable for cross-rails and obstacles of similar height in sand footing). This design is appropriate for smaller arenas (20 by 45 and 30 by 50 meters). If the course is used in a larger arena, the distances should be lengthened accordingly.

distance is another skill of significant importance to the rider, which requires repetition until it becomes automatic. (To review related distances, see the illustration
on p. 48.) In this example, the arena is sized 30 by 50 meters, the related distances
are measured for five normal strides with both of them being identical, and since
quality repetitions are the mother of skills development, this setup allows for easy
repetitions due to the continuous nature of the exercise.

As a preparation for the longer exercise, Obstacles 1 to 2 can be repeated
until the rider has the feel for which stride length is needed and how to react in
response to different takeoff spots at Obstacle 1 (normal, short, or long). Once this
is repeated on the opposite lead over Obstacles 4 and 5, the short course can be
ridden in one piece. Note that after Obstacle 6, the course can easily be started
again. Once the rider reaches a more advanced level of skill and feeling, the
course can be ridden three times in a row, for example, with the first round having
five strides in each related distance, the second round having six strides, then the
third round ridden again having five strides.

This exercise tests and educates rider skills such as control and feeling of
the canter stride. It is also a great way to evaluate the level of strength the horse
has developed through your dressage work. When riding an extra stride in the
related distance is very challenging, strengthening exercises in the form of flatwork should be revisited (see Part One) to avoid frustration and tension in the
jumping exercises.

▪ **Purpose:** To develop the rider's feeling for speed, rhythm, stride length, and
how different takeoff spots *into* the related distance affect the obstacle *out of*
the distance.

Introduction to Combinations

This introduction to combinations includes approaches in both trot and canter. The advantage with introducing combinations out of trot first is that a slower speed gives the rider more time to focus on steering and the position on top of the horse. Once the rider feels that steering and position are not problematic, it is usually only a minor progression to advance and approach combinations in canter. One major difference between combinations and related distances is the number of strides between the obstacles—combinations have only one or two strides between

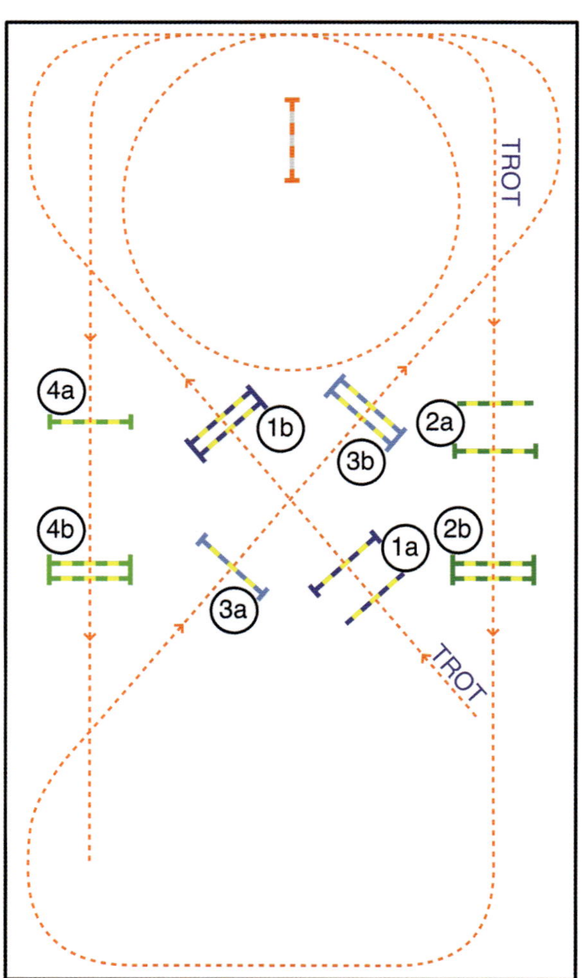

This exercise can also be built in many different arenas. The types of horses, height of the obstacles, and arena size are some factors that carefully need to be considered and adjusted for when setting the measured distances between the obstacles. In this arena with the obstacle height being about 0.5 meters (1.6 feet), the distances are set to the following measurements:

Trot poles in front of combinations: 2.2 to 2.4 meters (7.2 to 7.8 feet).

Obstacles 1a to 1b:
9 meters (29.5 feet).
2a to 2b: 5.5 meters (18 feet).
3a to 3b: 10.25 meters (33.6 feet).
4a to 4b: 6.75 meters (22.1 feet).

Note: The "b" obstacles are illustrated as oxers but can be replaced with verticals for less experienced horses and riders.

the obstacles, and the fewer strides found between obstacles, the less time the rider has for any necessary stride adjustments.

The vertical on the short side (at top of diagram) can be used as a warm-up obstacle so horse and rider do not have to start jumping with a combination as the first obstacle. After warming up over the vertical on the centerline, Obstacle 1a is jumped out of trot with two canter strides to 1b. Once horse and rider are comfortable with this trot combination, they continue down the long side and change direction across the diagonal over 3a and 3b, which is a two-stride combination approached in canter.

When comfortable with the two-stride combination, it is generally a good time to introduce a one-stride combination, and Obstacle 2a is then approached in trot with one canter stride to 2b. And after becoming familiar and comfortable with the one-stride combination out of trot, combination 4a and 4b are jumped out of canter with one canter stride in between.

Once the different combinations have been introduced separately, the exercise can be ridden in the numbered order as illustrated. Obstacle 1a is approached in trot with two canter strides to 1b, and approaching the corner, the rider checks which canter lead the horse is on, and if correction is needed, a simple or flying lead change is ridden.

Once a good rhythm and balance is established, a transition to trot follows, and a circle can be ridden if the rider needs extra time to get reorganized. Thereafter, the horse and rider continue to 2a and 2b, which is a one-stride combination jumped out of trot. The rest of the exercise is ridden in canter—3a and 3b is a two-stride combination on the diagonal, and 4a and 4b is a one-stride combination on the long side.

This exercise can easily be executed in sections over several sessions with the goal of finally combining them all in succession.

▪ **Purpose:** To introduce combinations in a systematic and pedagogic way that optimizes success and confidence-building in both horse and rider.

Combining Related Distances and Combinations

This exercise is not technically difficult but requires a significant amount of attention to details such as tracks, rhythm, and how stride adjustments are made in the combinations and related distances. The straight lines followed in the approaches to the obstacles require discipline and patience from the rider not to turn too early or too late (for a review of the approach lines, see p. 37) but also to maintain rhythm.

On long straight approach lines, it is easy to begin second guessing the rhythm and, therefore, change it without reason. This rarely leads to a better situation for takeoff at the obstacle.

The circle that follows on the short end allows for enough

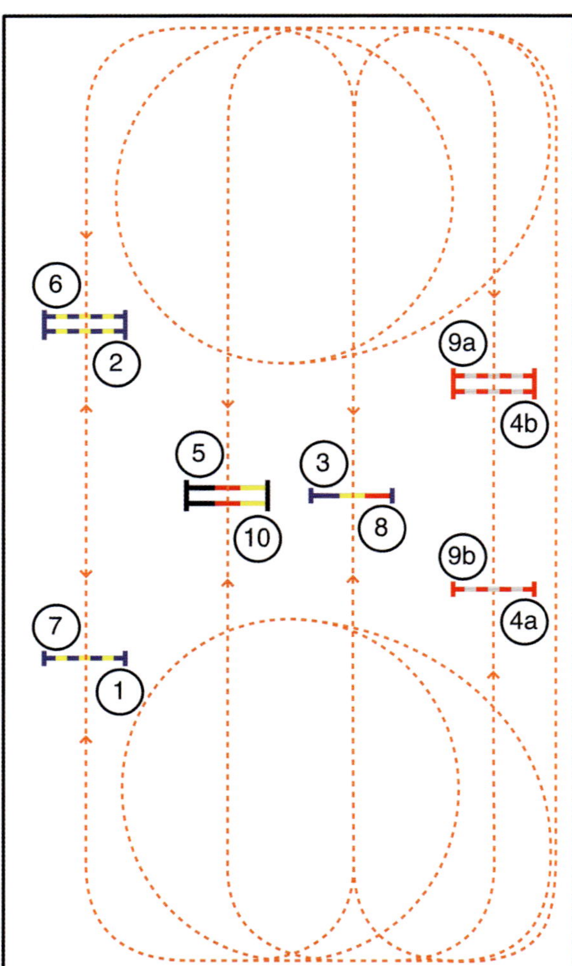

This exercise can be built in many different arenas. In a significantly narrower arena, the two obstacles closest to the centerline can be replaced with one obstacle and still follow the same principles of the illustrated exercise. For typical Warmblood horse types (in this arena with obstacle height set at about 0.5 meters (1.6 feet) the distances are set to the following: Obstacles 1 to 2—16.50 meters (64 feet) ridden in four strides, and 4a to 4b—10.00 meters (32.8 feet), a two-stride combination.

Note: Different types of footing, different arena sizes, and different heights of obstacles require adjustments to the measured distances.

time to evaluate the previous obstacle using self-directed questions like: *Was the horse straight? Was the horse relaxed? Was the rhythm the same before, over, and after the jump? Was the overall pace suitable—not too slow or too fast? How was the approach line? Was the straight line followed after the obstacle? How was the position of the rider?* For all these necessary assessments, the circle provides the rider with enough time to answer the questions and make any changes. After a few warm-up jumps, the exercise starts with Obstacles 1 and 2, which is a related distance. This means the rider has to choose and maintain a suitable canter for the measured distance immediately from the beginning of the exercise.

In the circle following the distance, the rider analyzes the canter and decides if any changes should be made to improve track, balance, rhythm, or stride length. The rider then continues to Obstacle 3, which is a vertical. After Obstacle 3 comes a slightly tighter turn into the corner, followed by a large circle that is used to prepare for the combination, Obstacles 4a and 4b. The combination is followed by another circle, which the rider can use to repeat the analysis of the canter and either make improvements or maintain good balance, stride length, and rhythm while continuing to Obstacle 5, an oxer.

After the oxer, the rider continues down the long side and starts the second part of the course, Obstacles 6 through 10, where the same principles are followed, using circles to analyze the canter quality between the obstacles.

The main goal with analyzing the canter on the circles between the obstacles in the course is to improve the jumping quality, with the obstacles being used as a feedback source to evaluate if the changes made to the canter bring horse and rider closer to or further from the goals of harmony and fluidity in the course. This practice provides valuable information for rider and trainer in determining which adjustments and techniques are working well and which are not.

Note: The exercise can also be separated into several segments. This option allows for more intensive work with a specific segment, and afterward, the whole course can be ridden again to determine what progress has been made.

▪ **Purpose:** Practicing discipline with tracks, rhythm, and combining related distances and combinations into a continuous exercise.

Introduction to Serpentine

This exercise requires the rider to be very disciplined with the rhythm and track due to the quick succession of obstacles following one after the other. This means that in order to maintain control, rhythm and track must be well-maintained. A rider who maintains a regular rhythm and good track with obstacles adjusted to a suitable height finds much benefit from this exercise, whereas poor rhythm and or track will create tension in the horse, often creating a stressful experience for both horse and rider. Under the latter circumstances, this exercise will not be beneficial from an educational standpoint and should be skipped until suitable control and discipline are in place.

The exercise *can* be executed in three stages to ensure competency:

Step One: Ride Obstacles 1, 2, and 3 (this short series of obstacles will demonstrate if horse and rider have good control over rhythm and track).

Step Two: Ride Obstacles 1 through 6 with the long side ridden between Obstacles 3 and 4 as illustrated in the diagram (the long side will provide the rider with extra time to analyze and reestablish a suitable rhythm should it prove necessary).

Step Three: Ride the obstacles in the following order,:1, 2, 3, 2, 1, 2, 3 and so on (the most advanced progression of this exercise) not only tests the rider's ability to remain disciplined and focused but also how quickly the rider is able to get the situation under control again if a change in track and rhythm do occur. This can only be done through quick analysis and equally quick reflexes in addressing the cause of an issue occurring within the exercise.

▪ **Purpose:** Maintain rhythm and track under the conditions of obstacles following quickly one after another.

This exercise can
also be used in many
different sizes of arenas
having a length over
40 meters (131.2 feet).
If the arena is signifi-
cantly over 60 meters
(196.8 feet) in length,
a *fourth* obstacle can
be placed on the
continued, symmetric,
serpentine-style line,
or alternatively, parts
of larger arenas can be
blocked off with cones.

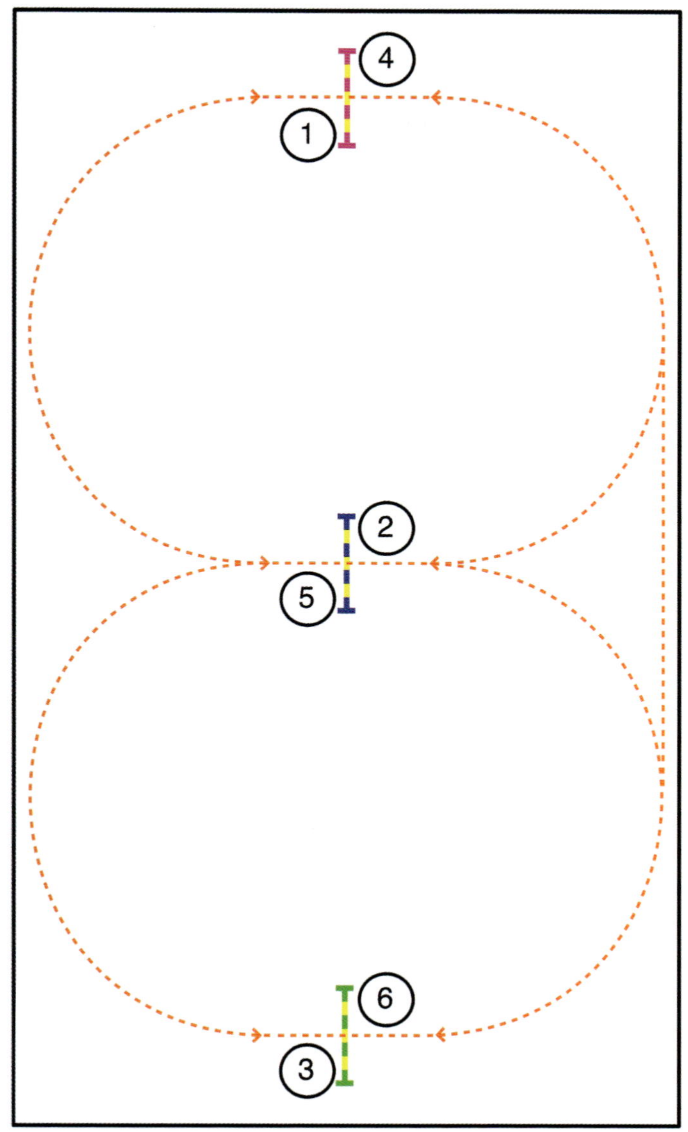

Long Course with Long and Short Approaches, Related Distances, and Turns

This course is an extension of the longer course with long and short approaches with Obstacles 1–10. (For a review of the course with long and short approaches see p. 47) Therefore, in this diagram, only the second part of the course, obstacles 10 to 17, are numbered and illustrated (that is, the course starts with Obstacle 10 and ends with Obstacle 17). A helpful way to prepare for combining the two parts into one course is generally to ride Obstacles 1 through 10 and Obstacles 10 through 17 separately, then combine the two parts when each is ridden at a satisfactory level.

The second part of the course as illustrated here includes related distances on a bending line, which have more variables (in addition to stride length and type of takeoff distance) than a related distance on a straight line. (For a review of takeoff and landing spots, see p. 35).

Jumping into the related distance, the track has a large impact on how the distance will ride—the *inside* track is significantly shorter than the *outside* track, which is very important to understand theoretically *and* be aware of during the exercise.

The skilled rider can use the bending line in a beneficial way (for example, with the short-striding horse, the distance can be ridden slightly to the inside, and with the long-striding horse, the distance can be ridden slightly to the outside), which supports a regular rhythm even on a course with a high difficulty level. Jumping bending lines can be introduced with great benefit through the use of poles—the poles allowing the rider to experience the effects of riding the inside, normal, or outside track while avoiding putting the horse in a difficult situation at the jump. (For a review of related distance on a bending line, see p. 79).

The turns on course after Obstacles 16 and 17 are very advanced and require good footing and a balanced rider that is able to give clear aids—without this combination of requirements being met, the turns can simply be left out and the course can end with Obstacle 15.

▪ **Purpose:** Exposure to a long course with various types of approaches.

This exercise can be used in many different sizes of arenas (with a minimum length of 40 meters (131.2 feet). In the diagram (with the length of 50 meters—about 164 feet), the distances are set for six strides with the measured distance of 23.50 meters (77.1 feet), which suits this kind of arena and footing well.

Note: The turns after Obstacles 16 and 17 only should be practiced with very balanced riders on good footing and with horses that have the suitable level of training.

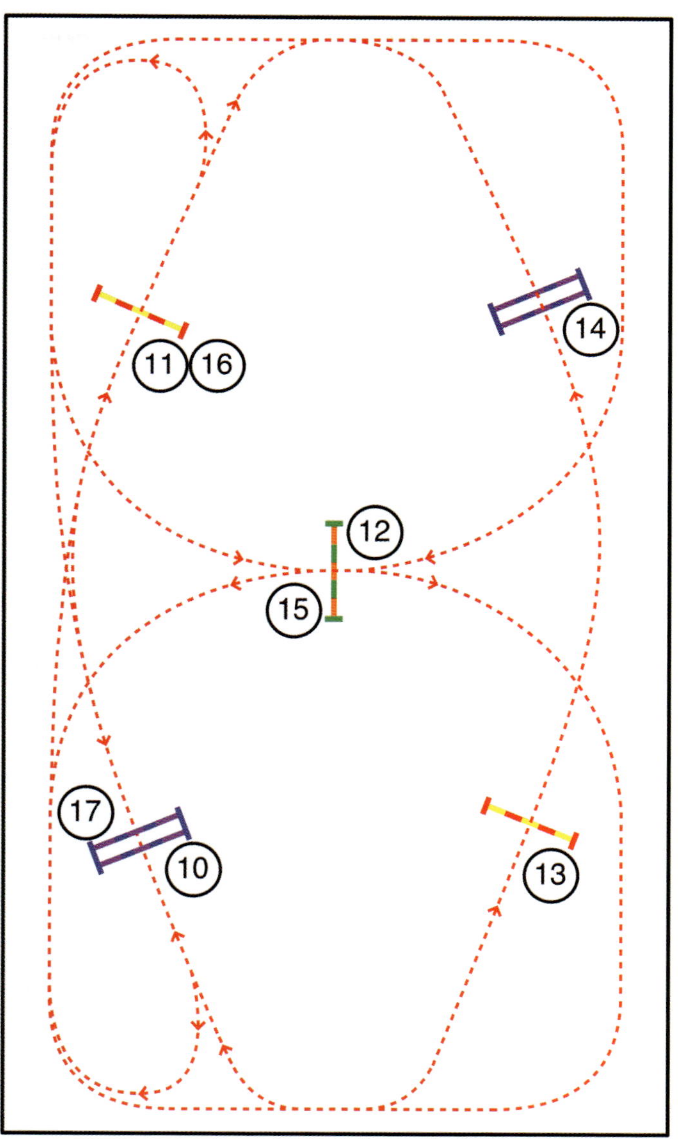

It All Comes Together—Assimilating Knowledge

This course assimilates many of the rider's skills that are required and practiced in the previous exercises. The course starts with Obstacles 1, 2, and 3, which are set on the familiar *serpentine-style line*. (For a review of the *serpentine-style line,* see p. 100). This is directly followed by Obstacles 4 and 5, which are set on two short diagonals. The course continues with a change of direction over Obstacle 6—a similar track to *change direction out of the circle*. (For a review of *change direction out of the circle over an obstacle,* see p. 45).

Obstacles 7 and 8 are a *related distance on a straight line*. (For a review of a *related distance on a straight line*, see p. 35). They are followed by another change of direction over Obstacle 9. The course then ends over 10a and 10b, which is a *combination* (you can review combinations on p. 96).

This fairly short jumping course combines many different elements, as most "real world" courses are also a variation of different elements (think jumping out of turns, diagonals, related distances, and combinations) and within these elements there are many variations as well. Certainly, there are more challenging situations than the ones occurring here in this course but the different elements of which the course is comprised will provide rider and trainer with an indication of strengths and weaknesses in the training—especially when combined with the appropriate obstacle height for horse and rider.

▪ **Purpose:** To combine assimilated knowledge into one course.

This course can be built in many different sizes of arenas (with a minimum length of 40 meters—131.2 feet). In this arena (with the length of 50 meters—164 feet) and height of the obstacles being 0.5 meters (1.64 feet), the related distance is set for four strides with the measured distance of 16.50 meters (54.1 feet); the combination is set for two strides with the measured distance of 10.00 meters (32.8 feet), which suits this kind of arena and footing well.

Note: Different types of footing, different arena sizes, and different heights of obstacles require adjustments to the measured distances.

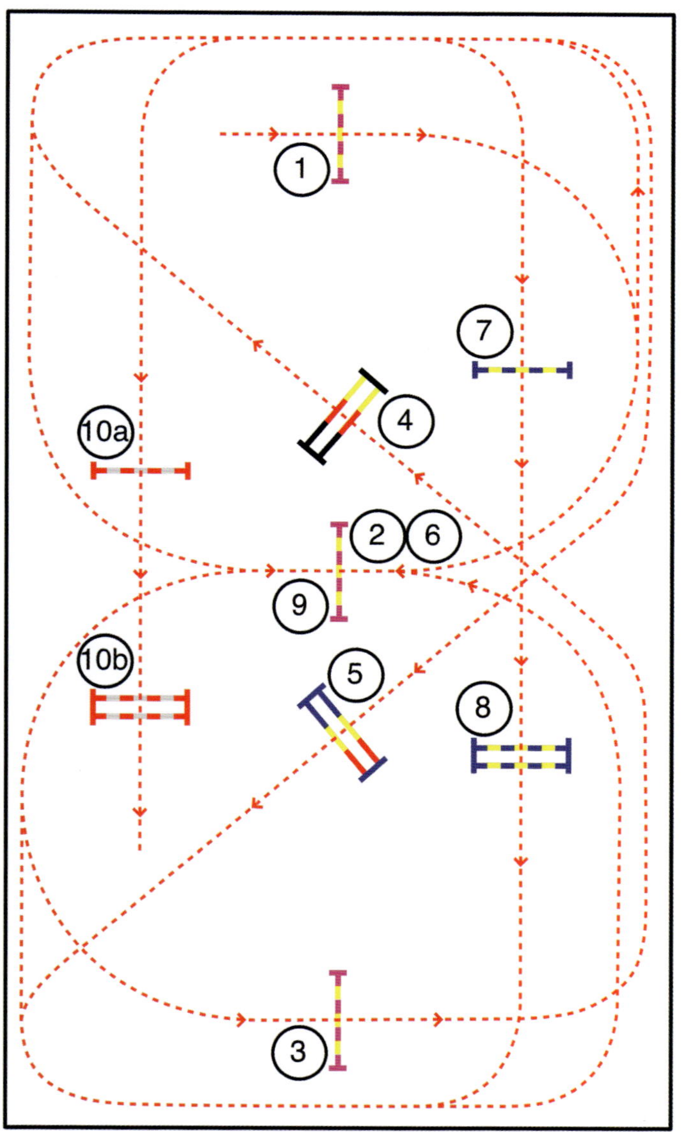

SUPPLENESS, RHYTHM, AND CONTROL— Jumping Exercises

These exercises can be used to incorporate more variety in training.

Canter Poles to Support Rhythm in the Approach

This setup of poles and obstacles builds on the basic exercise with canter poles on the long sides and diagonals. (To review canter poles on the long sides and diagonals, see p. 49.) Utilizing the canter poles helps the horse and rider not only determine suitable rhythm for the situation, but also maintain a suitable and steady rhythm in the approach to the obstacle. The canter poles provide the rider with valuable feedback to determine if the strides are too long and fast, just right, too short and slow, or if the rhythm is changing within the canter poles themselves.

The circles on the short ends can, if needed, be very helpful for horse and rider to make necessary adjustments to the canter stride length and balance to achieve a more ideal approach and rhythm to the next obstacle.

The tracks by themselves are very basic so when the understanding for these are established in dressage work (see Part One) as well as over poles, they should not cause any difficulties. When difficulties are present, the solution is generally to go back and review the dressage tracks again and practice them over poles to determine where the source of the problem is. Ideally, the horse should not have to change length of canter stride or speed over the canter poles, assuming the rider established an ideal rhythm for the measured distance between the poles. When the canter strides are a bit short, the horse will have to lengthen them to reach across the poles, and if the canter strides are a bit long, the horse will have to shorten them to fit the strides in before the obstacle.

▪ **Purpose:** Training rhythm in the approach to the obstacle while using canter poles for feedback regarding stride length and speed.

This course can be set in most arena sizes. Setting the poles and obstacles in a way that allows for circles to be ridden on the short ends (as illustrated) can be very helpful for horse and rider in establishing or reestablishing suitable rhythm. The distances used here are generally suitable for the typical Warmblood horse. Distances between the canter poles and the poles and obstacles are 3 meters (9.8 feet).

Note: Different types of footing, different arena sizes, and different heights of obstacles require adjustments to the measured distances.

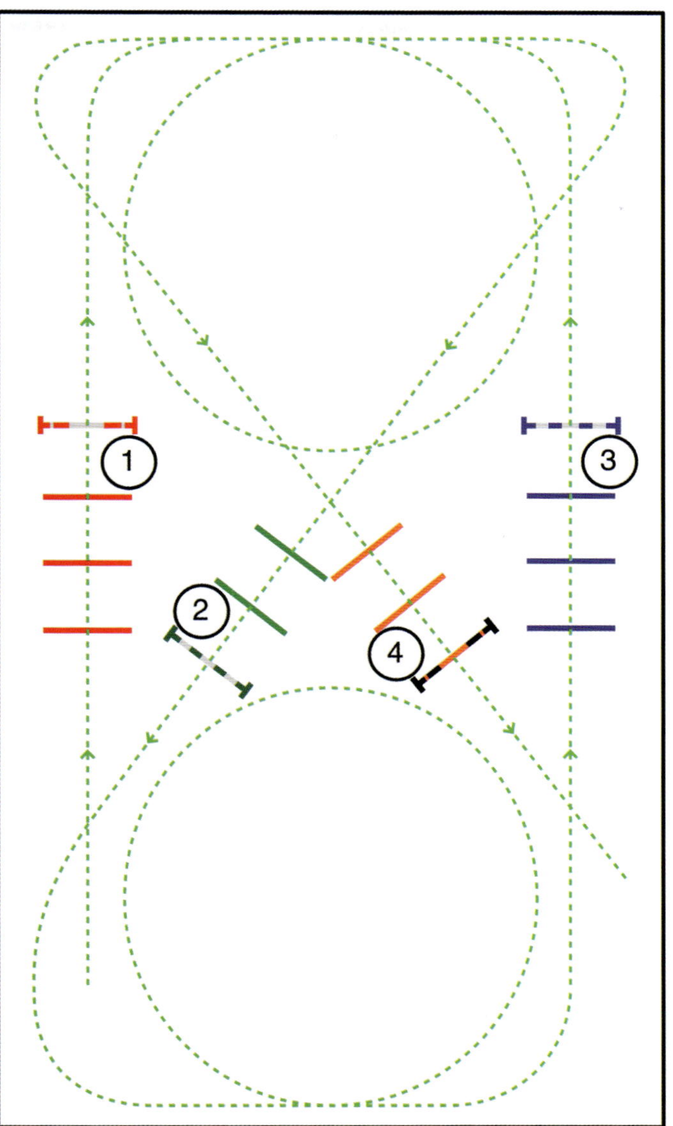

Canter Poles and Automatic Release

The core of this exercise is the obstacle on the long side with the canter poles placed before and after. Changing Obstacle numbered 1 and 4 to a canter pole on the ground makes the exercise suitable for warm-up over poles. Once the track, rhythm, and hands of the rider are at a satisfactory level, Obstacle 1/4 can be built up as a small jump. Raising it in the middle with canter poles before and after requires the rhythm to remain very steady.

If there is a significant change in rhythm linked to the middle pole being replaced with the Obstacle 1/4, a solution is to return to canter poles on the ground only and evaluate the quality again. Very likely, there will be a recognizable change in the rhythm, which is then more easily corrected over the canter poles on the ground without an obstacle, assuming the rider is not changing the way of riding because of the obstacle itself.

Special attention should be devoted to the rider's hands and the soft contact that follows the mouth of the horse over the canter poles.

Raising the obstacle in small increments will help the rider maintain a soft feeling of the mouth through the reins while the horse is jumping—this is the automatic release. When riders have difficulties controlling the hands, they should be evaluated in the dressage work without obstacles and then over a single obstacle with a long release. After determining where the problem lies, it can be corrected, and the rider can return to work with the automatic release.

Basic tracks continue this course, including different obstacle types like a triple bar, oxer, and vertical. Having the canter poles as obstacle number 1 and then repeated in the course again as number 4 can be very helpful for the rider for maintaining a steady rhythm throughout the course.

▪ **Purpose:** Improving the rider's feeling of rhythm and automatic release over obstacles.

This course can be set in most arena sizes. The distances used here for normal-sized Warmbloods between the canter poles and between the poles and the obstacle are 3 meters (9.8 feet). Note, however, that different types of footing, arena sizes, and heights of obstacles require adjustments to the measured distances.

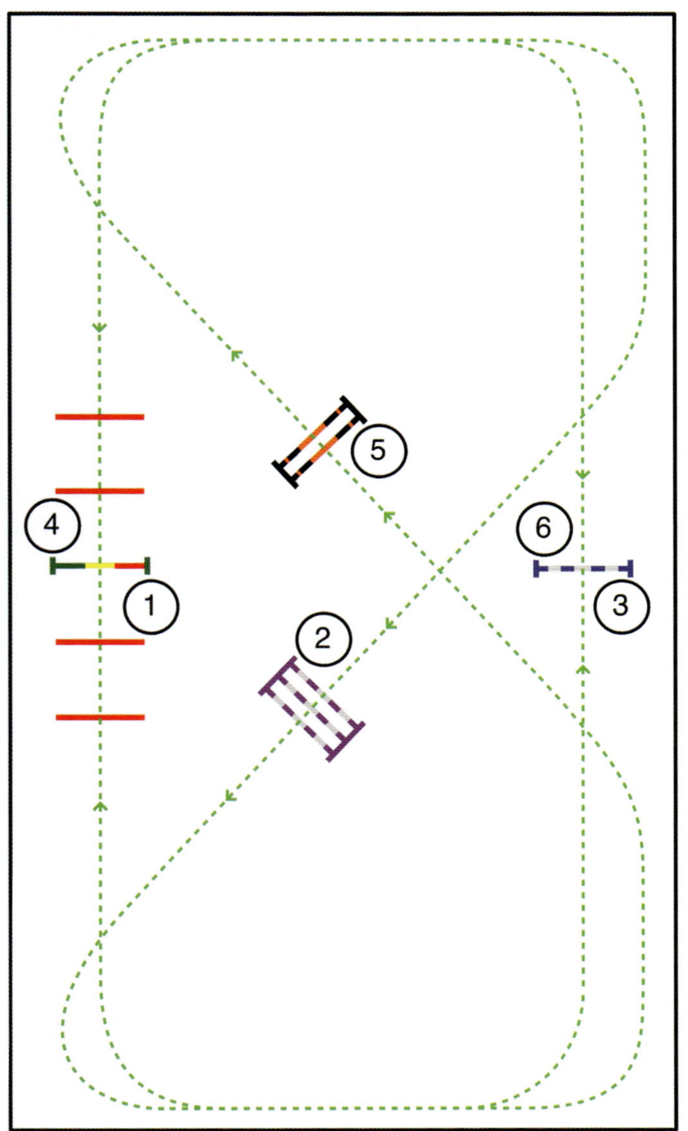

Awareness of Rhythm and Track

This setup of obstacles is a good checkup regarding how rhythm is maintained throughout the course without the help of canter poles as in the previous exercises. Here, instead, the related distance will be a gauge and source of feedback for how the rhythm and length of stride is managed by the rider. Good tracks are important for the course to ride in a harmonious way, while the placement of the obstacles in this course will help the rider in making appropriate choices in regards to the track without the use of cones. Thinking of this course in three sections, with each section teaching a different set of skills, will help with both warm-up jumping and the later work with the complete course. The first of the three sections of the course is basic level with two single obstacles on the long side, Obstacles 1 and 5, both of which should be built in a way that they are able to be jumped from either direction. The next section is the obstacle in the center that can be ridden on the circle and as change of direction out of the circle. The last described section is the related distance on the opposite long side from the two single obstacles, these are Obstacles 3 and 4, which also should be built in a way that they safely can be jumped from either direction.

The three sections can be used in any order, depending what is most suitable for horse and rider. The course itself can also be divided into two sections: Obstacles 1 through 5, and Obstacles 6 through 10. Dividing the course into sections as described can be very helpful for both the trainer teaching the course and the rider learning the course.

- **Purpose:** To demonstrate awareness of rhythm and basic tracks.

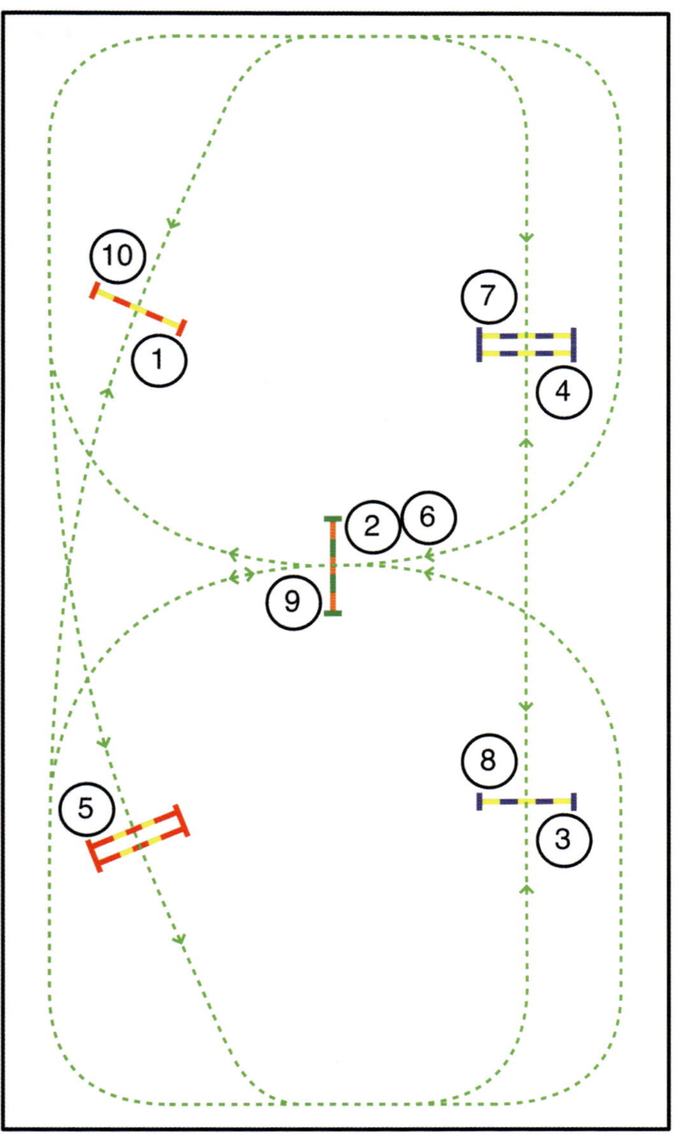

This course can be set in most arena sizes with only minor modifications. For a longer arena, lengthening the related distance and spreading obstacles 1 and 5 farther apart is recommended. The related distance as illustrated here measures 20 meters (65.6 feet) and is suitable for five strides if ridden with normal-sized Warmbloods over low obstacle height.

Note: Different types of footing, arena sizes, and heights of obstacles require adjustments to the measured distance.

Long and Short Approaches

This exercise is allowing the horse and rider practice for different types of approaches, such as riding straight before and after the obstacle, approach on the diagonal, and approach out of a turn. Obstacle 1 is set on the centerline and can be approached from left or right. In the diagram, it is approached in trot with a trot pole in front to support a suitable takeoff spot. This obstacle can be made more advanced through an approach in canter. In this case, the trot pole should be removed or the distance from pole to the obstacle lengthened. The fact that the rider can ride straight ahead with a relaxed horse after Obstacle 1 opens many options for advancement in the training. If the horse attempts to turn early due to lack of consequent training, most of the rider's effort and aids will necessarily be geared toward holding straight, and, therefore, any option of intentionally ridden short turns with a relaxed horse is eliminated.

Obstacle 2 is a fairly normal approach with roughly three straight canter strides to the obstacle following the turn. Obstacle number 3 is set toward the end of the diagonal with an approach of about six straight canter strides to the obstacle after the turn. Obstacles 4 and 5 are ridden with about one straight canter stride to them after the turn beforehand.

These are various scenarios in which the level of difficulty is greatly affected by the track and speed. If the exercise is ridden in regular speed with ideal track, it will provide rider and trainer with valuable feedback about the status of the current training. Answering the question, *Do the horse and rider struggle to maintain good tracks with good rhythm and suitable speed?* helps in determining what level of education horse and rider have achieved. If the horse and rider make the exercise look easy, it, in general, means that they are ready for the next step of advancement, which can be in areas of height, track, speed, or type of exercise. Should the exercise appear to be difficult for horse and rider, an analysis should be made to determine exactly where the areas of difficulties are, then once identified, they can be improved with suitable training.

▪ **Purpose:** Riding straight on the centerline and practicing a range of approaches (from long to short).

This exercise can be set
in many different arena
sizes, however, note
that a narrower arena
will make the shorter
turns more advanced.
If the arena is consid-
erably larger, it can
be helpful to block off
some space with cones.
The distance from the
trot pole to Obstacle 1 in
this diagram measures
2.20 to 2.40 meters (7.2
to 7.9 feet).

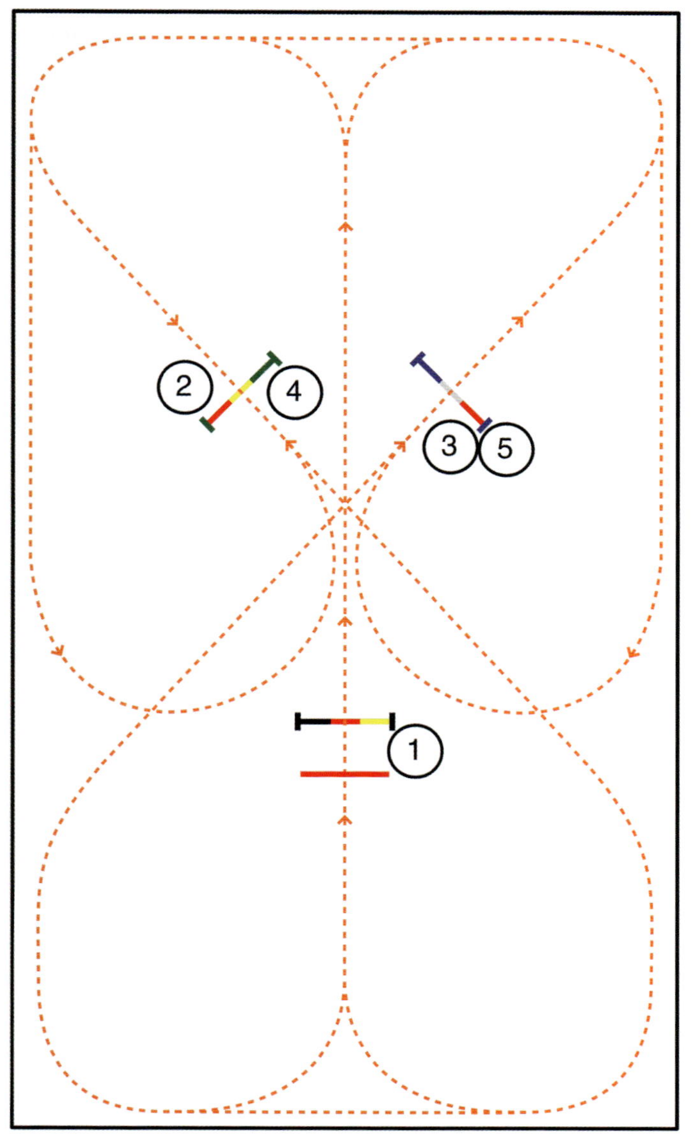

S-Line

This exercise with three applications (ranging from basic to advanced) is an excellent example of how one setup can serve various levels of training.

The *basic track* (marked in green) is exposing the horse and rider to several different types of approaches, ranging from short to long, as well as different types of tracks upon landing after the obstacle—from a short track with a quick upcoming turn to long straight tracks. This exercise can be used as a continual course as well—after Obstacle 4, the rider continues directly to Obstacle 1 to restart the course. This immediate repetition can be helpful for correcting minor mistakes regarding rhythm, track, or position. Repetition is a valuable tool for teaching horse and rider, especially when the rider has awareness of the cause of mistakes *and* understands the steps required for improvement. If a more in-depth explanation or analytical discussion is required between rider and trainer, or even for self-analysis, it is often more beneficial to do this during an aerobic recovery break for the horse.

The *intermediate track* (marked in orange and with the letters A and B) is an exercise that requires prompter changes of bend and flexion and is, therefore, a more intensive suppling exercise. When this track is introduced to horse and rider it is helpful to start with the track marked with A—it will ride similarly to change direction through the circle, and only includes one change of direction. Once track A is mastered and the rider can direct the change of direction with well-timed aids that support a correct change of bend and flexion, the horse and rider progress to the track marked B. This track includes the obstacles in the same direction and angles as track A but with a total of three changes of direction—the increased number of bend and flexion changes sets higher demands for the correct timing of the aids, which must be given in order to ensure correctly executed changes of bend and flexion throughout the exercise.

Once horse and rider are familiar with track A and B separately, the two tracks can be combined into a six-obstacle exercise: the rider rides track A and directly continues to track B. After track B, the rider has the option to continue and directly restart the exercise from track A when immediate repetition is considered beneficial.

This exercise can be set in many different arena sizes with a minimum length of 50 meters (164 feet); however, note that a narrower arena will make the shorter turns more advanced. If the arena is considerably longer, more obstacles can be added to the exercise by following the same pattern illustrated here. A helpful hint while building the exercise on low heights (0.5 meters—1.6 feet—and below), and for two strides between the obstacles on track C and three strides between the obstacles on tracks A and B, is to lay the poles straight on the center-line like a combination with 10 meters (32.8 feet) from center to center. The poles are then rotated from the center of the pole to a suitable angle (in this case roughly 45 degrees) and the distance from center to center is maintained.

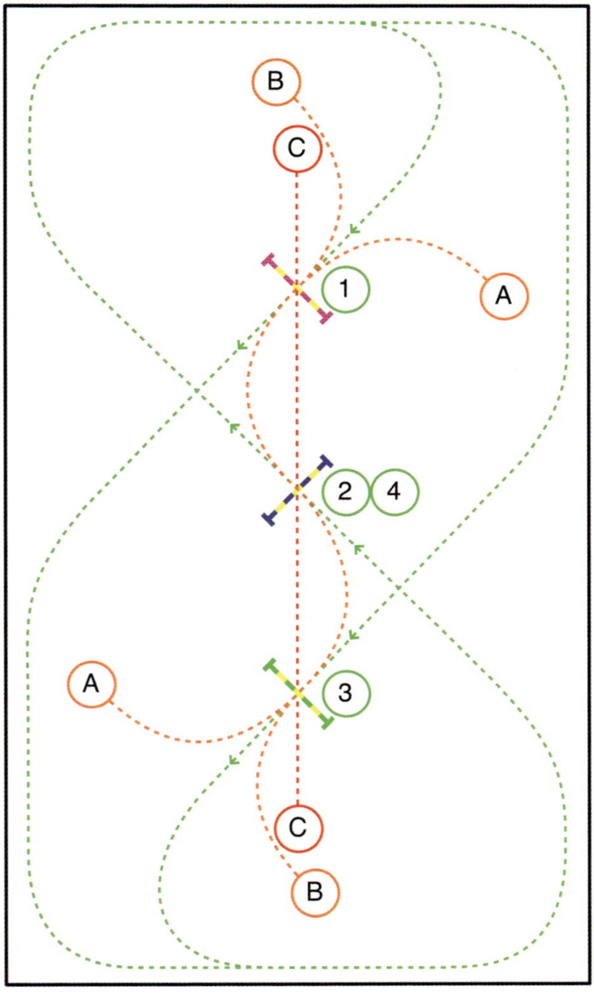

The *advanced track* (marked in red and with the letter C) aims to improve and train higher level control of the horse's body and stride while jumping the obstacles from an angle and successively on a straight line (similar to a combination with three elements).

The straight line over the angled obstacles requires a high level of straightness. Naturally, the opposite of a straight horse is a crooked horse. The crooked horse is naturally bent more in one direction (which most horses are to varying degrees); however, through the systematic training with correct suppling focus, the rider constantly works with the horse to become progressively more even in his left and right side.

The successful execution of all three exercises presented here requires good control over the horse, each on a different level. When introducing new exercises or unfamiliar situations, it is important for rider and trainer to introduce only one new major challenge at the time. If the rider or trainer introduces this exercise to a horse that already has difficulties in maintaining a good track and adds challenging height to the obstacles, the likelihood of rider and horse succeeding and having a good experience decreases drastically.

▪ **Purpose:** The *basic* (green) track has emphasis on rhythm and track. The *intermediate* (orange) track is focusing more on suppling. The *advanced* (red) track is intended to support high level control of the track with the added challenge of optics from the angled fences.

Transitions and Obstacles

This exercise works well for improving rider softness and control of the horse between obstacles. It is excellent practice for the rider to learn to refine the aids while eliminating unnecessary pressure that often leads to excessive forward energy and tension in the horse while jumping. The exercise begins with Obstacle 1 approached out of trot; after landing in canter, the rider gently rides a transition back to trot and continues to Obstacle 2, after which the rider transitions back to trot and continues to change direction over Obstacle 3 (trot poles placed on the centerline).

Obstacles 4, 5, and 6 are a mirror image of 1 to 3, and after Obstacle 6 (trot poles), the horse and rider are in a position for immediate repetition of the course when it's determined that repetition is beneficial for the best possible progress.

Circles can (with great benefit) be used after the obstacles to reestablish rhythm and balance should these be lost through jumping. Although the circles can be very helpful, the goal is to recognize the root cause of loss of rhythm or

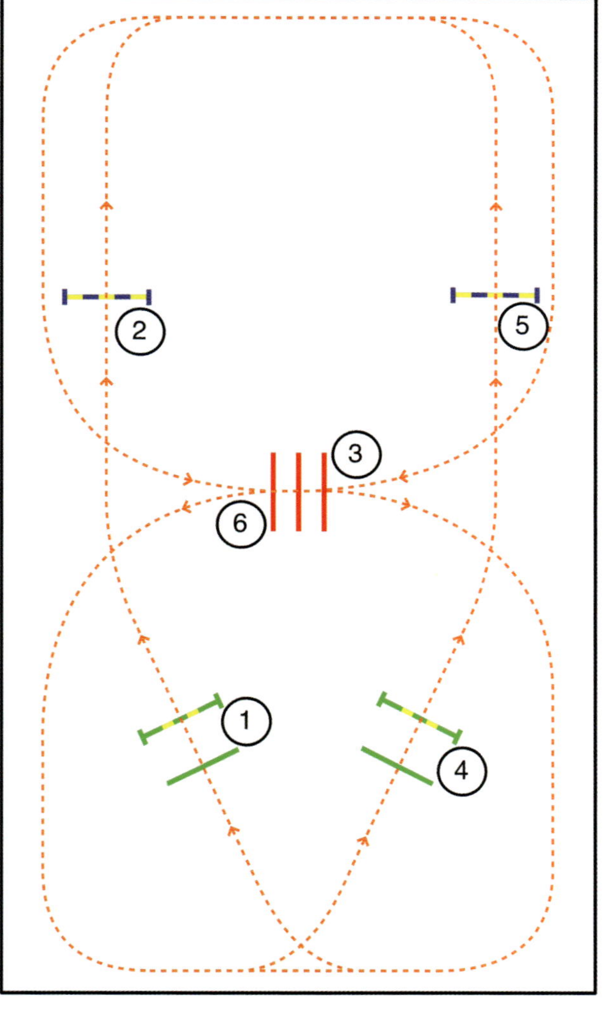

balance. With correct repetition, the need for utilizing the circles should slowly diminish.

This exercise is also a good tool for working with the position of the rider, which (before, over, and after the obstacle) has a direct correlation to how balanced and relaxed the horse is when landing after the jump. Obstacles 1 and 4 have a trot pole placed in front that helps with the timing of the takeoff. Obstacles 2 and 5 have no trot pole in front so require and train the rider's feeling for being balanced and in sync with the horse before, over, and after the jump *without being left behind or jumping ahead of the horse's motion.*

▪ **Purpose:** To support a relaxed and balanced horse between obstacles in addition to practice for the rider's position and timing of the aids.

Jumping Without Tension

This exercise continues training with transitions and obstacles (to review transitions and obstacles, see p. 116) as transitioning between trot and canter are very suppling and can serve as a great source for information about potential jumping-related tension in the horse. When tension is present, it is important to analyze where it could be stemming from. Among the various reasons for tension, there are two common sources: Either the rider has had previous stressful experiences that trigger a stressed state of mind (often leading to tense application of aids and a lower cognitive ability) or the horse has had them.

Note: Certain breathing patterns such as slow breathing through the nose are generally linked to a calm state of mind, whereas fast breathing through the mouth is often linked to

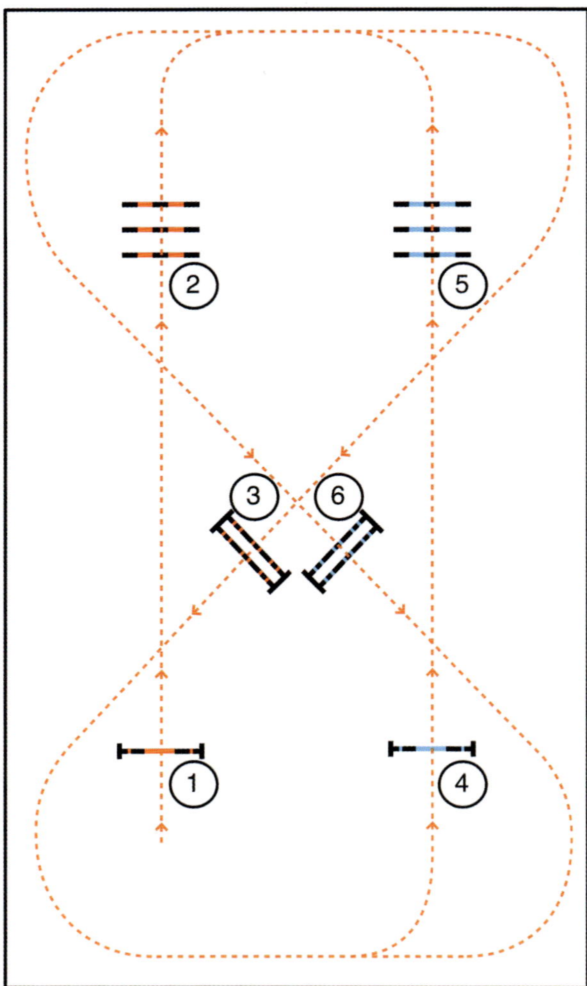

This exercise can be set in many different arena sizes. The distance from Obstacle 1 to the trot poles is in the setting depicted is 25 meters (82 feet); however, this measurement can be adjusted for different arena sizes and levels of difficulty. The trot poles are placed with 1.2 to 1.4 meters (3.9 to 4.6 feet) between each pole.

a more stressful state of mind. *If the rider is mindful of how to breathe, it is often possible to control the balance of the autonomic nervous system in a way that is beneficial for riding.*

In this exercise, it will make a noticeable difference if the rider is in a more relaxed state compared to a "fight or flight" state in which the muscles are usually tense and the fine-motor skills are less refined. This control over mind and muscles is very important since most of the rider's communication with the horse is kinesthetic.

This exercise starts with Obstacle 1, which is jumped out of canter, after which the rider gently transitions to trot and continues to Obstacle 2 (the trot poles). If tension is present (which could lead to difficulties with the transition) it can be of great help to ride a large circle around Obstacles 3 and 6, thus providing the horse and rider with more time in preparation for the trot poles. After the trot poles, the rider transitions to canter and continues to Obstacle 3 (an oxer on the diagonal). If the rider experiences difficulties in establishing a suitable canter for jumping after the trot poles, a large circle around trot poles number 2 and 5 can be beneficial.

The exercise then continues with Obstacles 4, 5, and 6—a mirror image of Obstacles 1 through 3. With a relaxed and responsive horse, the exercise can also be ridden in the reverse direction: the horse and rider begin over Obstacle 6 from the opposite direction, then continue to number 5 (the trot poles), then immediately transition to canter and jump Obstacle 4 (which comes up quickly after the transition to canter). The more relaxed and responsive the horse is to the rider's aids, the more harmonious this portion of the exercise will be.

The rest of the exercise (Obstacles 3 to 1 ridden in the reverse direction) is a mirror image of Obstacles 6 through 4 (obstacles should be built in a way that they are safely jumpable in both directions).

While riding this exercise, it is important to keep the emphasis on harmony and quality. Height is a factor that can be added when everything else is demonstrated at a satisfactory level. A good starting height is the height where horse and rider can make minor mistakes without causing stress, tension, or loss of confidence.

▪ **Purpose:** Riding transitions as a suppling exercise and as a gauge for determining levels of tension or relaxation in the horse related to jumping.

One Obstacle with Several Options

This is not so much a specific exercise as it is training and exposure to different arena tracks over a single obstacle. The horse and rider will almost certainly see these tracks or a variation of them while jumping against the clock on an intermediate to advanced level, and therefore, this type of training should be a natural part of the education for horse and rider. It is also important to consider that speed is a factor that generally influences the level of difficulty of any exercise, and so, awareness and practice of different speeds should be included as a part of regular training and be on an adequate level of mastery before being used in conjunction with jumping.

The track marked with number 1 is the centerline, which can serve as a valuable check to determine if the horse can remain relaxed on a straight line over an obstacle (for the horse to be able to stay straight and relaxed is an important prerequisite before starting to work on turns and angles). If these basic requirements are not met there is the possibility for the horse to become nervous and tense, which can lead to future loss of confidence.

Track number 2a introduces the use of angles in the approach to the obstacle—in this case the angle is about 70 degrees, which for most horses on an *intermediate* level does not cause any doubt to proceeding over the obstacle. Introducing angles should always be done with a lot of sensitivity as to how the horse is responding to ensure the best possible learning experience for both horse and rider.

Track 2b takes the track to a more *advanced* level with an angle of about 50 degrees. If the introduction to jumping out of angles has not been introduced gradually with specific focus on how the horse is responding, there is a risk the horse becomes insecure and loses confidence as the level of difficulty is increasing. It is important to remember that if signs of insecurity appear, it will generally be helpful to take a step back and make the task less challenging (this could mean changing fence height or the angle of approach). The degree of angles mentioned here is only for illustrating a gradual progression—slower advancements for creating the best possible learning environment for horse and rider is *never* incorrect.

This exercise can be set in many different arena sizes. If the arena is very large it can be helpful to use cones to guide horse and rider toward the desired tracks.

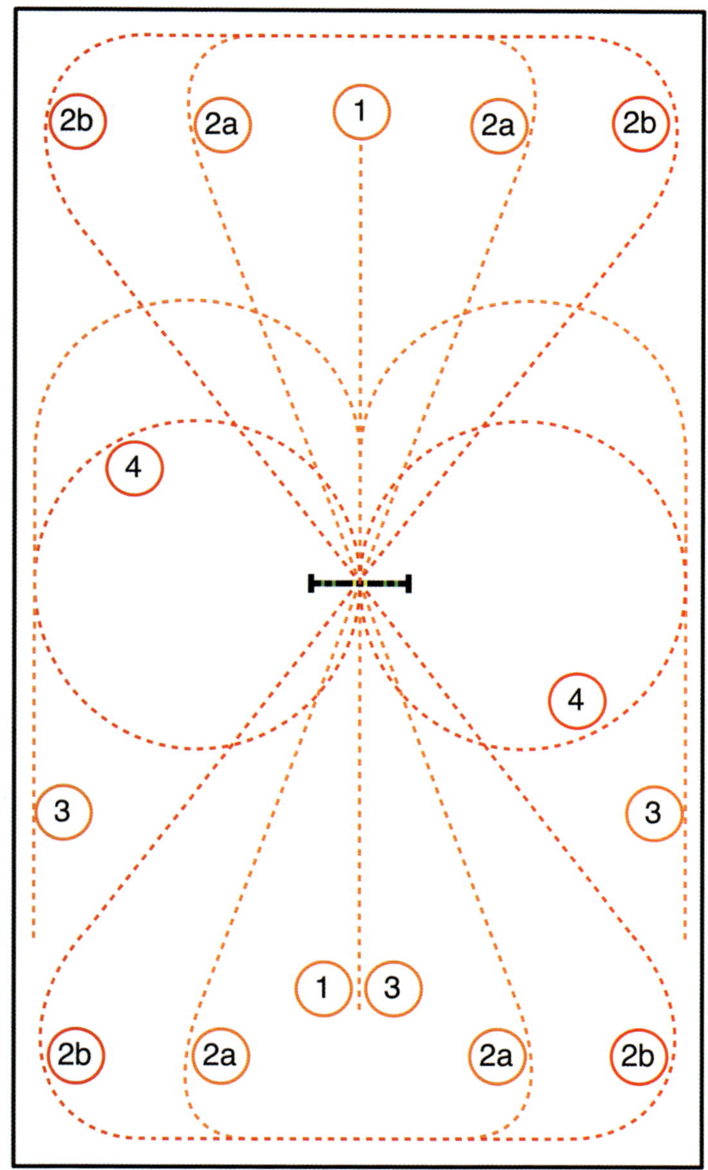

Track 3 is similar to a half-circle back, and the level of difficulty can be controlled by how early the horse becomes straight prior to the obstacle (the fewer straight strides the horse can take before the takeoff, the more the level of difficulty increases).

Track 4 is a smaller scale version of *change direction out of the circle* (see p. 45). This is considered an *advanced* track since the takeoff at the obstacle is out of a turn and the landing is directly into a turn. Also, the size of the arena and the height of the obstacle have a large impact on the level of difficulty.

Training with tracks like these in a safe and calm environment allows for a deeper development of the knowledge and awareness of what challenges are within the comfort zone for any horse-and-rider combination. The odds of success for horse and rider drastically improve when training tracks in a systematic, calm, and controlled environment, and therefore, their odds for success when performing under pressure improve as well.

Note: Once the horse and rider have developed enough experience and trust in this exercise, the vertical can be replaced with a spread obstacle.

▪ **Purpose:** Systematic practice and exposure to many common situations that occur in the *intermediate* and *advanced* levels of jumping competition courses.

Training the Unpredictable

In this exercise, the horse and rider are exposed to a very short approach out of the turn, due to the placement of Obstacles 2 and 5. In this situation, the possibilities to adjust the tracks for a different takeoff spot are very limited as the placement of the obstacle and the outside parameters of the arena significantly restrict possible track options for horse and rider.

Approaching the turn to Obstacles 2 and 5 in a higher speed is more advanced than approaching out of a slower speed; therefore, the triple bar on the centerline is placed as Obstacle 1, which encourages the rider to maintain a good forward pace. These two factors (speed and turn) create an excellent training experience for the rider, including learning how to support the horse appropriately

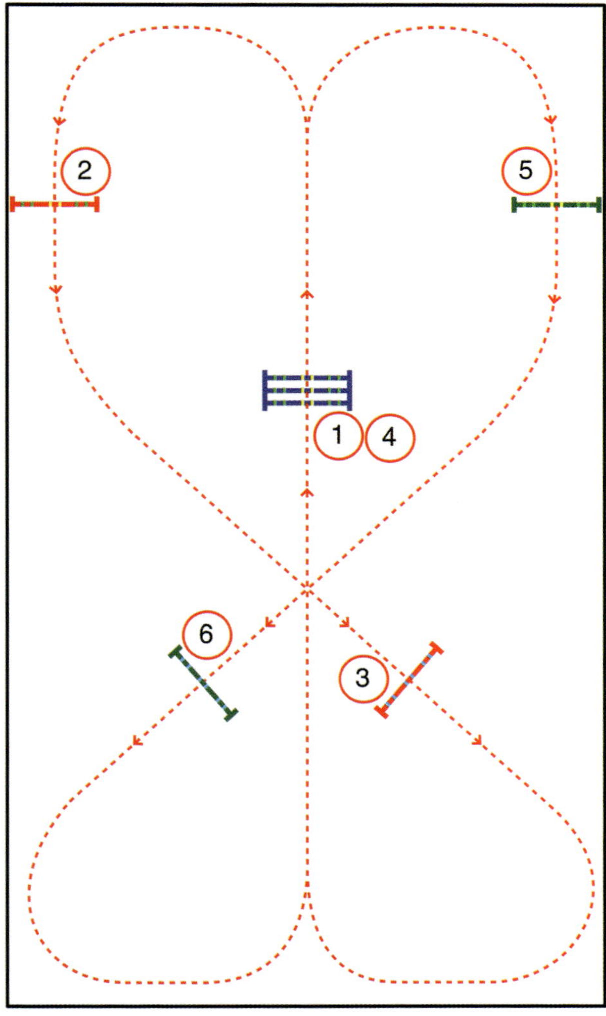

after slowing down and how to help the horse rebalance for a turn. The successful execution of this turn depends largely on fundamental skills (such as the ability of the rider to ride a good track and rhythm).

This exercise teaches best when ridden with a relaxed horse and a rider who only gives support for the takeoff spot that comes up at the jump. With a tense horse, it is difficult to maintain a good rhythm and track; therefore, this particular exercise is not suitable to be ridden until the horse is relaxed and strong enough to make balanced small turns.

A warmup can be ridden over Obstacles 3 and 6 in the reverse direction before starting the exercise. The exercise itself begins on the centerline over

Obstacle 1—the triple bar (in the rider's first round, this can be built as an oxer in order to gradually introduce an obstacle with increased spread). The types of obstacles and their exact placement in the arena are the factors that control the true purpose of the exercise.

The construction and placement of the triple bar serve two important functions: First, ensuring that horse and rider are engaged in an active forward canter (this can also be encouraged by utilizing canter poles set for a forward canter stride as an alternative to the triple bar). Second, controlling the diameter of the turn, since this will have a significant influence on the level of difficulty. Changing either of these components will largely change the nature of the exercise. The immediate task for the rider after the triple bar is to bring the horse back from a longer stride to a balanced, shorter stride suitable for the turn. Immediately thereafter, the rider must give correct support for the takeoff spot to the obstacle coming up next.

Over Obstacle 2, the rider looks to Obstacle 3, which requires the rider to turn shortly after the landing from Obstacle 2. Obstacle 3 is placed in its exact location in order to check that no tension or disturbance to the rhythm occurs due to the previous short turn ridden to Obstacle 2. It is common for tension to arise in a situation that is thought of as difficult, and this tension often carries through the rest of the course—often with a negative impact on performance.

After Obstacle 3, the rider continues directly to Obstacle 4 (unless a circle is determined to be beneficial), then rides the mirror image of the exercise in the opposite direction. Obstacles 3 and 6 can eventually be replaced with oxers; however, this change should only be made after determining that the horse and rider are handling the current task in a manner that supports their skillset improvement and dual confidence.

Starting the exercise over lower height obstacles can be very helpful in determining how to progressively increase the level of difficulty in the most suitable way for each horse-and-rider combination.

▪ **Purpose:** Practice for the rider to support the horse out of a very short approach for any takeoff spot that the situation provides.

Jumping Serpentine

This exercise serves not only to improve the skills and understanding necessary in order to turn (before, over, and after the obstacle) but also to broaden the horizon of the horse and rider's capability to be efficient with number of strides ridden and time taken between obstacles. While minimizing the number of strides between obstacles through well-controlled change of track is an important skill, the rider and trainer should always critically analyze the task they expose the horse to—constantly determining what is fair and directed to building confidence.

The center obstacle is a good choice for warm-up as it can be used for jumping on the circle in both directions, and for *change direction out of the circle* (see p. 45).

To begin the exercise, the height of the obstacles should be adjusted so it is not creating unnecessary difficulty for horse or rider. Once the horse and rider are familiar with the exercise, the obstacles can be raised but only with a feeling for maintaining trust and confidence in the horse.

In this diagram, the approach to the first obstacle starts from the left lead canter, but for balance in the training, it is important to repeat the exercise beginning from the right lead canter as well.

Track number 1 serves as an introduction for horse and rider to this serpentine track. As the first and last loops are slightly smaller than the two loops in the middle, it is helpful to review 10-meter canter circles before riding these smaller loops (ensuring that the horse is balanced and strong enough for these types of turns—see p. 17). Once horse and rider are familiar with the concept of the exercise, the size of the loops can gradually be reduced as track 2 illustrates. In this phase it will generally become clear to the rider and trainer if the level of difficulty should be increased (or not).

Riding this exercise highlights how important the straightness of the horse is—with a horse that is very crooked in the body, his shoulder usually falls in on the turning direction one way and drifts out away from the turning direction the other way, making the track unwillingly narrower or wider. When this is recognized and not controllable, it is important *not* to proceed to the more challenging phase of the track—instead it will be more helpful to revisit the suitable dressage training.

Using exercises as a source for feedback and as an advisor for what training milestones are missing or in need of improvement can be very helpful for the development of both rider and horse. Note that acknowledging and recognizing strengths are equally as important as pointing out what needs to be better. Often a rider goes away from a training session thinking of it not being successful when in reality, only a small part of the training was at issue. Commonly this "small part" ends up being only about 10 percent of the session, and with 90 percent being a success in the training, there is often far more positive than negative. Thinking of the session this way can be helpful for the rider to keep the level of confidence up. Remembering the phrase, *"When in doubt, just zoom out,"* can help both rider and trainer see the overall picture of the training and not place too much focus on what is lacking.

Track number 3 is the most challenging version of this serpentine track, it has the most angled approach while riding the least number of strides between the obstacles. Without a horse that is straight, balanced, and responsive to the aids, this track could dissolve existing confidence from horse and rider rather than being educational and confidence-building for them both. Executed correctly and at the right time in the educational journey, this exercise is excellent practice for horse and rider.

▪ **Purpose:** For the rider to feel how to reduce the number of strides between the obstacles by changing the track with a high level of control.

This exercise can be adjusted for many different arena sizes; however, if the arena is longer than 65 meters (213.3 feet), another obstacle can be placed using the same pattern as illustrated to maintain equal level of difficulty. Increasing the distance between the obstacles and from the obstacles to the short sides, instead of adding an additional obstacle, decreases the exercise's level of difficulty. In this arena, the distance from center of the obstacle to center of the next obstacle is 15 meters (49.2 feet), measured on the centerline. From both short sides to the center of the closest obstacle is 10 meters (32.8 feet), also measured along the centerline.

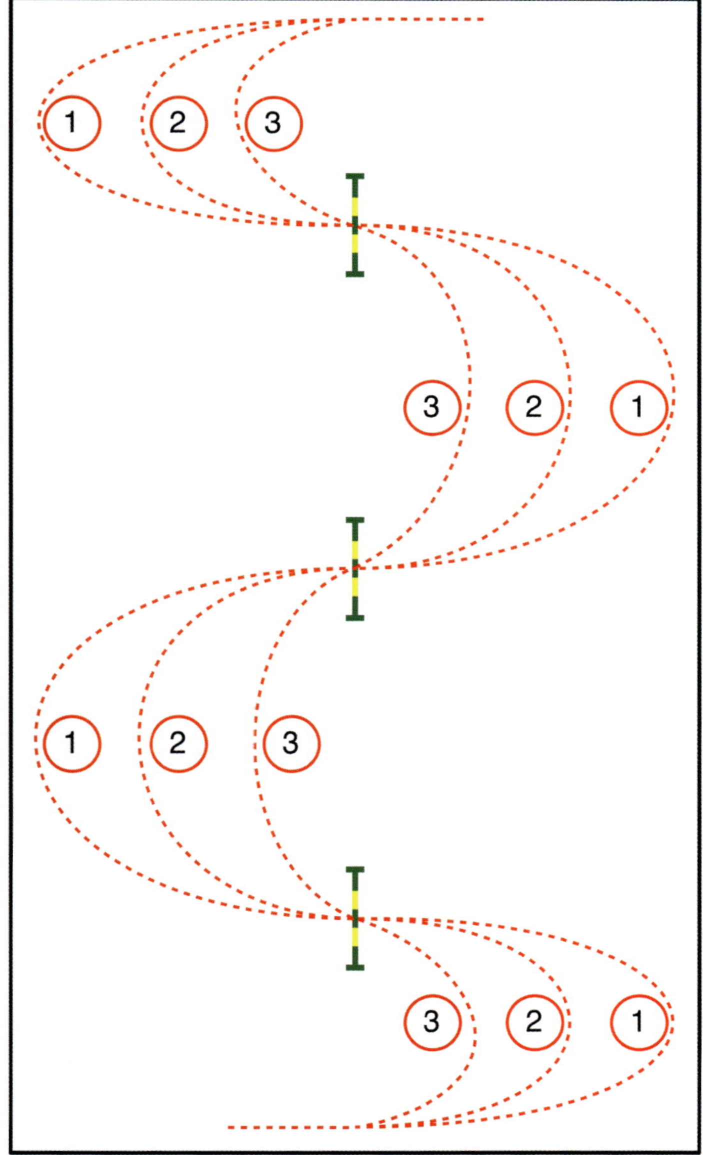

Awareness in Turns

The exercise is meant to increase the rider's capacity for riding and improving turns. It is an important assessment for both rider and trainer to evaluate the present level and for determining future goals. To be successful in various turns before and after the obstacle requires a lot of practice, and without this systematic practice, it is difficult to know the comfort zone of horse and rider regarding training and performance. Being self-critical in a positive but realistic way is crucial for reaching new levels of confidence and harmony between horse and rider. This self-assessment in conjunction with the exposure to a systematic and pedagogic training environment, are critical for true success in horse sport.

In this exercise, one option for a warm-up over fences that supports good rhythm is jumping Obstacle 3 from the right,

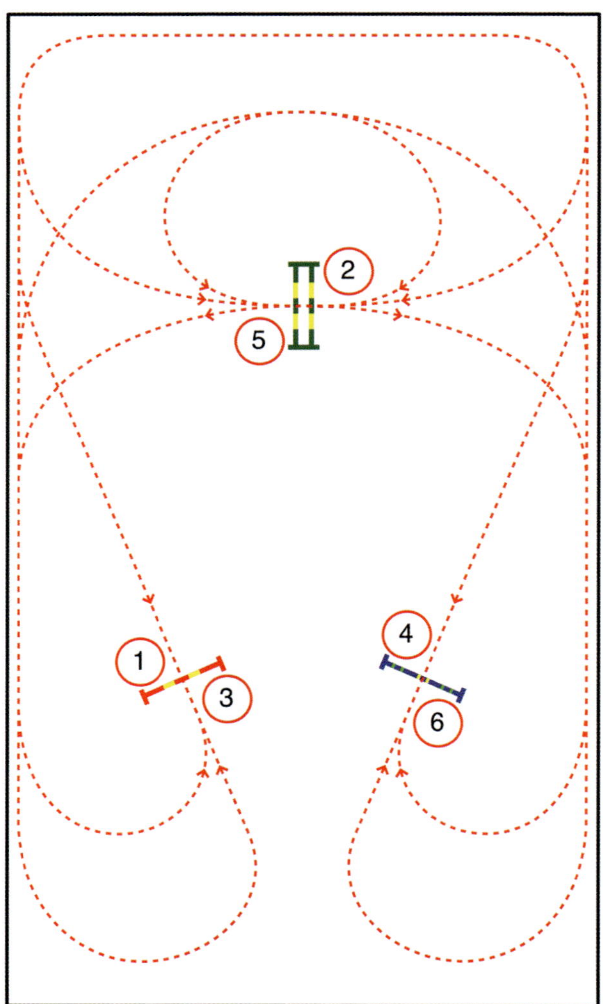

This exercise can be adjusted for many different arena sizes. The center of the oxer in this arena is placed 15 meters (49.2 feet) away from the short side and the center of the verticals are placed 16 meters (19.7 feet) from the short side.

and Obstacle 6 from the left. Encouraging the horse to be in a good rhythm while *thinking forward* before starting the practice with turns is beneficial for both horse and rider.

The exercise starts with Obstacle 1, a vertical from a long approach immediately followed by a short turn upon landing. Placement of the obstacle in the arena allows for options to either turn immediately or after a few canter strides. The common factor for both turns is that the rider must fully commit to the track and be in balance with the horse. The moment the rider doubts the turn, the horse will receive mixed signals for where to go and often end up confused about the choice of track.

Obstacle number 2 is an oxer ridden out of the turn, and while introducing these turns, it can be helpful to choose the wider track option and gradually work toward the tighter turn option. In jumping Obstacle 2 (the oxer out of the turn), the spread of the obstacle forces the rider to plan the turn more precisely when compared to jumping a vertical out of the same situation.

After this oxer, the rider continues to Obstacle 3 (a vertical ridden out of a short turn, which almost is identical to a *half-circle back*—see p. 20). With the fence set on the track *half-circle back*, the rider has to plan the turn in a way that makes it a fair task for the horse. Among other factors, how tightly the turn is ridden contributes greatly to the level of difficulty. Precise planning from the rider is crucial in regards to making the turn into a fair task for the horse. The turns in this exercise are similar to some of the turns in *training the unpredictable* (see p. 122) with the variation that, in this exercise, the rider has the option to use the track to allow for more straight strides before the takeoff.

The second part of the exercise continues over Obstacles 4 to 6 and is an exact mirror image of the first part of the course. For progression, speed should become a natural part of the exercise on an *advanced* level, and the amount of the speed should always match the level of training (meaning the horse must be able to remain relaxed and in balance). Tension and loss of balance will make it significantly more challenging for the horse to jump the obstacles comfortably.

When using this exercise as a source of feedback for analyzing strengths and areas in need of improvement, it can be helpful to divide the analysis of the exercise into the three following sections: *long approaches, short approaches*, and *short turns upon landing*. This sectional analysis can be helpful in deciding which specific areas are in most need of improvement. After making necessary improvements, the repetition of this exercise can serve as a continuing tool to gauge progress in horse and rider.

- **Purpose:** Train awareness and precision in riding various turns.

Walk Jumping

This is a strengthening exercise for the experienced horse. The slow pace used in the approach decreases momentum, creating a situation where the horse must push off with more strength in the takeoff as compared to a standard approach in trot or canter (where more momentum is carried).

The exercise is generally not suitable for the young or inexperienced horse. Due to the increased effort in the takeoff, the horse can quickly become insecure and lose confidence. The intended outcome of the exercise is a horse that is quicker and more powerful in the takeoff once regular speed is reestablished. This exercise is *not* suitable for the horse that is already quick in the takeoff because he will often become rushed and have a difficult time staying relaxed in an exercise requiring more power off the ground.

For the advanced rider, this exercise is excellent training for improving position over jumps. The slower-paced approach with less momentum, which transitions to normal momentum on top of the fence, is a substantial change in acceleration. This change in acceleration brings to light even very minor weaknesses in the position that might otherwise not be felt or seen during a regular approach with normal momentum, and are, therefore, often unknowingly ignored.

The warm-up can be done tracking left and right over the trot obstacles on the long sides, allowing the horse to gently use the muscles for jumping before increasing the difficulty and strength that is required from jumping out of walk. After warming up, the rider begins the exercise, and by alternating the approaches to the obstacles from left and right on the long sides, the training is kept well

This exercise can be adjusted for almost all arena sizes. The trot pole used in front of the obstacles on the long sides are placed 2.2 to 2.4 meters (7.2 to 7.9 feet) in front of the jump. Note that since this distance serves as a starting point for a typical Warmblood, the distance should be adjusted accordingly to ensure best suitability for different horses.

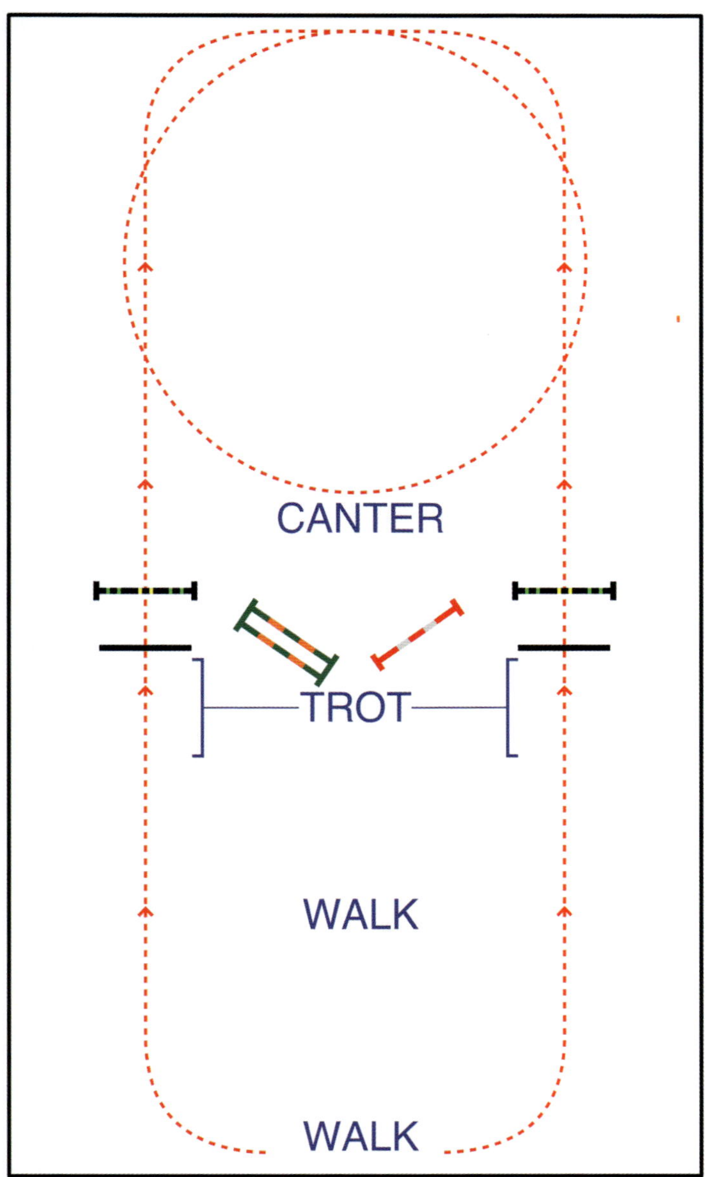

balanced. The rider approaches the obstacle out of walk and transitions to trot a few steps before the trot pole in front of the jump, as in this initial phase of jumping out of walk, it is often very helpful to start the trot a few steps prior to the pole (making it easier for the horse to understand his task).

As the horse and rider build confidence over the initial low obstacle, the transition to trot can be ridden just as the horse is about to step over the trot pole. Raising the height of the obstacle increases the difficulty level of the exercise significantly, and should, therefore, be done very gradually and with attention to how horse and rider are responding.

If the horse hesitates or rushes the obstacle, the level of difficulty should immediately be evaluated and adjustments made—for example, lowering the height or transitioning to trot earlier. It is important to remember that the exercise should build confidence and trust in both horse and rider—making the exercise too difficult often leads to the opposite result and should be avoided.

The goal in this exercise is for the horse to land in canter and continue toward the short side on a straight line. Using the circle as illustrated can be very helpful in establishing a well-balanced and forward canter. The obstacles on the diagonals are ridden out of canter and set for the rider to feel the change in the horse—typically jumping with more energy and quickness.

▪ **Purpose:** Strength training for the horse and seat training for the rider.

GRIDS AND COMBINATIONS

Grids are supplemental to regular training and can be a great help with building strength, providing gymnastic effects, and helping the rider improve the position over fences. As with combinations, they should be built in a way that encourages confidence and trust. Utilizing distances or obstacles that are unsuitable will reduce confidence and trust in both the horse and rider.

Trot Combinations

This exercise serves as a first step toward jumping combinations and grids. It is common for a horse with little or no experience in this area to doubt or question the task of jumping another obstacle with only one or two strides in between. With the inexperienced horse, the rider often feels the horse slowing down or attempting to go to the left or right side of the second obstacle, instead of staying in rhythm and jumping it in the middle.

A pedagogic way to start jumping combinations or grids with the inexperienced horse is to jump Obstacle "b" as a small warm-up vertical out of trot first (in this situation the poles from Obstacle "a" are placed on the side so that horse and rider can ride through the standards of obstacle "a"). In this situation, the cups on jump standards are removed and placed in a safe location where they cannot cause injury from the horse stepping on them.

Once the horse jumps this Obstacle out of trot and canter in a relaxed manner, the poles from Obstacle "a" are added back with Obstacle "b" remaining on low height. In this way, as the horse lands after Obstacle "a," the Obstacle "b" is familiar and does not seem to appear suddenly or surprise the horse.

Many problems can be avoided if the horse is confident with jumping single obstacles and related distances prior to starting the training with combinations and grids. The rider needs to be able to stay in good balance with the horse and have the skill and feeling for both a quick adjustment of the track and the necessary confidence to provide support if the horse would slow down or speed up.

Note: A rider that reacts strongly or abruptly while adjusting track or speed often causes resistance and tension; under these conditions, it is more difficult for the horse to concentrate on the upcoming task. A horse operating from the sympathetic nervous system (also known as "fight or flight" state) has very little overview of the situation and his learning progress is, therefore, limited.

Once the horse is familiar with jumping two obstacles in a row with one or two strides between Obstacle "a" and "b," the exercise can be ridden from beginning to end. In the diagram, the Obstacles marked "b" are set as oxers, but for the inexperienced horse it can be helpful to keep them set as verticals.

The exercise begins by approaching 1a out of trot; upon landing, the horse canters two strides to Obstacle 1b, then

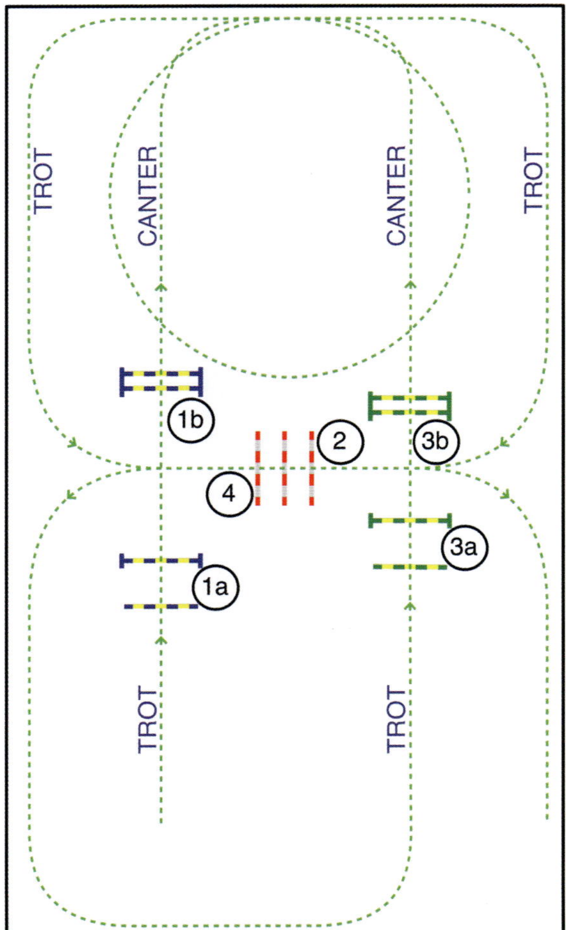

This exercise can be adjusted for almost all different arena sizes. The trot pole used in front of the obstacles on the long sides are placed 2.2 to 2.4 meters (7.2 to 7.9 feet) in front of the jump. The distance used for two strides in this illustration is 9 meters (29.5 feet) and for one stride is 5.5 meters (18 feet).

Note: These distances serve as starting points for a normal Warmblood, and the distances should be adjusted accordingly to ensure best suitability for different size and type horses.

continues in canter on a straight line to the short side where the circle is used to establish a balanced and rhythmical canter. Once this is accomplished, the rider transitions to trot and continues straight ahead, then turns across the arena over the trot poles marked Obstacle 2.

From here the rider continues in trot to the second part of the exercise starting with Obstacle 3a; upon landing, the horse canters one stride to 3b and continues straight ahead in canter where, on the short side, the circle is once again used to establish a balanced and rhythmical canter. The rider then transitions to trot and finishes with the trot poles. If an immediate repetition of the exercise is beneficial, the rider is now on track to continue to Obstacle 1 and begin again. Starting the exercise with a trot combination set for two strides instead of one stride is generally easier for horse and rider as two strides give the rider more time to respond to any change in speed or track, and allows the horse more time between obstacle "a" and "b" to study the upcoming task.

▪ **Purpose:** Introduction to jumping two fences in a row with one and two strides in between.

Trot and Canter Combinations

The goal with this exercise is to expose horse and rider to jumping a combination in canter. For the rider, one of the most important key skills in jumping combinations is the ability to select and maintain a suitable length of the canter stride. A stride that is *too short* for the measured distance in the combination will lead to the horse having to reach to get across the second obstacle or even cause him to put an extra short stride in. A stride that is *too long* will make it difficult for the horse to fit the stride in comfortably before the second obstacle. Both of the described scenarios can easily lead to horse and rider becoming insecure and losing confidence; therefore, the height of the obstacles should be carefully chosen to avoid any additional challenges during the initial learning phase.

Another factor that affects the way combinations ride is the takeoff spot at the first obstacle in the combination. (To review takeoff and landing distances, see

p. 35.) In a combination the adjustment of the stride following the landing after a short or long takeoff spot at the "a" obstacle, does require a prompt reaction from the rider since there are a maximum of two strides to work with.

For warm-up, the trot and canter poles can be included in the work, which will encourage a suitable rhythm from the outset of the exercise. As a warm-up, jumping Obstacle 3b is one option for allowing the horse to become familiar with the "b" obstacle prior to jumping the combination out of canter later in the exercise. (When jumping 3b as a single obstacle, the poles and cups should be removed from 3a and placed in a safe location to avoid injury.)

The exercise begins with Obstacle 1a and 1b, a one-stride combination ridden out of trot. This combination will encourage horse and rider in finding a suitable rhythm. Obstacle 2 is canter poles set for a regular stride, which serves as an indicator of suitability of the canter stride in preparation for Obstacle 3a and 3b, a one-stride combination ridden out of canter. The rider then establishes a balanced and rhythmical canter, if not accomplished by the short side, a circle is encouraged. Once a balanced and rhythmical canter is established, the rider transitions to trot, then proceeds to Obstacle 4, which is trot poles. The trot poles provide the rider with valuable feedback regarding relaxation and rhythm after the transition back to trot.

After Obstacle 4, the horse and rider are set to continue and repeat the exercise again should this be beneficial. Note how the combinations are set in the diagram: by framing each other in, they help in guiding the horse to the second element of the combination.

▪ **Purpose:** Canter a combination.

This exercise can be set in many different arena sizes. The trot pole used in front of Obstacle 1a is placed 2.2 to 2.4 meters (7.2 to 7.9 feet) in front of the jump and the distance between 1a and 1b is 5.5 meters (18 feet). The distance used between each canter pole is 3 meters (9.8 feet), which matches the stride length needed for 3a and 3b, the one-stride combination jumped out of canter with measurement of 6.75 to 7.25 meters (22.1 to 23.8 feet, depending on obstacle height). Obstacle 4, the trot poles, is set with 1.2 to 1.4 meters (3.9 to 4.6 feet) between each pole, which generally is a normal distance for most horses. Remember that these distances serve as starting points for a normal Warmblood and should be adjusted accordingly to ensure best suitability for different horses.

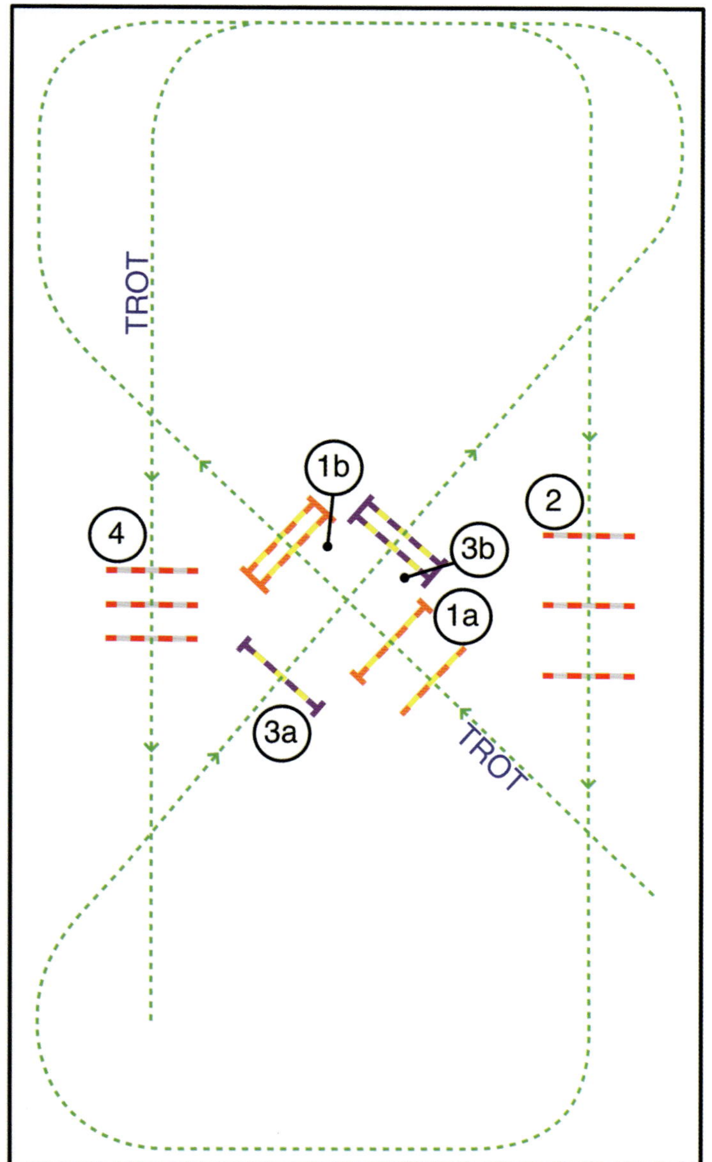

The Y Exercise

This exercise combines several different segments of training into one exercise including: *combination ridden out of trot, counting strides in related distances, jumping out of turns, awareness of speed,* (and last but not least) *transitions to trot for demonstrating control after the obstacle.* The exercise is fairly short, and each segment leads directly to the next without much time for adjustments between the obstacles. If the intensity of this exercise feels stressful to the rider or overwhelming to the horse and their harmony is disrupted, the situation should be analyzed to determine which training segment needs more practice. Once that difficulty is improved, the exercise can then be repeated in its entirety to determine if holistic progress has been made.

When riding exercises and using the result as a source of feedback about the status of training, it is important to think of the feedback as information only—not necessarily good or bad—because this hinders fair analysis and constructive thinking. For example, if the horse has to take off short or long at the jump, and the rider only thinks of this as a bad situation or failure, not only will it be harder to analyze what to change for an improvement, it will also often negatively affect the following obstacle due to the negative thinking and frustration. The rider or trainer must point out what is in need of improvement, but the priority should be to describe ideal situations and find ways and alternative ways of getting there. If a rider cannot do a task, it simply means that the rider does not yet know *how* to do that task, and continued education is the key for further progression.

Among many options for warming up is to jump Obstacle 2 on the diagonal in the reverse direction, then continue to Obstacle 4, also jumped in the reverse direction. The warm-up can be started from the opposite canter lead as well, beginning over Obstacle 3 in the reverse direction on the diagonal, then continuing over Obstacle 8, also in the reverse direction. These two parts of the warm-up can also be ridden as a continual exercise, which can be helpful to find a flowing state of harmony in horse and rider. (Before using certain obstacles for warm-up, they should always be checked and, if necessary, adjusted in a way so that they are suitable for jumping in the intended direction.)

This exercise can be set in most arenas with a length of 50 meters (164 feet) or more. The trot pole used in front of Obstacle 1a is placed 2.2 to 2.4 meters (7.2 to 7.9 feet) in front of the jump and the distance between 1a and 1b in this diagram is 5.5 meters (18 feet). Obstacle 1b to 2 is ridden in three strides with the measurement of 13.5 meters (44.3 feet). Obstacle 5b to 6 is ridden in four strides with the measurement of 16.5 meters (54.1 feet). As before, these distances serve as starting points for a normal Warmblood, and the distances should be adjusted accordingly to ensure best suitability for different horses.

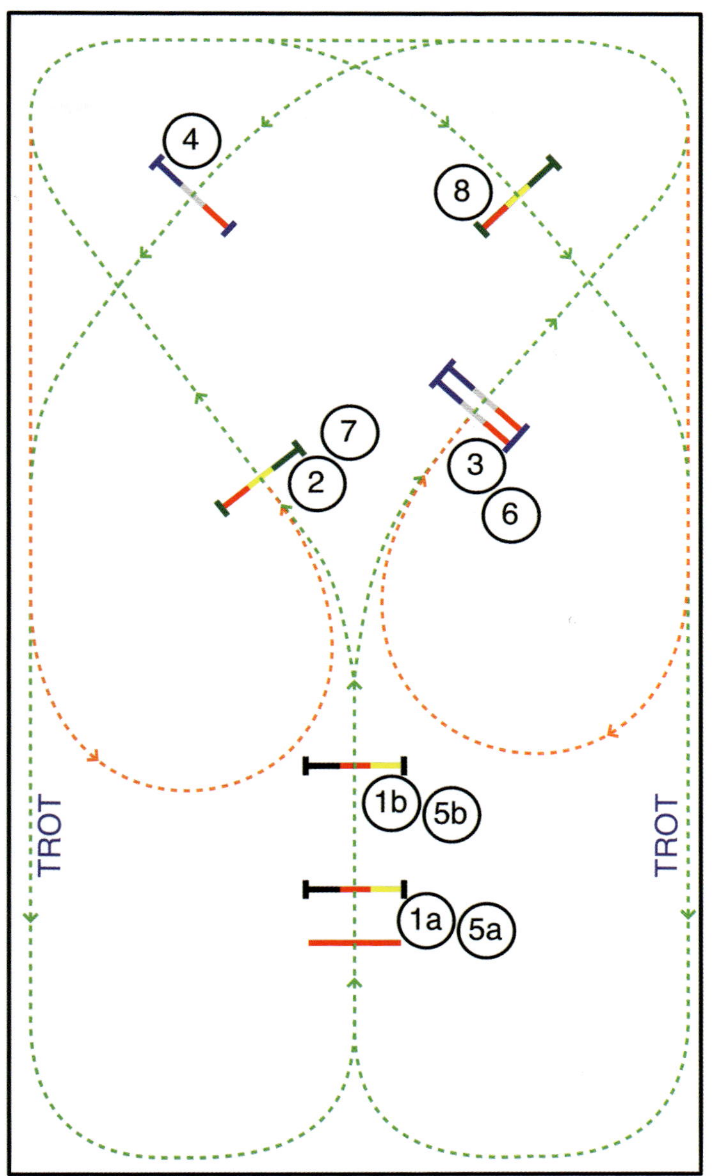

The exercise itself starts with 1a and 1b, a one-stride combination approached out of trot. This combination is helpful in establishing a rhythm for the upcoming Obstacle 2, a vertical into the related distance for three strides, set on a bending line. The awareness of number of strides ridden is critical because it provides the rider with valuable information about speed, stride length, and track. Review the section on bending lines if necessary (see p. 76).

After Obstacle 2, the rider continues to Obstacle 3, an oxer set on a track identical to a half-circle back. (To review the *half-circle back*, see p. 20). Here, the awareness of the track is very important, and frequently, the less experienced rider will mistakenly ride a tighter turn than necessary unintentionally increasing the level of difficulty.

Obstacle 4 serves to encourage the rider to quickly reestablish good rhythm, balance, and control over the track upon landing after Obstacle 3. After Obstacle 4, the rider transitions to trot, with the quality of the transition largely dependent on the horse's level of training, relaxation, and balance.

If a circle is not necessary, the horse and rider continue directly to 5a and 5b, another one-stride combination out of trot. After this combination, the rider continues to Obstacle 6, the oxer into a related distance for four strides, set on a bending line.

Thereafter, the rider continues to Obstacles 7 and 8, which is almost a mirror image of Obstacles 3 and 4.

Note: Keeping the center of the arc of the bending line halfway between the related obstacles helps the track to ride smoothly. If the center of the arc is placed more toward the second obstacle in the related distance, it increases the level of difficulty, and also makes it more difficult to maintain a good rhythm.

▪ **Purpose:** Jumping combinations, counting strides, and riding turns.

Grid Introduction

This basic introduction to jumping a grid can serve as a continuation from the *trot and canter combination exercise* (see p. 135). Approaching the grid out of trot and continuing in canter can help in establishing a good rhythm. The approach out of trot also gives the horse more time to study the upcoming task making the horse less likely to become surprised, which could lead to difficulties in maintaining a good rhythm and track.

Approaching the grid in trot also eliminates large variations in the takeoff spot. The approach in trot with a trot pole in front of the obstacle encourages the horse to take off at an ideal spot for the given obstacle, and the rider now has fewer variables to focus on, giving more of the attention to rhythm and track. With insecure horses the obstacles can be replaced with a pole on the ground and ridden in walk and trot the first few times. Thereafter, the obstacles can gradually be built up one by one, starting from the back with Obstacle 2d, then 2c, 2b, and lastly 2a.

When introducing the grid in this way, it is helpful to leave the obstacles at a low height for two reasons: First, so the height is not an additional difficulty factor, and second, the distances in the grid are set for a horse building momentum through the grid, which means that the distances are becoming slightly longer as the horses progresses from 2a toward 2d. This means jumping 2c to 2d out of trot would require an active forward trot for the horse to cover the distance. Even if the striding is not perfect, it is still of great benefit for the horse to be able to jump the grid with only one obstacle added at a time.

The advantage of introducing the last obstacle in the grid first is that the horse is now jumping toward a familiar obstacle, compared to adding obstacles from front to back, which would mean that the horse is faced with an unfamiliar obstacle in the landing (the latter scenario often leads to the less experienced horse slowing down and changing track).

A warm-up for the horse that is confident may consist of Obstacle 3 (initially a vertical and later an oxer), and the grid may also be included on a lower height and without breaking it down.

The exercise itself starts with number 1, a set of trot poles, intended to encourage the horse and rider to be in a suitable rhythm when continuing to Obstacle 2a, the first obstacle in the grid.

The trot pole in front of Obstacle 2a encourages horse and rider to a suitable takeoff spot, and the distances to 2b, 2c, and 2d are all set for one stride (with the distances being progressively longer to accommodate the increased momentum gained through the grid).

The goal with Obstacle 3, the oxer, is to serve as a good feedback opportunity in evaluating how well horse and rider manage to maintain the steady rhythm created through the grid.

Note: Regarding the placement of the grid and how it allows the horse and rider to pass through the corner before and after the grid, it is important the grid is not pointing straight into the corner, which would lead to a very sharp turn afterward and does not encourage a rhythmical and balanced canter after the landing.

- **Purpose:** Introducing a basic grid to horse and rider.

This exercise can be set in most arenas with a length of 50 meters (164 feet) or more. Number 1, the trot poles, are set with 1.2 to 1.4 meters (3.9 to 4.6 feet) between each pole (which is generally a normal distance for most horses). The trot pole used in front of Obstacle 2a is placed 2.2 to 2.4 meters (7.2 to 7.9 feet) in front of the jump, and the distances between 2a and 2b is set at 5.5 meters (18 feet), 2b to 2c is set at 6 meters (19.7 feet), and 2c to 2d at 6.5 meters (21.3 feet). These distances serve as starting points for a normal Warmblood, and the distances should be adjusted accordingly to ensure best suitability for different horses.

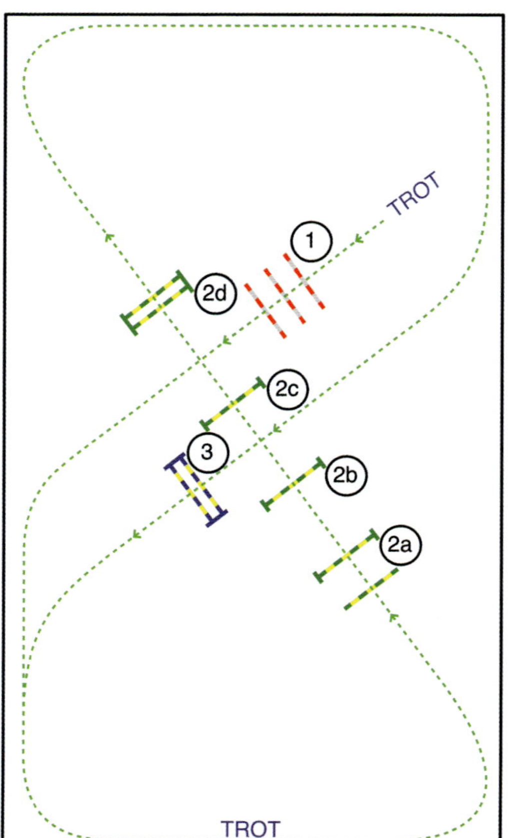

Bounce Introduction

Bounces can be a valuable exercise for both horse and rider. For the horse, they can serve as excellent gymnastic and strengthening exercises, and for the rider, they can be very valuable in improving and maintaining a good and balanced position while jumping.

Bounces can be included in courses, grids, and gymnastic exercises, with great advantage. For the bounces to have beneficial effects, it is important the horse is relaxed and not stressed or nervous while approaching and jumping them. Therefore, a gentle and systematic introduction is important.

To introduce the bounces as illustrated here, the poles from number 1a, 1b, and 1c can be replaced with single poles on the ground, and the horse can go over them at the walk. The next step is to trot over them and once the

This exercise can be set in most arenas. The distances between 1a and 1b are set at 2.8 meters (9.2 feet) and 1b to 1c is set at 3 meters (9.8 feet). The trot pole in front of 1a is placed 2.2 to 2.4 meters (7.2 to 7.9 feet) out. The canter poles, number 2, are set with 3 meters (9.8 feet) between each pole. Number 3, the bounces, is set with 3.2 meters (10.5 feet) between each bounce. These distances serves as starting points for normal Warmbloods, and the distances should be adjusted accordingly to ensure best suitability for different horses. A normal distance for most horses ranges from 2.8 to 3.5 meters (9.2 to 11.5 feet).

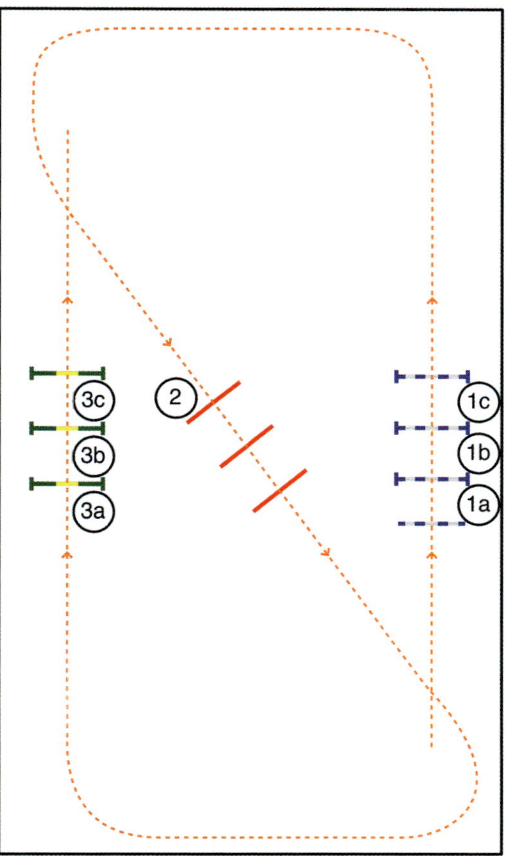

horse is relaxed doing that, number 1c can be built up as a small obstacle.

When the horse is comfortable with jumping Obstacle 1c, Obstacle 1b can be built up on a low height, and the first bounce is now ready to be jumped. When the horse does not jump the obstacles and instead just trots over them, the jumps can be raised by a small amount and the rider can gently support the horse forward in the takeoff to encourage the horse to land and continue in canter. Once the horse jumps 1b and 1c while remaining relaxed and thinking forward, Obstacle 1a can be added together with the trot pole in front.

To introduce Obstacles 3a, 3b, and 3c (the bounces out of canter), each obstacle can be replaced with a single pole on the ground. Once the horse and rider are familiar with the canter poles, the obstacles are built up one by one, again starting with 3c—numbers 3b and 3a are still left as canter poles on the ground.

Next, number 3b is built up, and now the horse is jumping a canter pole to a bounce. Finally, Obstacle 3a is added and all three bounces are ridden out of canter. Once the horse and rider are introduced to the bounces out of trot and canter separately, they can be combined into a continual exercise.

The exercise itself begins with numbers 1a, 1b, and 1c—bounces with a trot pole in front. The trot pole in front encourages the horse to a suitable takeoff spot. The bounces are helpful to establish a steady rhythm in canter, which then is maintained to number 2, the canter poles. The canter poles provide the rider with valuable feedback about the length of the canter stride after jumping the bounces, and based on this feedback, the rider can determine if it is necessary to make adjustments to the canter stride in preparation for number 3, bounces out of canter. If the horse shows signs of insecurity, it is generally a good idea to go back to the previous steps where the rider feels the horse is gaining confidence again.

- **Purpose:** Introducing bounces to horse and rider.

Gymnastic Grid

Gymnastic grids with bounces and a variety of strides between jumps are a good training tool for improving balance and position of the rider between and over fences. Simultaneously, they are great gymnastic and strengthening exercise for the horse. The precisely measured distances between the elements in the grid are, in general, what determine how it will ride (for example, as a bounce or with one or more strides between the obstacles). Changes in speed and stride length are also factors that play a large role in how the grid will ride. Most grids are set on a suitable stride for the situation and speed unless a specific purpose is mentioned and explained that requires measurements outside of the ordinary.

For the horse, jumping a bounce and continuing with one and two strides to the following obstacles requires a high level of attention—this attention is important for the horse to be successful in jumping on a higher level. For the horse that has not yet learned to pay close attention to his situation while jumping, grids and pole exercises can be very helpful in developing this skill.

The more the rider's balance and position is improved between and over fences, the less of a distraction the rider is to the horse—the horse can then increase focus on the upcoming task, which in this case is jumping clearly and cleverly. It is important to understand that any movement of the rider is in fact an aid to the horse, and the horse does not generally understand the difference between voluntarily and involuntary aids. The grid can be very helpful for improving the position of the rider because when the rider receives an instruction in the beginning of the grid, there are several jumps left for the rider to put the instruction into action as compared to single jumps where the next opportunity to correct a certain habit is several strides away and another approach has to be made.

One option for starting the warm-up over fences is to adjust Obstacle 4 to a vertical or a small oxer, depending on which option best suits the specific horse and rider. Number 1, the three bounces, is also a good addition to the warm-up before starting to jump the grid.

The first obstacle of the gymnastic grid, numbered 3a through 3d, is set to be approached out of trot. In this way, the takeoff spot can be controlled, and

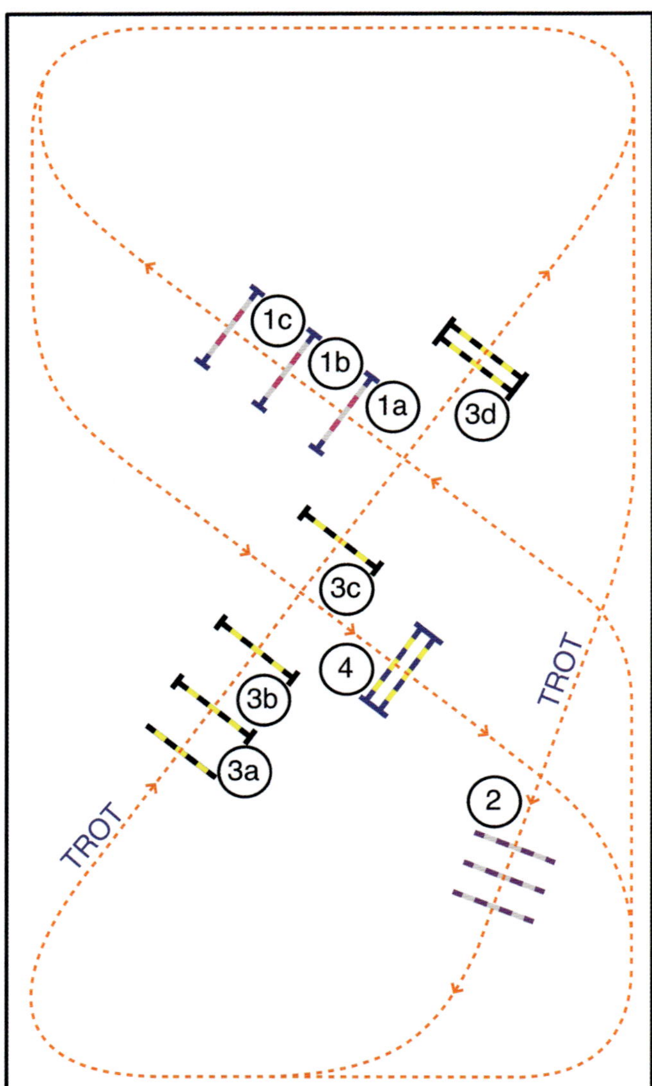

This exercise can be set in most arenas with a length of minimum 50 meters (164 feet). The distance between each bounce in Obstacle 1 is measured at 3.2 meters (10.5 feet). The trot poles are set at 1.2 to 1.4 meters (3.9 to 4.6 feet) between each pole. The trot pole in front of 3a is set at 2.2 to 2.4 meters (7.2 to 7.9 feet), 3a to 3b is a bounce with a distance of 2.8 meters (9.2 feet), 3b to 3c is set for one stride at 5.75 meters (18.9 feet), 3c to 3d is set for two strides and measured at 9.75 meters (32 feet). These distances serve as starting points for normal Warmbloods, and the distance should be adjusted accordingly to ensure best suitability for different horses.

more focus can be devoted to the main purpose of the exercise. The trot pole is a helpful tool that, in this case, leads the horse and rider into 3a and 3b, a bounce, followed by a one-stride distance to 3c, immediately followed by a two-stride distance to 3d.

The obstacles set in this arena can be combined into an exercise starting with Obstacle 1, the three bounces out of canter, after which the rider transitions to trot and continues to number 2, the trot poles. The transition and the trot poles serve as good tests to determine if the horse is in a suitable rhythm and balance. After the trot poles, the horse and rider continue in trot to the grid, 3a through 3d, and the exercise finishes over Obstacle 4, an oxer, with the goal of maintaining to the oxer the rhythm established through the grid.

▪ **Purpose:** Introducing a longer grid to horse and rider including a bounce, and one and two strides between jumps.

The K Exercise

This exercise builds on skills gained in grids ridden on a straight line and will have many of the same benefits (to review the *gymnastic grid*, see p. 145). The addition of turning within the grid requires the horse and rider to turn over and in between the obstacles, which for the horse is a valuable gymnastic exercise that has many applications while jumping bending lines and courses against the clock. For the rider, it is a great opportunity to check, and if necessary, improve how the eyes are used while jumping. By looking in the direction of the next obstacle and stepping down in the inside stirrup, the rider is automatically applying the weight aids, which can be supported by the rein aids in the case that the horse does not turn enough. When stepping down and distributing weight in the inside stirrup, it is important to not push against it with so much force that the rider's weight is shifting to the outside instead. In these situations, horses often become confused due to the counteraction of the weight aids and rein aids. If not totally confused, the horse will most likely respond to the most dominant of the two aids, additionally becoming more resistant to maintaining correct flexion and bend in his body.

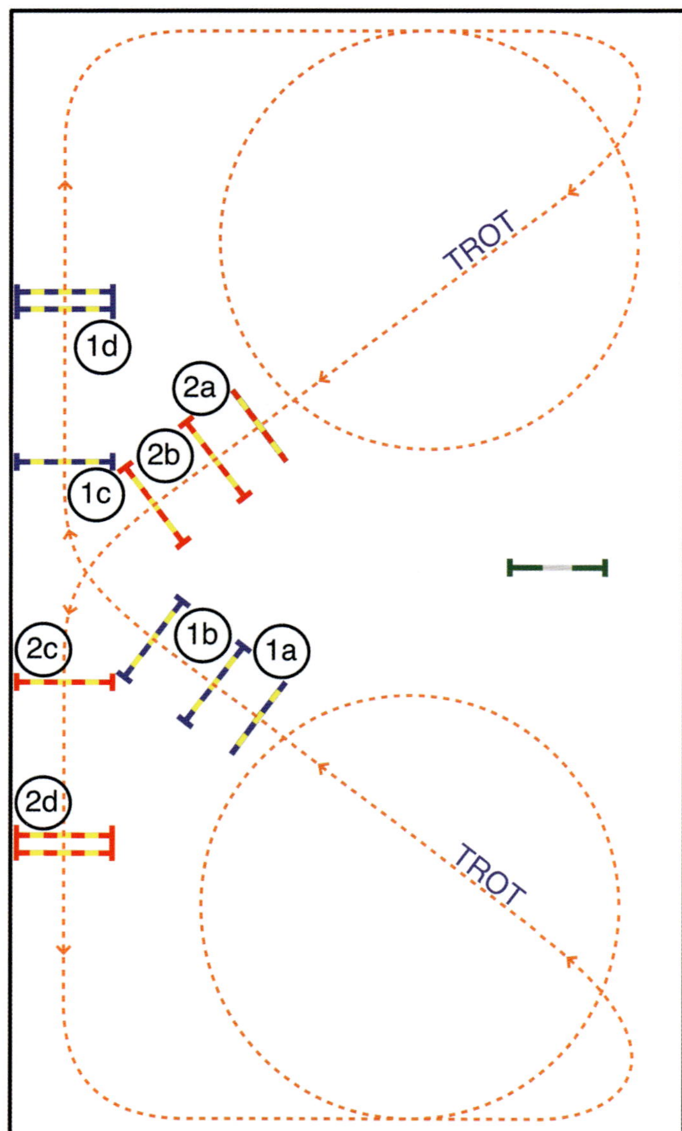

This exercise can be set without modification in most arenas with a length of minimum 50 meters (164 feet). The trot pole in front of Obstacle 1a is set at 2.2 to 2.4 meters (7.2 to 7.9 feet); 1a to 1b is a bounce with a distance of 2.8 meters (9.2 feet); 1b to 1c is set for two strides at 9.25 meters (30.3 feet); 1c to 1d is set for one stride with the distance of 6.25 meters (20.5 feet). These grids are identical, and the same measurements are used for both. As before, these distances serve as starting points for normal Warmbloods over low height, and the distances should be adjusted accordingly to ensure best suitability for different horses.

Before starting to jump the grid on a low height, the single obstacle on the long side can be used in both directions for warm-up. Both grids are set identically to one another, so they will ride exactly the same from left and right.

The *first grid* starts in trot toward the bounce, Obstacles 1a and 1b (with a trot pole in front of 1a to encourage a suitable takeoff spot). Over the bounce, the rider looks toward Obstacle 1c, and by looking toward 1c in combination with stepping down slightly into the inside stirrup, the weight aids are telling the horse in which direction the rider is planning to continue, and the rein aids are then used to support the weight aids with the turn, if needed. The wall of the arena will be helpful with the turn and, in addition to the rider's aids, make it more obvious for the horse to continue over obstacle 1c after doing the planned two strides between 1b and 1c.

In the takeoff at Obstacle 1c, it is important for the rider to look at the next obstacle. Without doing so, it will more likely be difficult to stay on a good track and jump the middle of Obstacle 1d, which here is set on a one-stride distance.

After the grid, the rider evaluates the canter and stays on the circle if necessary—a suitable rhythm and balance should be reestablished before transitioning to walk where the horse can have a brief rest before starting to trot and approaches the *second grid* marked Obstacles 2a through 2d.

Note: The obstacles along the long side in the grid are set next to the wall, and it is very important there is no space for the horse to consider going through; therefore, the use of wall standards would be ideal since they eliminate any space between standards and wall.

▪ **Purpose:** For the horse, mainly a gymnastic and strengthening exercise. For the rider, training of weight aids and rein aids over obstacles.

Bounces on the Circle

This exercise assimilates some of the skills learned and practiced in previous grids (to review a *gymnastic grid*, see p. 145, to review a *gymnastic grid on a bending line*, see p. 147). Turning while jumping bounces is an advanced exercise and should generally be reserved for the more experienced horse and rider. The practice of the exercises, from *basic* to *advanced,* in a systematic order as described in this book will help the horse and rider, to a large degree, gain the necessary skill to make bounces on the circle a valuable exercise that can be practiced on a regular basis.

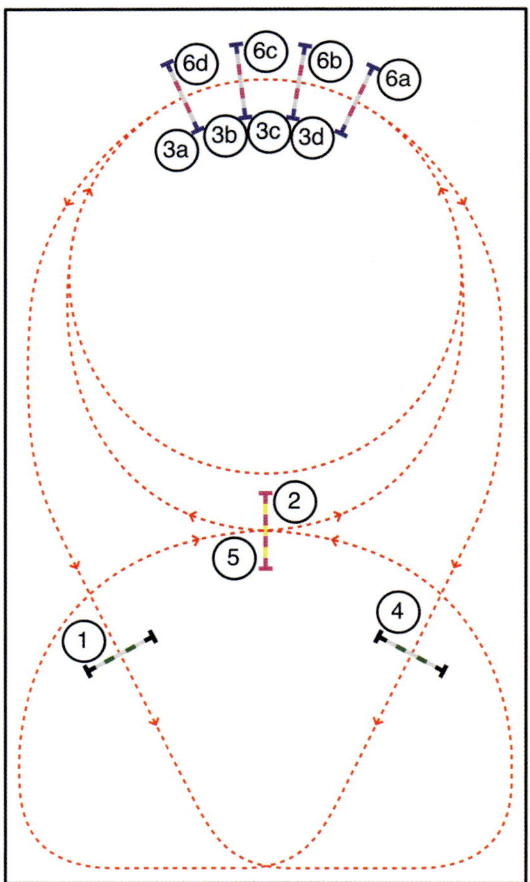

The position of the rider is (as always) very important, as the rider who sits correctly on the horse between and over the jumps maximizes the potential for the correct and fine use of weight and rein aids. Additionally, this rider will also take in and be able to analyze more of the feedback received from the horse while jumping through the bounces. Some of the important feedback the rider receives has to do with the strong and the weak side of the horse's body. To the *weak side* (also known as the *concave*

This exercise can be set in most arenas, as the bounces are placed on the circle track with a distance of 3 meters (9.8 feet) between each obstacle measured on a curved line from center to center of each pole. Any distance between 2.8 and 3.5 meters (9.2 and 11.5 feet) is generally considered to be within the normal range for bounces for a normal Warmblood, and the distances should be adjusted as needed.

side), the rider will often feel the horse drifting out over the outside shoulder, which makes the distances between the bounces feel longer. To the *strong side* (also known as the *convex* side), the rider will often feel the horse falling in over the inside shoulder making the distances between the bounces feel shorter.

The information that the rider receives here can be helpful in determining which dressage exercises to utilize for improvement in the horse's body (see Part One, p. 3). Every horse is unique and to maximize improvement, the dressage exercises should be individually tailored to suit each one specifically. Simply executing certain exercises or dressage movements with the horse should not be the goal; instead the exercises and dressage movements should be done with the goal of developing a healthy, strong, and supple horse that will last and perform happily, well into an old age.

A great metaphor for the way that dressage impacts the horse is this: generally, we don't buy a quarter-inch drill because we want a quarter-inch drill, we buy it because we want a quarter-inch hole. In this case, the exercises found here, and the classical dressage work they are based on, are simply the tools we use to create the result that we want—a strong, healthy, and rideable horse.

There are several options for warming-up over fences before jumping the bounces on the circle. One is jumping Obstacles 2 and 5 on the circle, followed by the bounces (which can be adjusted to canter poles on the ground for the warm-up phase). While the bounces are the main purpose of this exercise on the circle, it is important not to make it too challenging for the horse in the initial learning phase. Instead of increasing the difficulty level of the obstacles through raising the height, an alternative is to increase the level of difficulty of the technical aspect instead and ride the course-like exercise numbered 1 through 6. (After Obstacle 6 the rider can continue directly to Obstacle 1 and repeat the course, should this be considered beneficial.) The session is then ended on a positive note and the next time these types of bounces occur in training, the horse will associate them with this previous positive experience and more progression can be made.

▪ **Purpose:** Turning while jumping bounces as strengthening and gymnastic exercises.

Oxer Grid

This grid will generally benefit the experienced horse the most, and for the slightly less experienced or insecure horse, a similar grid with four verticals set at a low height could be used instead. The goal in any case should always be to create training sessions that are having maximum benefit for the horse at a given moment in time. Three common ways to increase the level of difficulty in this exercise are: First, to increase height; second, increase spread; or third, increase height and spread simultaneously.

1. Increasing the *height* of the obstacles requires the horse to push off harder in the takeoff. As the height increases, the canter stride between the obstacles will feel shorter, which encourages the horse to come back and take more weight on his hind end.

2. Increasing the *spread* of the oxer causes the horse to push off harder in the takeoff to achieve more reach. The spread also requires the horse to jump higher in order to maintain a round curve over the obstacle. Adding spread should be done through moving all elements, both front and back of the oxers, an equal amount. This way the distance to the poles on the ground is kept equal and no repositioning is necessary.

3. Adding increased *height and spread* simultaneously is the most advanced of the options described here to increase the level of difficulty as the horse now has to jump up and forward in order to maintain the round curve over the obstacle. Between the fences, the horse must take more weight on the hind end as the canter stride is shortened in preparation for the obstacle following immediately.

The poles on the ground are helpful for encouraging a suitable rhythm: for the slow horse, they support enough ground coverage, and for the fast horse, they will be helpful in slowing the horse down.

In regards to training jumping technique, the shape of the oxers can be

This exercise can be set in most arenas with a length of 50 meters (164 feet). The oxers are placed 6.5 meters (21.3 feet) apart, with the poles on the ground being placed 3.25 meters (10.7 feet) away from the oxers.

changed between being ramped to encourage increased bascule and square to support faster front legs. The goal with changing the shapes of the oxers is to encourage the horse to study the obstacles. This training, however, should always be done with the goal of creating a good experience for the horse and never with the intent of leading the horse into mistakes.

This grid is not numbered, only marked "a" through "d" from both directions, which means that the grid can be approached and ridden both from the left and right. This is possible because the distances are set exactly the same from both directions, and as a consequence, the horse has to come back a significant amount between the obstacles.

Many grids and combinations are usually measured to accommodate the horse gaining momentum throughout. One factor of great importance and *why* this exercise is most suitable to the more advanced rider, is the skill of how precisely the rider is able to bring the horse into the grid. This should ideally be done from a suitable rhythm for the grid, and also a suitable stride length. If the horse has to take off from a situation that is not ideal (due to errors in track, speed, rhythm, or relaxation) many of the benefits from the grid will be lost for the horse due to the immediate adjustments he needs to accommodate the less-than-ideal situation.

For the warm-up over fences, the single vertical on the long side can be used; it can be ridden on a straight line as well as on an angle.

- **Purpose:** Strength and technique training for the horse.

Oxer Bounce

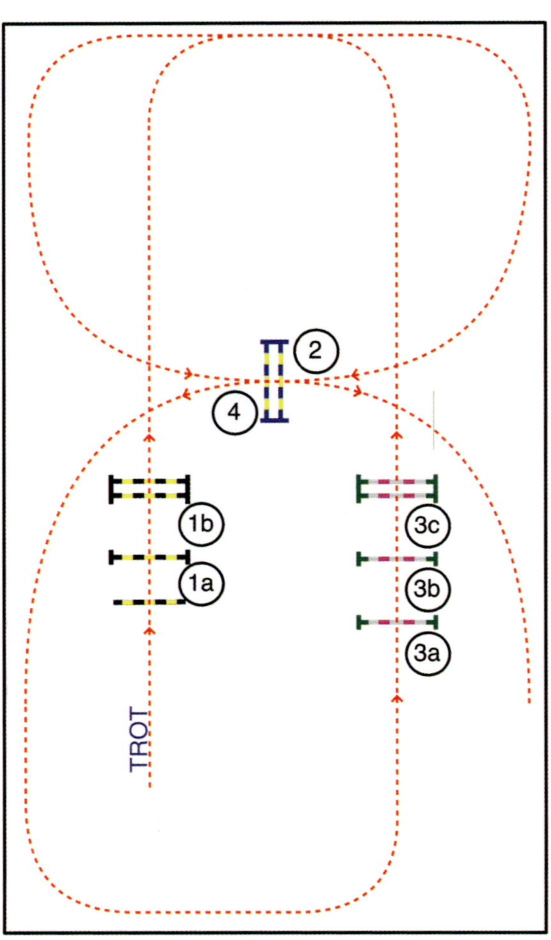

Using one or more oxers in bounces is an exercise that is mainly suitable for the advanced horse and rider. The inclusion of oxers in bounces requires the horse to push off stronger in the takeoff since more forward momentum is needed compared to verticals. Due to this increase in push off the ground, this is also an intensive strength-building exercise, which is important to understand as it is possible that the horse will feel tired sooner compared

This exercise can be set in most arenas. The trot pole in front of Obstacle 1a is placed at a distance of 2.2 to 2.4 meters (7.2 to 7.9 feet). The distance between 1a and 1b is 2.8 meters (9.2 feet). The two distances in Obstacle 3a to c are both measured at 3.25 meters (10.7 feet). These distances serve as starting points for a normal Warmblood and should be adjusted accordingly to ensure best suitability for different horses.

to riding a less-intensive bounce exercise. When the horse shows signs of being tired, the rider should consider taking a break or ending the training session, allowing the horse to keep a positive mental state. It also helps to avoid injuries (which the horse is more prone to when performing while tired). The stronger push-off at the oxer is what makes this exercise also valuable for the rider's position over fences: the increased momentum will bring out weaknesses in the rider's position which then can be identified and improved. This is a similar situation to jumping out of walk (see p. 130).

This exercise exposes the horse and rider to two different scenarios while incorporating an oxer in a bounce. Obstacle 1a and 1b is a bounce approached out of trot, requiring the rider to ride an engaged rhythmical trot in the approach, as the horse that is approaching 1a in a slow disengaged trot often struggles to reach over the oxer, which easily could lead to loss of confidence. Obstacle 3a through 3c is a three-bounce with an oxer as the last effort, which is set to be approached in an engaged rhythmical canter, as one too slow or disengaged will have the same consequences as described in trot. There are many options to utilize oxers in the bounces depending on the horse, the situation, and what the rider intends to accomplish.

Besides *height and spread,* the oxers can also be *ramped or square,* which have significantly different purposes. (To review the different purposes with training oxers, see p. 31.) The warm-up over fences can be done over the bounces with the oxer pole removed (note that jump cups should be removed together with the pole and placed in a safe location to avoid injury).

If determined to be beneficial, the obstacles can be ridden as a course-like exercise starting with Obstacle 1a out of trot. After 1b, the rider continues in canter and changes rein over Obstacle 2, the oxer on the centerline (this track rides very similarly to *change direction out of the circle* (see p. 15). After the change of rein, the rider continues in canter to Obstacle 3, the bounces out of canter. The bounces are followed by another change of rein over Obstacle 4, the oxer. If determined to be beneficial, the option for an immediate continuation from Obstacle 1 is possible.

▪ **Purpose:** Strength training for the horse and improving the position of the rider.

JUMPING COURSES

The following courses are meant to serve as a source of inspiration and awaken interest for further studies into the art of training the horse and rider. Designing courses and exercises is where you will develop your own creativity using the classical dressage tracks as the foundation for your creations. There are many variations and combinations to use; by evaluating each individual horse and rider, in order to ensure that the tracks are of a suitable level, you will promote good riding and a confident horse.

The distances are not listed on the course plans because of the large variation in footing from arena to arena. Riding in a small indoor arena on sand compared to riding in a large outdoor arena on modern fiber footing are worlds apart when it comes to measuring and setting distances; therefore, calculating the measurement is always relative to the situation.

Course with Quarterline

- **Arena Size:** 20 by 40 meters

- **Purpose:** Using quarterlines within the course.

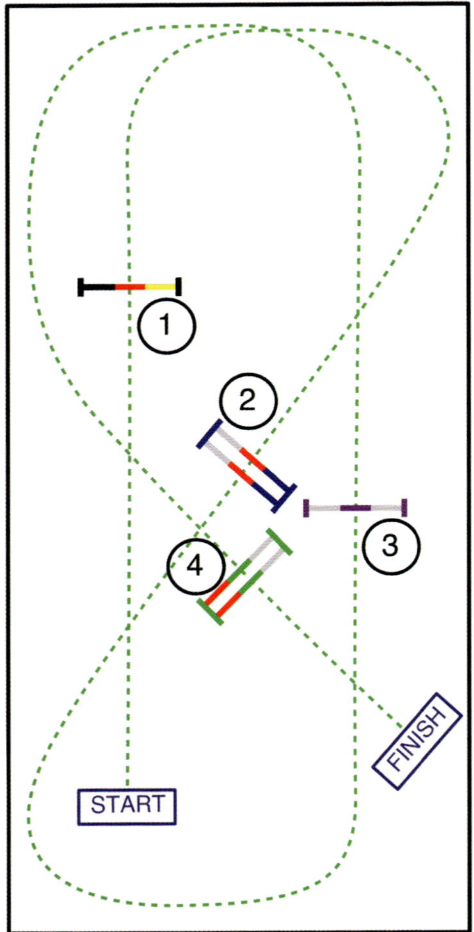

Basic course in a small arena.

Course with a 20-Meter Circle

- **Arena Size:** 30 by 50 meters

- **Purpose:** Incorporating a 20-meter circle type track in the course.

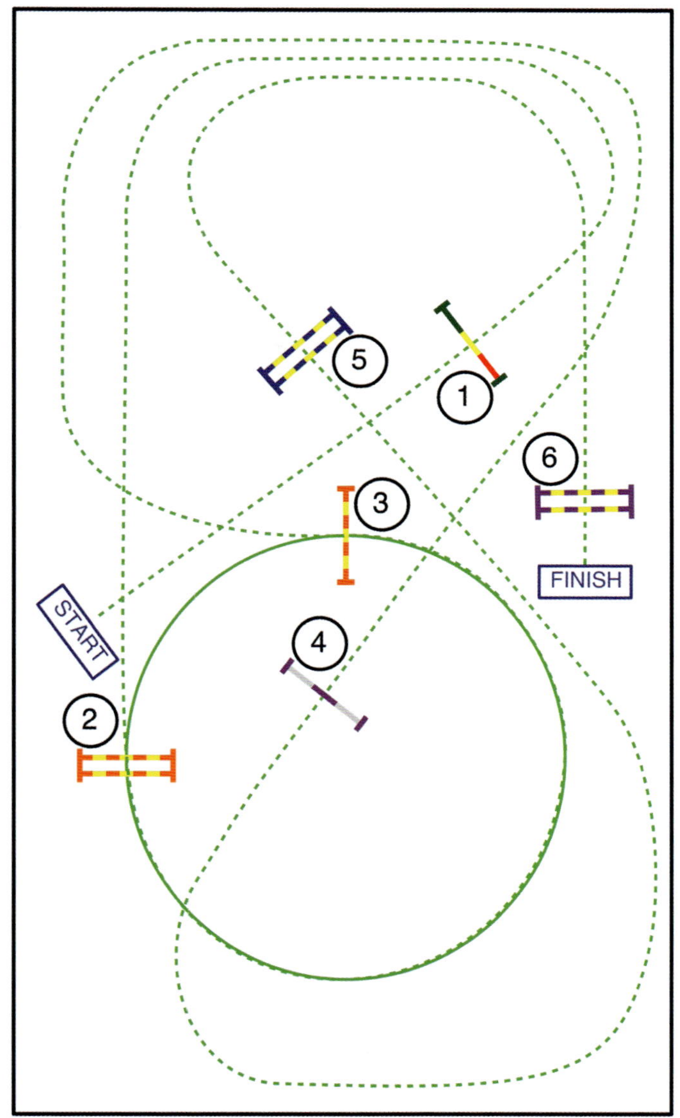

Basic course in a small arena.

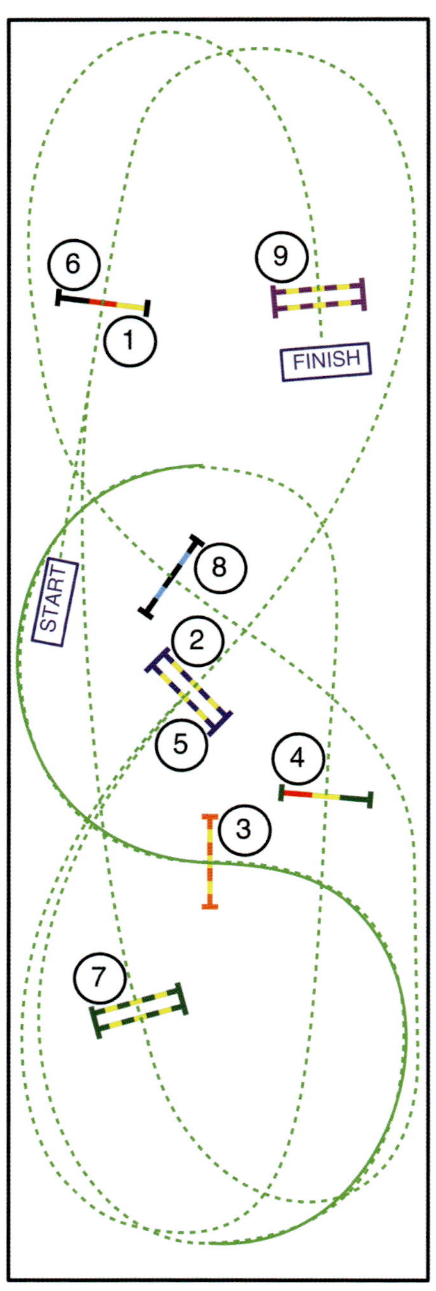

Course with Change of Direction Out of the Circle

- **Arena Size:** 20 by 60 meters

- **Purpose:** Example of how *change direction out of the circle* can be used within a course.

Basic course in a 20- by 60-meter arena.

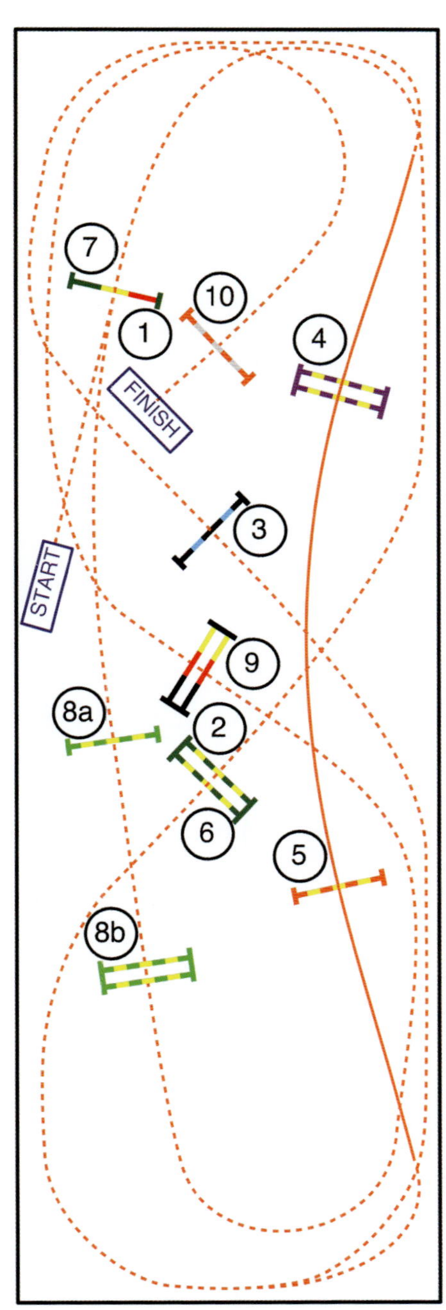

Course with One-Loop Serpentine

- **Arena Size:** 20 by 60 meters

- **Height:** 1.00 meter (3.3 feet)

- **Purpose:** Example of how a single-loop serpentine can be incorporated in a course.

This is an *intermediate-level* course in a 20- by 60-meter arena. Obstacle 4 to 5 is set on five normal strides with the distance of 21.50 meters (70.5 feet); Obstacle 7 to 8a is set on five normal strides as well with a distance that measures 21.50 meters (70.5 feet); the two-stride combination 8a to 8b is set on 10.25 meters (33.6 feet). As usual, these distances serve as starting points for a normal Warmbloods and should be adjusted accordingly to ensure best suitability for different horses, arenas, types of footing, and height of obstacles.

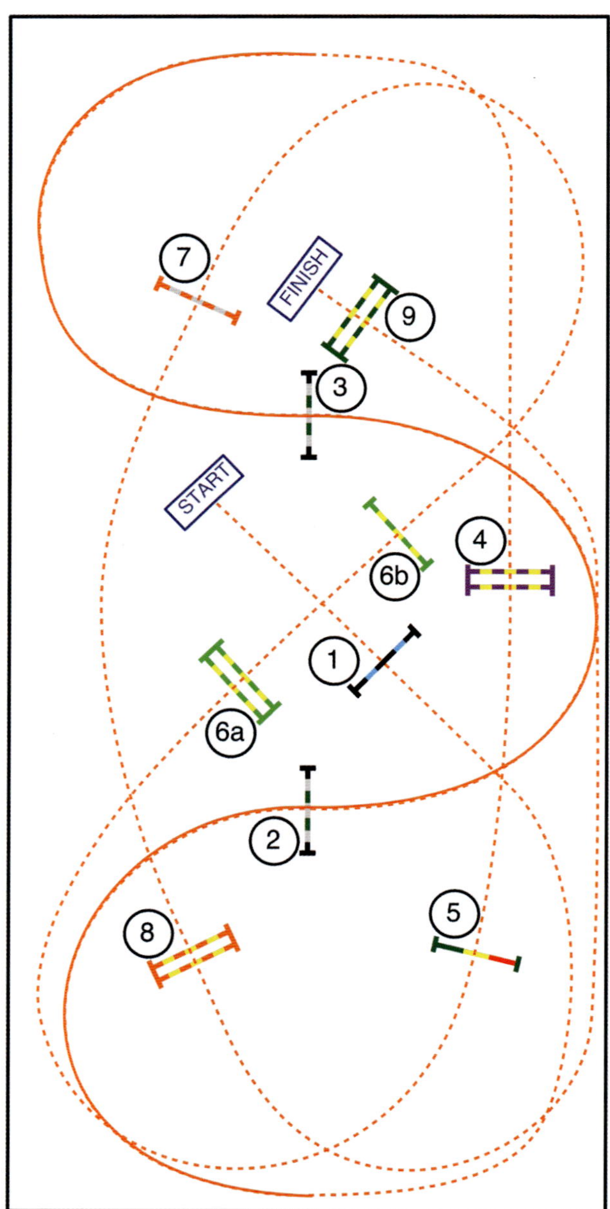

Course with Three-Loop Serpentine

- **Arena Size:** 30 by 60 meters

- **Height:** 1.00 meter (3.3 feet)

- **Purpose:** Example of how a three-loop serpentine can be included in a course.

An *intermediate level* course in a 30- by 60-meter arena. Obstacle 4 to 5 is set on four normal strides with the distance of 17.25 meters (56.6 feet). The combination 6a and 6b is measured for two strides with the distance of 10.25 meters (33.6 feet). These distances serve as starting points for normal Warmbloods and should be adjusted accordingly to ensure best suitability for different horses, arenas, types of footing, and height of obstacles.

Course with Short Diagonals

- **Arena Size:** 20 by 40 meters

- **Height:** 1.00 meter (3.3 feet)

- **Purpose:** An example of how short diagonals can be included in a course built in a small arena.

This is an *intermediate level* course in a 20- by 40-meter arena. The measured distance from Obstacle 3 to 4 is set at 16.75 meters (55 feet) for four strides. Obstacle 6a and 6b is a two-stride combination with the measured distance of 10.25 meters (33.6 feet). Note that these distances serve as starting points for a normal Warmbloods, and the distances should be adjusted accordingly to ensure best suitability for different horses, arenas, types of footing, and height of obstacles.

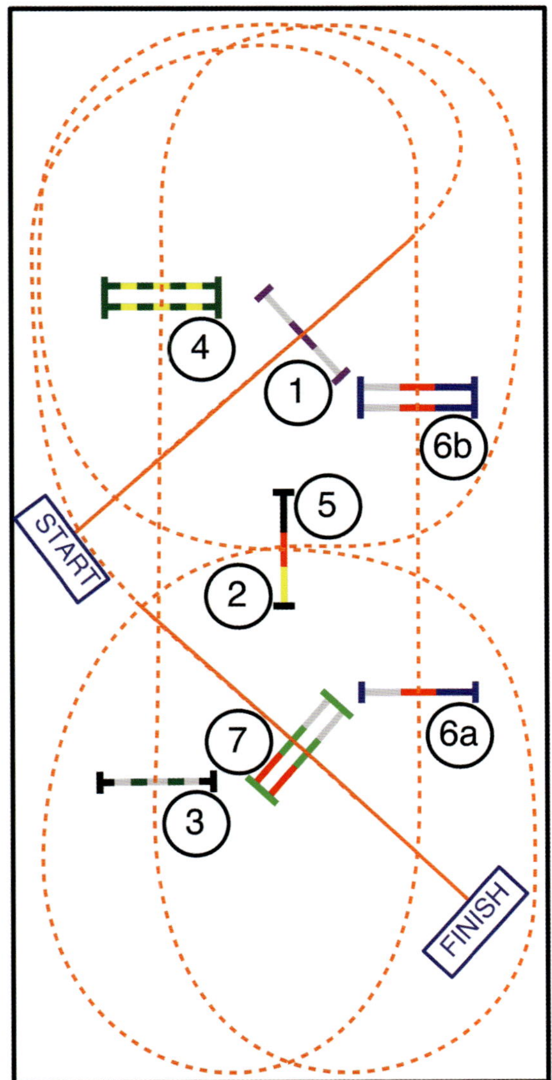

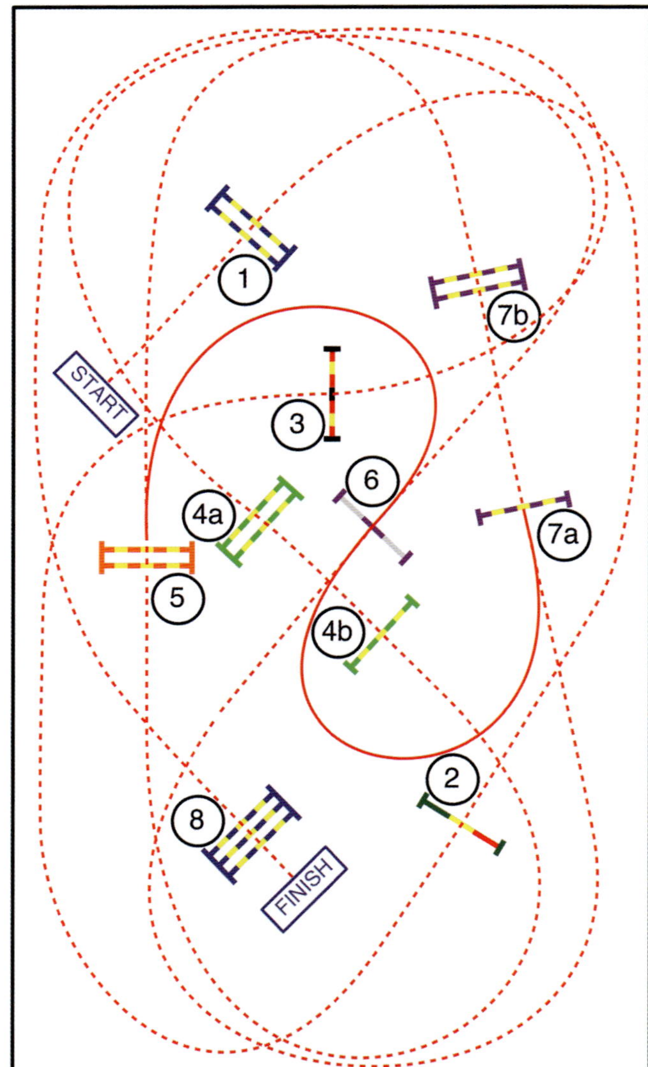

Course with Change of Direction Through the Circle

- **Arena Size:** 30 by 50 meters

- **Height:** 1.20 meters (3.9 feet)

- **Purpose:** Example of how a similar track to change direction through the circle can be used in a course. In this course, the red line illustrates how this specific track can be applied to save time while riding against the clock.

This is an *advanced level* application of an *intermediate level* course in a 30- by 50-meter arena. Obstacle 4a to 4b is set for one stride with the distance of 7.25 meters (23.8 feet). The second combination 7a to 7b, is set for two strides with the distance of 10.50 meters (34.4 feet). Again, these distances are starting points for a normal Warmbloods and should be adjusted as needed.

Course with Half-Circles Back

- **Arena Size:** 35 by 55 meters

- **Height:** 1.30 meters (4.3 feet)

- **Purpose:** Example of how half-circles back can be ridden as optional tracks while riding a course against the clock. The red lines illustrate a commonly occurring option.

This is an example of an *advanced level* course in a 35- by 55-meter arena. Obstacle 5a to 5b is a one-stride combination set at 7.30 meters (24 feet). Obstacle 6 to 7 is a related distance normally ridden in three strides with the measured distance of 14.00 meters (46 feet). Obstacle 8a to 8b is a two-stride combination set at 10.60 meters (34.8 feet). Note that these distances serve as starting points and should be adjusted to ensure best suitability for different horses, arenas, types of footing, and height of obstacles.

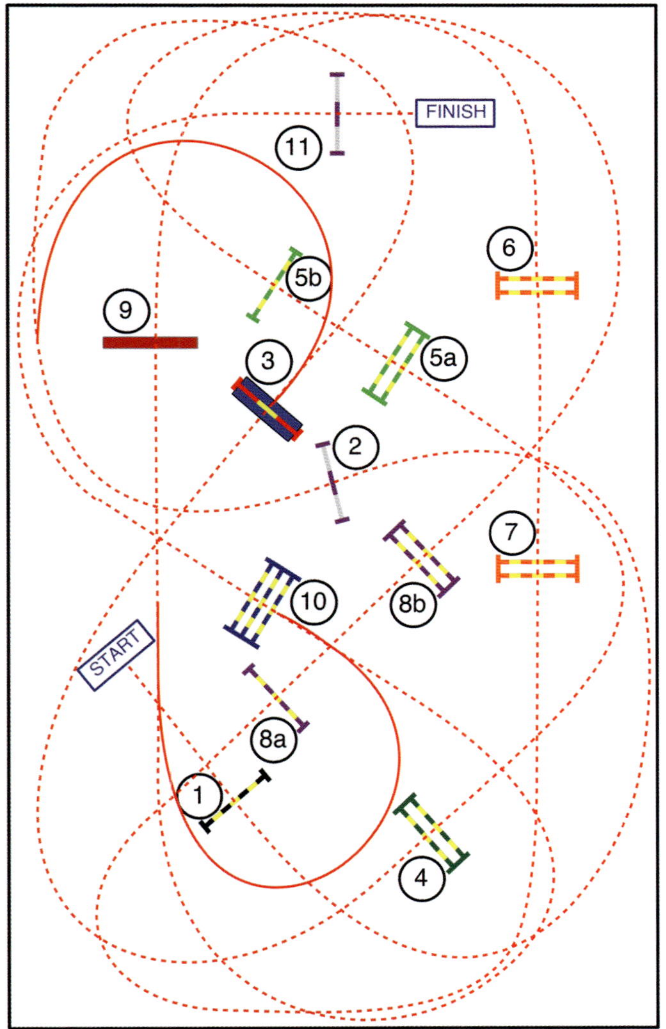

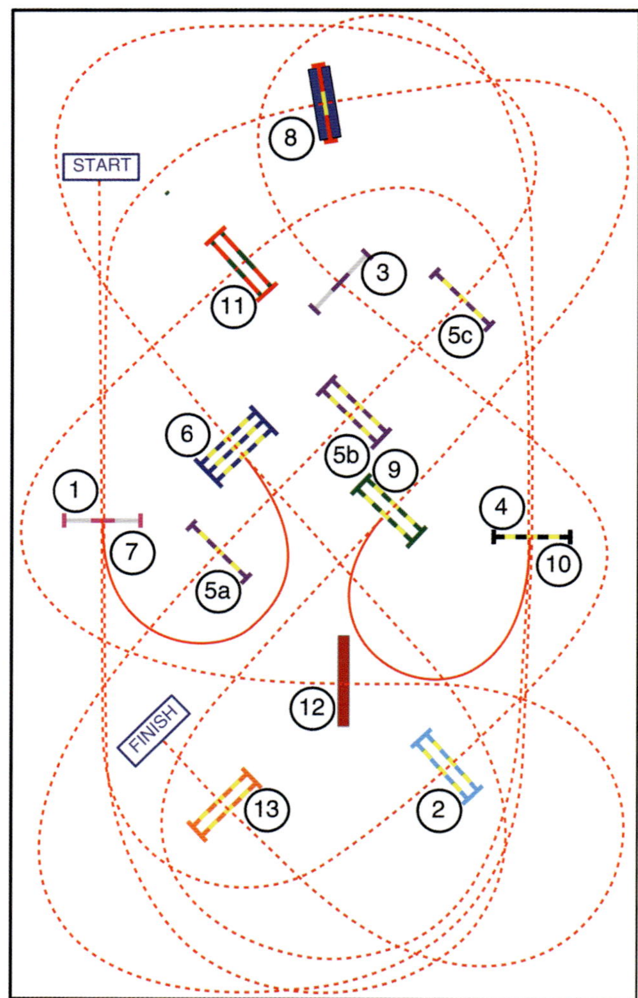

Course with Half-Circles Back in Reverse

- **Arena Size:** 35 by 55 meters

- **Height:** 1.40 meters (4.6 feet)

- **Purpose:** Example of how half-circles back in reverse can be used while riding a course against the clock. The red line from Obstacles 6 to 7 and Obstacles 9 to 10 illustrates the track as a time-saving option.

This is an example of an *advanced level* course in a 35- by 55-meter arena. Obstacle 5a, 5b, and 5c is a treble combination with the distance from 5a to 5b being set for two strides and measured at 10.75 meters (35.3 feet), and 5b to 5c for one stride and measured at 7.75 meters (25.4 feet). Obstacle 7 to 8 is measured at 28 meters (91.9 feet), which for many will ride in seven strides, but any stride number between six and eight would be considered normal due to the alternatives provided by the bend in the track (distances should be adjusted to ensure best suitability for different horses, arenas, types of footing, and height of obstacles).

WORLD-CLASS EXPOSURE WITH INTERNATIONAL COURSE DESIGNERS

The following courses are some examples from high-level competitions created by world-class course designers. A few selected course designers were asked to submit one of their favorite course plans with a comment, which resulted in a remarkable selection of elite-level course designs from around the world to include in this book. These courses can be studied in depth for deeper understanding of the artful way course designers can use lines and tracks in the show jumping competition arena.

Ali Mohajer (Iran)

- **Location of competition:** United Arab Emirates

- **Arena Size:** 85 by 55 meters

- **Height:** 1.45 meters (4.6 feet)

- **Course designer comments:** "The reason I sent this course as the favorite is that this arena is a special small grass arena (almost 85 by 55 meters with good footing) in the middle of a residential area, so it's always very challenging to design a big course in this arena as there are lots of visual effects and other factors are involved. So, for me as a course designer, it is very important to have a fair, safe course that presents good sport to non-horsey people and professionals at the same time. It's the only grass arena in UAE at the moment."

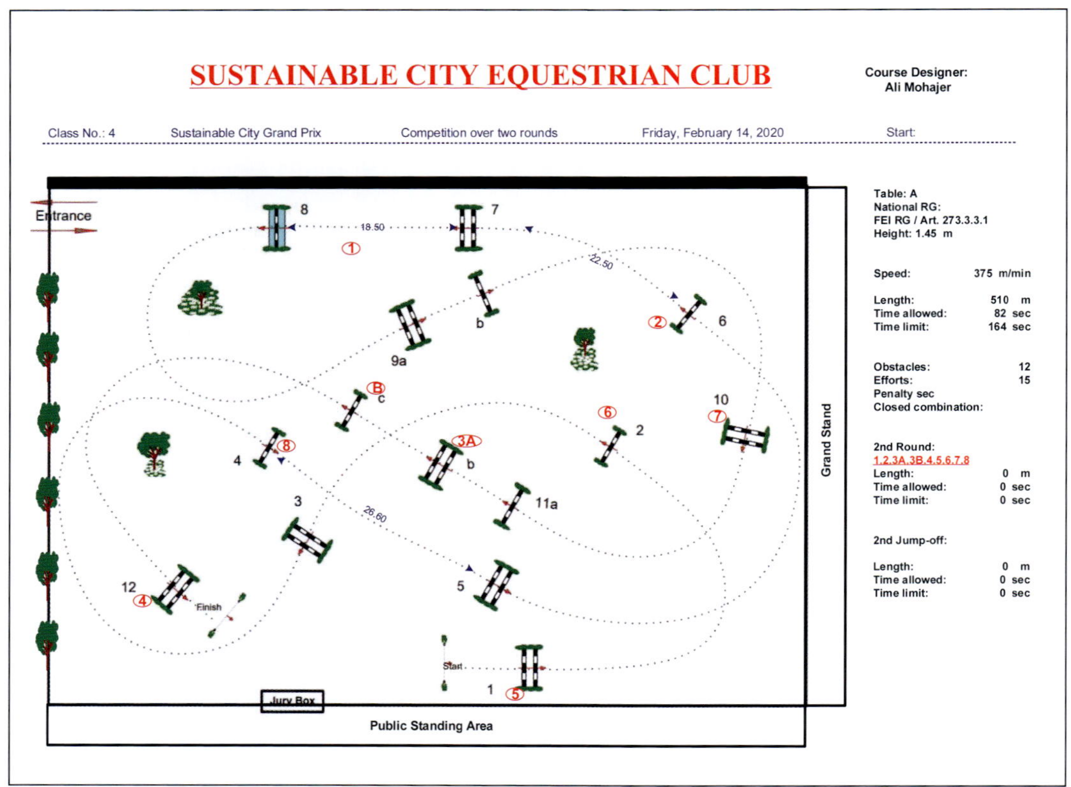

This is an *advanced level* course. Studying the lines will help you understand how smooth and rhythmical the course will ride—in this course, the lines are very smooth and encourage a free, forward canter and good rhythm.

Murat Batur (Turkey)

- **Location of competition:** Turkey

- **Arena Size:** 77 by 44 meters

- **Height:** 1.35 meters (4.4 feet)

- **Course designer comments:** "There are variety of reasons why this course plan is my all-time favorite. First of all, it is a classic event that has been organized every year for more than 35 years, and I have had the honor to be the course

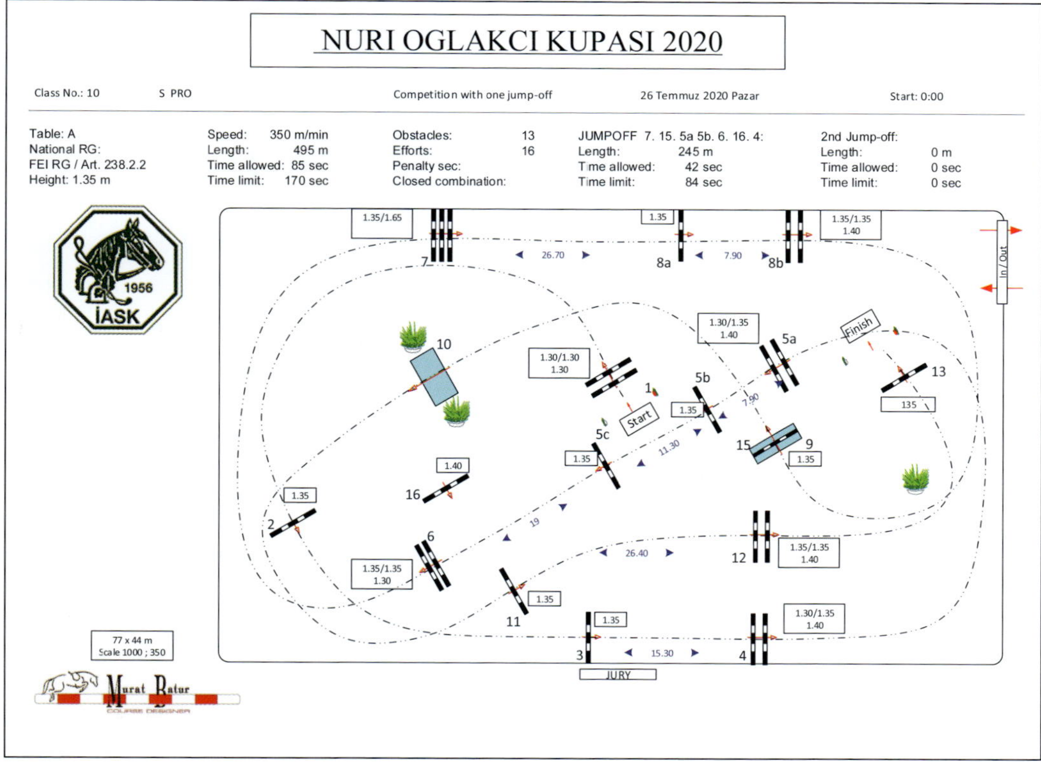

This is an *advanced level* course and a great example of how to use different types of tracks within the course.

designer. During the years I was competing myself, my best result in this competition was second place with less than a split-second time difference at the jump off in 1996.

"The course shown here is well-balanced, demanding, and technical, requiring power and scope. The obstacles are placed evenly in the arena, starting with an inviting ramped oxer. The questions start for the riders at an early stage of the course between Obstacles 3 and 4, with a forward three strides from vertical to a large spread oxer, which obliges the athletes to find a correct forward gallop before they turn to a treble combination that is away from the entrance of the arena. The first element of the treble combination is again a large spread oxer with one- and two-stride verticals. Following the combination is a committed line with a forward four strides to an oxer. This line surprisingly did not cause a lot of problems for the riders.

"The line from Obstacle 7 (triple bar) to 8a (vertical-oxer double combination) toward the in-gate caught some riders with one pole down in the combination. The rider has a fair distance and a nice angle before the approach to Obstacle 9 and 10 (the open water).

"After the open water, the rider has the option to turn inside to the next obstacle or gallop behind obstacle 2. The time allowed was limited, therefore, the inside turn was really the only option if the rider did not already push the time factor from the start of the course. The major problem was caused at Obstacle 13 with four faults or even some refusals.

"Out of 72 entries, we had: four eliminated, two retired with 12 time faults, and the rest within four to eight faults, ending with eight horses and riders in the jump-off. The jump-off course has all kind of questions in it. It offers a fast, forward start with left and right short turns in the course and a spectacular finish with a long-distance gallop to the last oxer."

Steve Stevens (United States)

- **Location of competitions:** United States

- **Arena Size Saugerties:** 114 by 114 meters

- **Height Saugerties:** 1.50 to 1.60 meters (4.9 to 5.2 feet)

- **Arena size Kentucky:** 124 by 93 meters

- **Height Kentucky:** 1.30 meters (4.3 feet)

- **Course designer comments:** "The Saugerties $1,000,000 Grand Prix in 2015 only had one clear round. The stadium jumping for the Land Rover Three-Day Event in Kentucky, which I designed in 2021, is one of only a handful of 5-star competitions in the world of eventing, so both courses are very important to me."

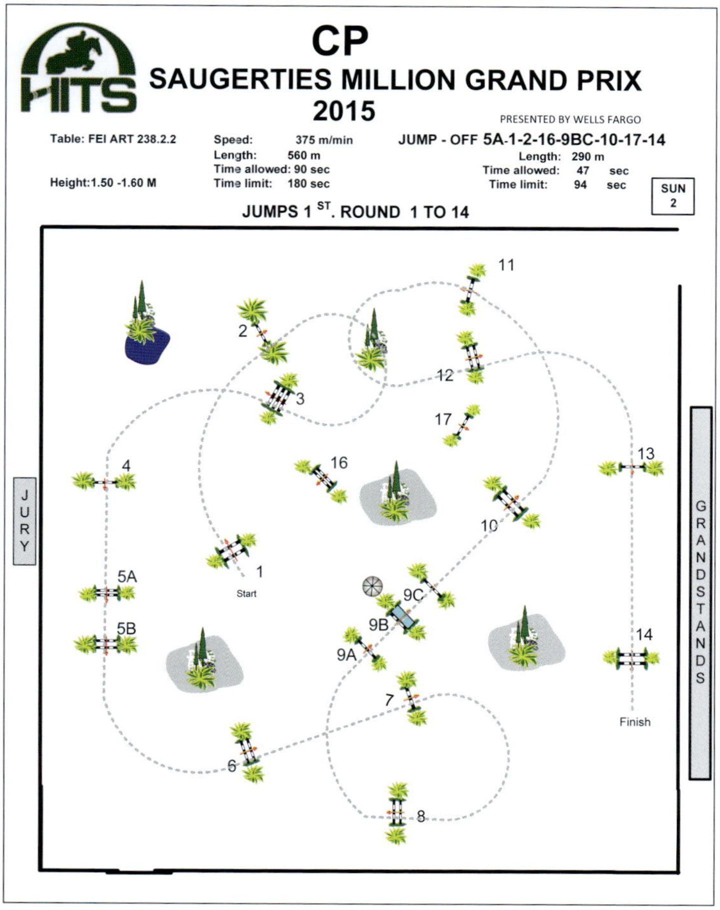

This is an *advanced level* course with a beautiful track in a large arena (note the *half-circle back* shaped tracks within the course).

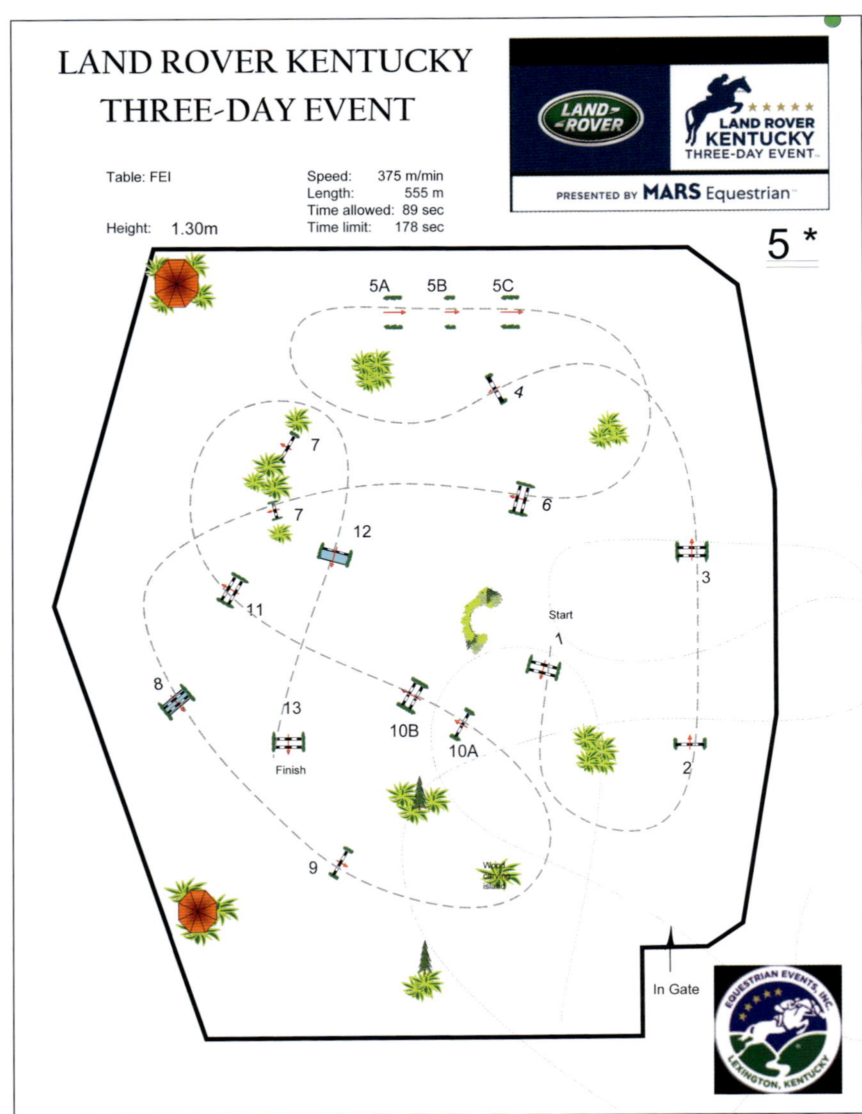

A very harmonious track set in the Grand Prix arena in Lexington, Kentucky (note the serpentine-style shaped track from Obstacles 4 through 9).

Guilherme Jorge (Brazil)

- **Location of competition:**
Brazil

- **Arena Size:** 110 by 90 meters

- **Height:** 1.60 meters (5.2 feet)

- **Course designer comments:**
"I've been fortunate enough to have built quite a few courses that I would say would be my favorite, each for a different reason, but since I must pick one, being able to design for the Olympic Games in my home country of Brazil makes it extra special. The course proved demanding yet fair, and the level of competition was outstanding, with the best teams winning their coveted Olympic medals. I had a fantastic team behind me. We had beautiful fences showcasing the culture and history of Brazil, and we were all very proud of the way we presented our sport."

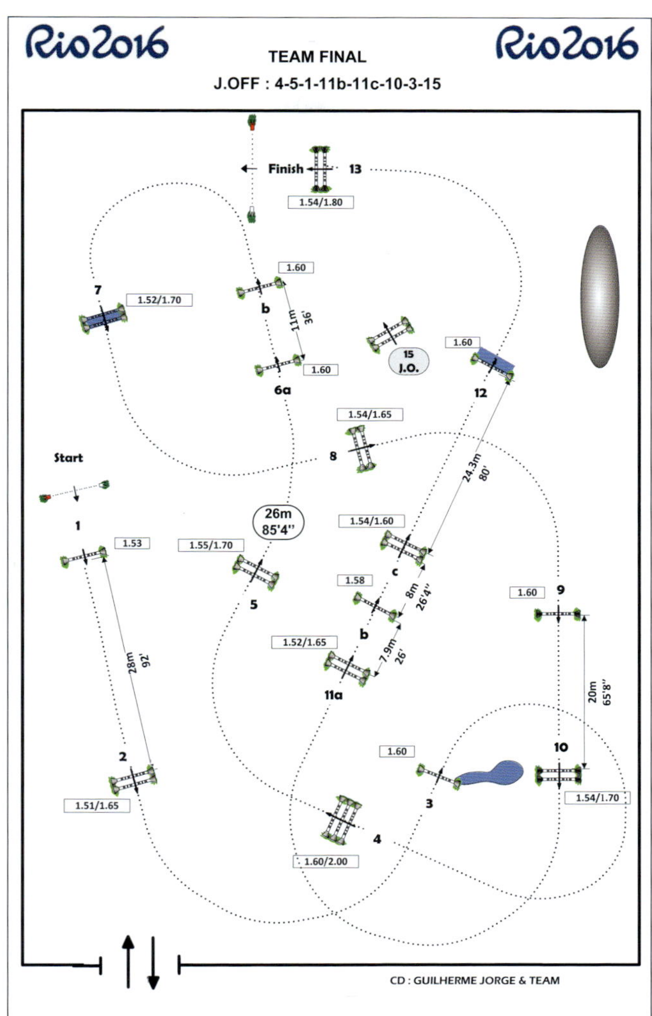

Team final, Olympic games in Rio de Janeiro, Brazil, 2016.

Christa Heibach (Germany)

- **Location of competition:** United States

- **Arena Size:** 110 by 84 meters

- **Height:** 1.60 meters (5.2 feet)

- **Course designer comments:** "This is my course designer's plan from the World Cup Qualifier and Olympic Team Qualifier in Wellington, Florida, in 2008."

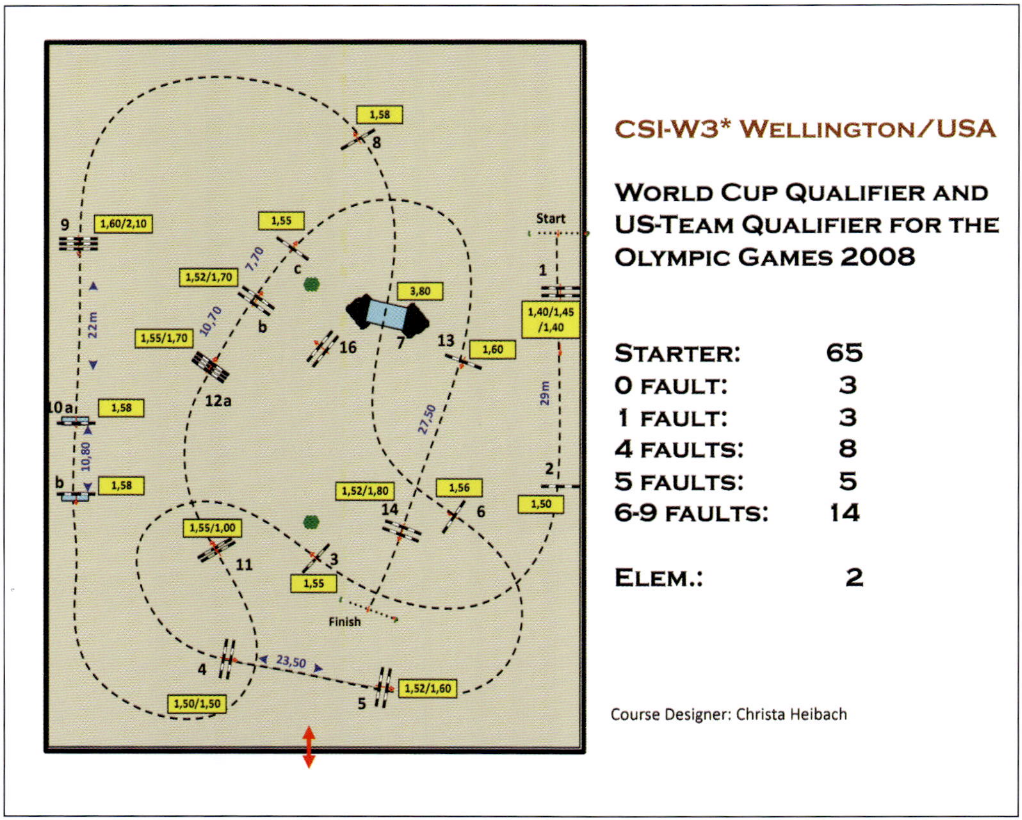

The course with distances and dimensions listed on it.

Arno Gego (Germany)

- **Location of competition:** Germany

- **Arena Size:** 150 by 125 meters

- **Height:** 1.60 meters (5.2 feet)

- **Course designer comments:** "Here is my hand-drawn course plan of the Grand Prix in Aachen, 2002. This was my last competition in Aachen as a course designer after 38 years" (Arno Gego, 1938–2022).

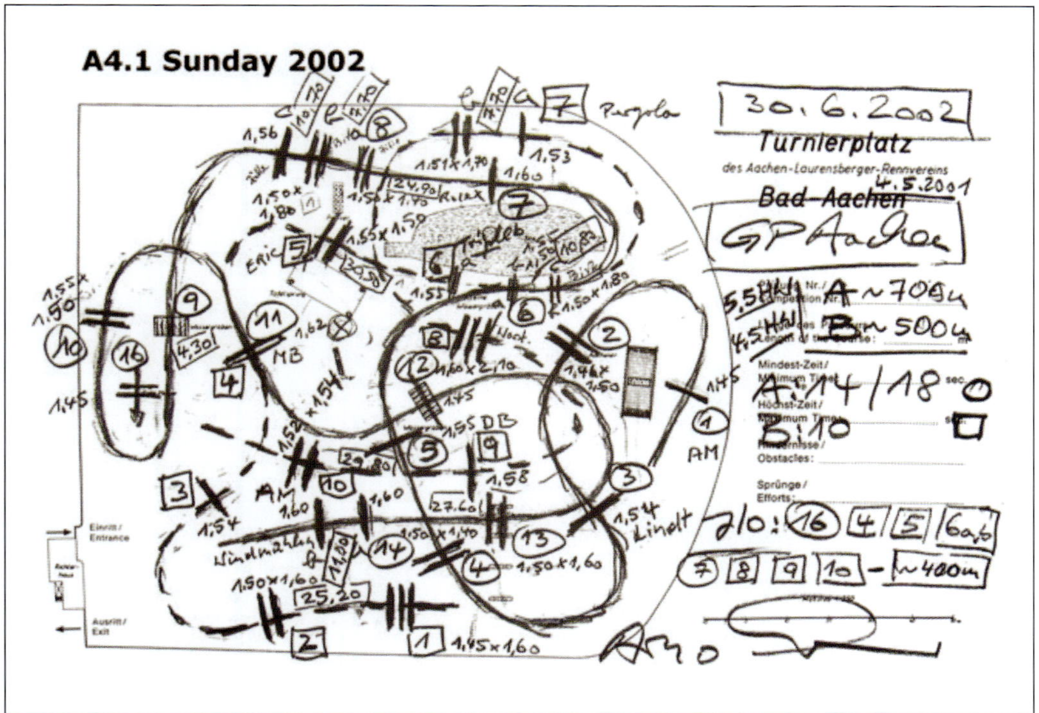

A true work of art with a wealth of information included on the course plan.

Linda Allen (United States)

- **Location of competition:** United States

- **Arena Size:** 100 by 100 meters

- **Height:** 1.60 meters (5.2 feet)

- **Course designer comments:** "This is the course plan of the team competition from the 1996 Olympic Games in Atlanta with the breakdown of how the competitors fared over the two rounds (same course, same day under the rules of 1996).

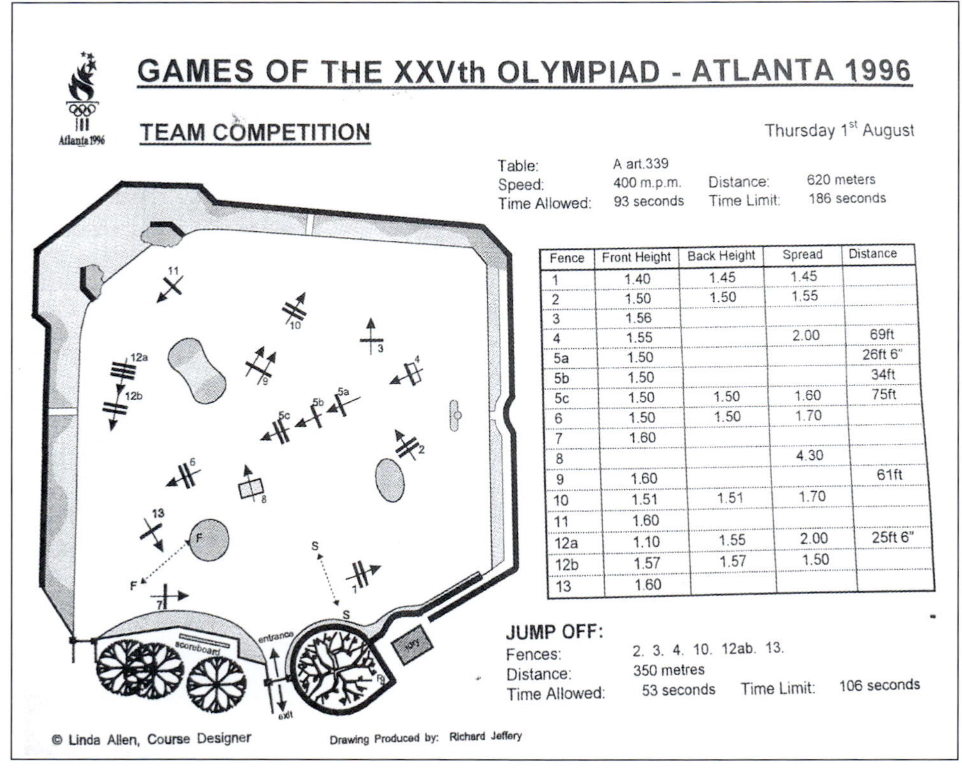

Fence	Front Height	Back Height	Spread	Distance
1	1.40	1.45	1.45	
2	1.50	1.50	1.55	
3	1.56			
4	1.55		2.00	69ft
5a	1.50			26ft 6"
5b	1.50			34ft
5c	1.50	1.50	1.60	75ft
6	1.50	1.50	1.70	
7	1.60			
8			4.30	
9	1.60			61ft
10	1.51	1.51	1.70	
11	1.60			
12a	1.10	1.55	2.00	25ft 6"
12b	1.57	1.57	1.50	
13	1.60			

Original course plan printed in 1996.

It is the result that I am most proud of as it was quite a mixed group of riders and horses.

"All the tracks at the Games were long! This one at 620 meters is very long. Also, distances are shown in feet, but they reflect the days before today's composite footing and thus are much shorter than what is typical today. This was natural sand, carefully selected, installed, and maintained by Hermann Duckek from Denmark, rated excellent by the riders but without the characteristics of today's products used everywhere. A later Games was on grass (Athens) that did not prove satisfactory, with several horses sustaining serious injury.

"A big part of my pride in the courses in Atlanta was the jump construction.

GAMES OF THE XXVth OLYMPIAD - ATLANTA 1996

TEAM COMPETITION - Round 1

Thursday August 1st

NUMBER OF STARTERS: 81

TABLE OF FAULTS

FENCES	1	2	3	4	5a	5b	5c	6	7	8	9	10	11	12a	12b	13
TYPE*	O	O	V	V l'pool	V plank	V plank	O	O	V wall	W	V wall or plank	O	V	T	O	V
KNOCKDOWNS	4	9	1	2	18	10	7	13	13	24	10	9	9	21	30	17
REFUSALS			1	1	2	5	1	1	1		3	1	3	1		2
FALLS											1					
ELIMINATION'S				1							1					
RETIREMENTS											1					
FENCES WHERE RIDERS WITH SINGLE PENALTIES INCURRED FAULTS	-	1	-	-	-	-	1	3	-	2	1	-	-	3	1	3

* V = vertical, O = oxer, T = triple bar, W = water.

ANALYSIS OF INDIVIDUAL ROUNDS

Clear	Clear/time	4 faults	4 faults/time	7 faults/time	8 faults	8 faults/time	12 faults	12 faults/time	Others
8	2	11	4	1	13	4	13	1	24
9.9%	2.5%	13.6%	5%	1.2%	16%	5%	16%	1.2%	29.6%

% OF RIDERS WITH TIME FAULTS (not counting those with refusals): 15%

Statistics of the team competition, Round One.

I designed them and they were built by various incredible builders in the United States and abroad. The track represented a trip across the United States with stops in the South, New York, Mt. Rushmore, Dallas, and Hawaii, among others, and ending with the space shuttle. I am happy to say that I was able to sell all the jumps for the Organizing Committee and that many of them are still in use today at competitions such as La Silla (Mexico) and Spruce Meadows (Canada)."

GAMES OF THE XXVth OLYMPIAD - ATLANTA 1996

TEAM COMPETITION - Round 2

Thursday August 1st

NUMBER OF STARTERS: 79

TABLE OF FAULTS

FENCE	1	2	3	4	5a	5b	5c	6	7	8	9	10	11	12a	12b	13
TYPE*	O	O	V	V on back l'pool	V plank	V plank	O	O	V wall	W	V wall or plank	O	V	T	O	V
KNOCKDOWNS	3	3	3	5	13	7	10	11	7	21	9	13	13	10	16	11
REFUSALS				3	2	2									1	1
FALLS				1		1									1	
ELIMINATION'S																1
RETIREMENTS																1
FENCES WHERE RIDERS WITH SINGLE PENALTIES INCURRED FAULTS		1		1			2	1	2	1			1		4	4

* V = vertical, O = oxer, T = triple bar, W = water

ANALYSIS OF INDIVIDUAL ROUNDS

Clear	Clear/time	4 faults	4 faults/time	8 faults	8 faults/time	11 faults/time	12 faults	12 faults/time	Others
10	4	14	3	15	2	2	5	2	22
12.7%	5.1%	17.7%	3.8%	19%	2.5%	2.5%	6.3%	2.5%	27.8%

% OF RIDERS WITH TIME FAULTS (not counting those with refusals or falls): 17.7%

Riders with double clears: NIL   Riders with one clear and one clear plus time: 3   Riders with clears plus time: 1

Statistics of the team competition, Round Two.

AFTERWORD

Training is simple—this does *not* mean to say that it is easy. What "simple" means in the context of training the horse and rider is "plain, basic, or uncomplicated in form, nature, or design; without much decoration or ornamentation; humble and unpretentious" (*Oxford English Dictionary*).

Many may argue this point, but the fact remains there *is* a straightforward path to success in training horses, and it has been used and expanded upon for thousands of years. In this time, there have also been many deviations from the path that respects both the natural functioning of the horse and his rider. Many riders have had success with horses by following different paths, some more and some less fair to the horse's part of the partnership.

The horse is responsible for any and all of our successes as a rider, because without the horse, no rider could participate in this, the most unique of all sports. This sport is possible for *any* rider to do well, because the horse is the athlete, and the rider is simply the pilot.

It is completely up to the rider to decide how much or how little he or she is willing to disturb the horse while sitting on top. It is also up to the rider (both while training and in competition) to always have the game plan in mind. This plan begins with the rider calmly and confidently steering the horse

Albert Voorn is a native of The Netherlands and was a regular member of the Dutch National Team for show jumping for many years. One of Albert's most important influences is the legendary Canadian show jumping rider Ian Millar, whose philosophy about working in harmony with horses greatly shifted his own training practices. Additionally, Albert continues to this day to be greatly affected by his very first riding instructor, MISTER BOEF (known only as this, in bold capital letters, out of respect!), whose elegance and work ethic were crucial in pushing Albert to become the horseman he is today.

Albert is himself an individual Olympic silver medalist in show jumping from the 2000 Olympic Games held in Sydney, Australia. He was recently awarded the highest national distinction as a show jumping coach by his national federation. Although he had no formal education or licensure within the parameters of his federation, Albert's success with many horses and riders over his career led to this exception, which honors his incredible understanding and exceptional contributions to the sport of show jumping, both within Holland and worldwide.

Albert has an enormous passion for sharing his experience and knowledge with others, even those riding at an introductory level. Several of the best riders currently in the sport credit Albert as their most influential mentor. When Albert is not traveling to teach or train, he can often be found grooming for his wife, Irma. They both enjoy carriage driving and the preservation of its art and history through participation in local and international carriage-driving shows. You can read more about Albert at www.albertvoorn.com.

to the track of the training exercise or competition course they face together. The flatwork and jumping exercises used in correct training are successful for all horses and riders because they are based on friendly lines and progress to the more challenging tracks required in our sport. A horse is most successful on any level with a confident pilot, and I have found great success with my students by using only those exercises based in fairness to the level of education of both the horse and rider.

We as trainers and riders must allow for the time and repetitions necessary for each to gain confidence in one level of training before progressing to the next. This is always based in the simplicity or complexity of the line that I have horse and rider follow in any given moment in the training. My advice to you as riders, trainers, and fans of the sport, is to look for simplicity and reward it, because simplicity is what the horse is looking for, and without it, there will be no path to success remaining for the future of equestrianism.

Albert Voorn

ACKNOWLEDGMENTS

This book would not exist if not for the many mentors and masters in their fields who have imparted on me the inspiration, drive, and curiosity to never stop learning. Some of them are from the past, some of them might be unaware how much impact they have had on me, and some of them have been very close to me over many years. They all have one factor in common—a tremendous amount of passion for what they do or did.

A huge thank you to my most recent and important mentor Albert Voorn—without him, I would not have been able to assimilate my knowledge to the extent I have today. When I first met Albert, I rode all the classical dressage exercises with the horses I trained, but the *lightness*, which is described in all classical books about riding, never appeared in the same way it was explained. Albert taught me much about this lightness, and once you have experienced the difference it creates in your partnership with horses, you can never go back. I am also very grateful to him for sharing his jumping exercises with me, which have influenced much of the content of this book. Thank you, Albert.

A special thank you to Ulf Wadeborn, as he has always been there for me by reviewing and discussing the true purpose of the classical dressage tracks. Thank you, Ulf.

A very special thank you to the Aachen School of Equestrian Art and Design. Professor Arno Gego and Christa Heibach have been both fantastic friends to me personally and my exquisitely knowledgeable and passionate teachers in the art of course design. They changed the trajectory of my life—it would never have been the same if I had not been able to attend their school and then been able to count them as both dear friends and irreplaceable mentors. Thank you, Arno and Christa.

A big thank you to the course designers that shared their favorite courses with me to use in this book. Each one of their courses is a true piece of art with a lot of thought and knowledge behind their design. Equestrian art brings people from all over the world together, and I consider myself very lucky to have course designer friends that are so supportive and helpful. Thank you to Murat Batur, Ali Mohajer, Steve Stevens, Guilherme Jorge, Christa Heibach, Arno Gego, and Linda Allen.

Thank you to Trafalgar Square Books for supporting me through this process; without them, this book would not exist. Rebecca Didier is just fantastic to work with—always there to talk and answer questions in such a positive way. Thank you so much for your help, Rebecca.

Thank you to everyone who helped and taught me at the local riding school when I first started to ride. A special thank you to Staffan Lindh for treating me as a family member and letting me spend most of my childhood in the stable. Thank you, Mette Henriksen and Ann-Karin Bitterlich for awakening my interest in dressage and letting me observe so many of your lessons.

I would like to acknowledge and thank Gilbert and Yvonne Böckmann who took me on as a working student on their family farm with 400 horses when I was only 17 years old. I had never seen so many horses in one location before and they gave me so many valuable experiences in riding, hard work, and discipline. Thank you, Gilbert and Yvonne.

A large thank you also to the entire Swedish University of Agricultural Sciences in Uppsala, who always supported my curiosity. I am especially grateful for my friendship with Anna-Lena Holgersson who, as a program director, has stayed in contact with me from my start of the equestrian studies program in 1994 until today. She continually shares new science with me and is always supportive and helpful when I come to her with a question or an idea. Thank you, Anna-Lena.

A big thank you to Per Fresk, who rode for Sweden in the Rome Olympic Games of 1960 and who was the first person to awaken my interest in course design. His educational courses that I attended as a student at the National Riding School in Strömsholm, Sweden, were inspiring, and his attention to detail truly made him stand out as a person and as an educator. Thank you, Per.

I would also like to extend thanks to my instructors in jumping at the University for Agricultural Sciences: Peter Eriksson, K-G Svensson, Jan Jönsson, Tony Oscarsson, Jens Fredricsson, Sylve Söderstrand, and Lars Bilock. All have tremendous accomplishments within equestrian art and sport and anyone that knows their teaching and training will recognize their influence in the exercises within this book as well. Thank you all for teaching me with such passion.

Just as important as my instructors in jumping were also my instructors in dressage, who always pointed out the importance of the track, making these important foundations so ingrained in my mind that I will never forget them. Thank you Bo Jenå, Kyra Kyrklund, Richard White, Göran Lindström, EvaKarin Oscarsson, and Marianne Esseen Söderberg for never letting me get away with riding a poor track!

A last thank you to all my friends and my family who have always been supportive—especially to my wife McKrell.